THE ROLE OF KNOWLEDGE BROKERS IN EDUCATION

This ground-breaking book comprehensively addresses an area of major and sustained concern: how to improve the use of research evidence and enhance educators' research engagement as a route to the improvement of educational practice. It focuses on the topic of knowledge brokering and mobilization in education, and its role in fostering evidence-informed practice.

Divided into three sections, each addressing a different role of knowledge mobilizers, the book is based in clear evidentiary grounding. The chapters:

- Explore payoffs and challenges of connecting research to practice
- Provide recommendations in relation to practice and decision-making
- Present organized and professionally-enhancing tools, strategies, and insights

Written by internationally recognized leaders and expert contributors, *The Role of Knowledge Brokers in Education* brings together extensive and global perspectives in an accessible yet comprehensive volume. This book is an invaluable resource for educational leaders worldwide who are interested in using or generating research for school improvement, as well as researchers, academics, and students in schools of education.

Joel Malin is Assistant Professor of Educational Leadership at Miami University-Oxford, Ohio.

Chris Brown is Professor of Education in the School of Education and Childhood Studies, University of Portsmouth.

THE ROLE OF KNOWLEDGE BROKERS IN EDUCATION

Connecting the Dots Between Research and Practice

Edited by Joel Malin and Chris Brown

Routledge
Taylor & Francis Group

LONDON AND NEW YORK

First published 2020
by Routledge
2 Park Square, Milton Park, Abingdon, Oxon OX14 4RN

and by Routledge
52 Vanderbilt Avenue, New York, NY 10017

Routledge is an imprint of the Taylor & Francis Group, an informa business

British Library Cataloguing-in-Publication Data
A catalogue record for this book is available from the British Library

Library of Congress Cataloging-in-Publication Data
Title: The role of knowledge brokers in education : connecting the dots
between research and practice / edited by Joel Malin and Chris Brown.
Description: Abingdon, Oxon ; New York, NY. : Routledge, 2019.
Identifiers: LCCN 2019013854 (print) | LCCN 2019019631 (ebook) |
ISBN 9780429462436 (Ebk) | ISBN 9781138616134 (hbk) |
ISBN 9781138616141 (pbk)
Subjects: LCSH: Educational research.
Classification: LCC LB1028 (ebook) | LCC LB1028 .R535 2019 (print) |
DDC 370.21—dc23
LC record available at https://lccn.loc.gov/2019013854

ISBN: 978-1-138-61613-4 (hbk)
ISBN: 978-1-138-61614-1 (pbk)
ISBN: 978-0-429-46243-6 (ebk)

Typeset in Bembo
by Swales & Willis Ltd, Exeter, Devon, UK

Printed and bound by CPI Group (UK) Ltd, Croydon, CR0 4YY

Joel dedicates this book to his wife Nicole and his parents, Jan and Steve, each of whom in his mind exemplifies key qualities/characteristics that are detailed in many parts of this book.

Chris dedicates this book to Professor Judy Sebba and Professor David Gough. Two wonderful colleagues who have been instrumental in guiding my thinking in the area of Knowledge Mobilization.

CONTENTS

ACKNOWLEDGEMENTS

Joel and Chris would like to thank the contributors for working so hard to help create what we believe is a state-of-the-art text, and one that provides a truly innovative contribution to the field of knowledge mobilization. We feel fortunate to have been able to work with all of you.

ABOUT THE EDITORS

Joel R. Malin (Miami University-Oxford, OH): Joel Malin is an Assistant Professor of Educational Leadership at Miami University. His research interests include research use and engagement, cross-sector collaboration, and leadership and policy (e.g., surrounding ambitious high school college and career readiness reforms). In the research use area, Joel has been especially focused on: (1) understanding the nature of educators' research use and engagement; (2) understanding the nature and influence of educational intermediaries/brokers that seek to support the use of research and professional ideas in practice; and (3) considering how to leverage existing networks to enhance research engagement. Joel is currently the Treasurer of the American Educational Research Association's (AERA) Research Use Special Interest Group, and was recently honored with the University of Illinois at Urbana-Champaign's Young Alumni Award.

Chris Brown (University of Portsmouth, UK): Dr Chris Brown is Professor of Education in the School of Education and Childhood Studies, University of Portsmouth. With a longstanding interest in how evidence can aid education policy and practice, Chris has written four books (including *Leading the Use of Research* and *Evidence in Schools*), several papers and has presented on the subject at a number of international conferences in Europe, and North America. Chris has extensive experience of leading a range of funded projects, many of which seek to help practitioners to identify and scale up best practice, and was recently awarded a significant grant by the Education Endowment Foundation to work with 100+ primary schools in England to increase their use of research. Other projects include an evaluation of England's progress towards an evidence informed school system (funded by England's Department for Education). In 2015 Chris was awarded the American Educational Research Association

'Emerging Scholar' award (Education Change SIG). The award is presented to an individual who, within the first eight years of the career of an educational scholar, has demonstrated a strong record of original and significant scholarship related to educational change. Chris was also awarded the 2016 AERA Excellence in Research to practice award and the UCEA Jeffrey V. Bennett Outstanding International Research award.

ABOUT THE CONTRIBUTORS

Nina Bremm, (Dr. phil., University of Hamburg, is Senior Lecturer at the Department of Educational Sciences, Institute of Education at the University of Duisburg-Essen. Her projects and publications focus on school development in disadvantaged communities, system transfer and sustainability in school development processes, learning networks, questions of social justice and inclusion as well as teaches attitudes and beliefs towards marginalized students.

Carol Campbell, Ph.D., is Associate Professor of Leadership and Educational Change and Co-Director of the Knowledge Network for Applied Education Research (KNAER) Secretariat at the Ontario Institute for Studies in Education (OISE), University of Toronto. She is an appointed Education Advisor to the Premier and the Minister of Education in Ontario and a member of the International Council of Education Advisers to the First Minister and Deputy First Minister in Scotland. Carol has held education, academic and policy roles in Canada, USA and UK, including Executive Director of the Stanford Center for Opportunity Policy in Education (SCOPE) at Stanford University, Chief Research Officer for the Ontario Ministry of Education, Policy Advisor to the Commissioner for London Schools and a faculty member at the Institute of Education, University of London. Carol's recent co-authored books are: *Teacher Learning and Leadership: Of, By and For Teachers*; *Empowering Educators in Canada*; and *Empowered Educators: How High-Performing Systems Shape Teaching Quality Around the World*.

Vincent Cho, Ph.D., is an Associate Professor in educational leadership at Boston College. His research addresses issues relating to school leadership in the digital age. A former teacher and administrator, Cho's aim is to help schools and educators make the most of their knowledge about students. Recent projects have examined administrators' uses of social media, 1:1 computing initiatives, and districts' implementation of computer data systems. Cho has earned American Educational

Research Association (AERA) best paper awards for his work relating to data use, as well as organizational theory. He serves as Assistant Editor for *Educational Policy* and on the editorial board of *Teachers College Record*. In addition to works appearing in leading academic journals, Cho is also co-author of *Supervision: A Redefinition* (9th edition) with Thomas J. Sergiovanni and Robert J. Starratt.

Amanda Cooper, Ph.D., is an Assistant Professor in Educational Policy and Leadership at Queen's University in Canada. Her interests professionally and academically revolve around improving research use in public services, efforts called knowledge mobilization (KMb) in Canada. She is the Principal Investigator of RIPPLE—Research Informing Policy, Practice and Leadership in Education (www.ripplenetwork.ca)—a program of research, training, and KMb aimed at learning more about how knowledge brokering (KB) can increase research use and its impact in public service sectors by facilitating collaboration between multi-stakeholder networks.

Caroline Creaby is a Deputy Headteacher at Sandringham School, a secondary school in England. As a school leader, Caroline has led on several strategic areas including teaching and learning, teacher professional learning and research use. Since September 2017, Sandringham has been designated as an EEF/IEE national Research School and Caroline is its Director.

Kristen L. Davidson, Ph.D., is a postdoctoral fellow for the National Center for Research in Policy and Practice at the University of Colorado Boulder. Using empirical and theoretical methods, she primarily investigates how consequential education policies play out in districts, schools, and communities, with central attention to advancing an equitable, democratic educational system. She has conducted research on research–practice partnerships, research and data use in education, parental choice of schools, family and community engagement, and community dialogues. Davidson earned her Ph.D. in Educational Foundations, Policy and Practice at the University of Colorado Boulder.

Elizabeth Farley-Ripple, Ph.D., is an Associate Professor of Education and Public Policy in the School of Education at the University of Delaware. Her research expertise is in policy analysis and evidence-based decision-making, and she has worked on a range of educational and social policy issues, including research use in at all levels of the system, administrator mobility, school and teachers' use of data, teacher quality and effects, and issues of equity in a variety of student outcomes. Currently, Dr. Farley-Ripple serves as the Director for the University of Delaware Partnership for Public Education and co-leads the IES-funded Center for Research Use in Education.

George Gadanidis, Ph.D., is Professor of Mathematics Education at Western University. He works at the intersection of mathematics education, technology and the arts, and spends at least 50 days each year in research classrooms, collaborating with educators to develop better ways of engaging students with beautiful ideas of mathematics. He is Co-Director of the KNAER Math Knowledge Network (mathnetwork.ca).

Joaquín Gairín is full professor of educational management at department of Applied pedagogy—Universitat Autònoma de Barcelona. He is currently the head of the research group EDO (organizational development team) and leader of projects on social and educational development, inclusion in higher education, educational change and assessment of programs and institutions.

Sara Grajeda, Ph.D. is a Research Associate at the Center for Research in Education and Social Policy (CRESP) at the University of Delaware. She earned her doctoral degree from Brigham Young University in Educational Inquiry, Measurement and Evaluation and her master's degree in Educational Psychology from the University of Virginia. Her dissertation focused on modeling growth in academic achievement for 3rd, 4th and 5th graders in math, reading, and English language arts. Her research experience and interests also include measurement development and validation through factor analysis, item response theory, and generalizability theory. Dr. Grajeda is involved with item writing, survey development and data analysis for the center.

Jonathan Haslam is the Director at the Institute for Effective Education. For the last ten years, he has been working to get research evidence out to practitioners and policy makers in an easy-to-understand format. He is the editor of *Best Evidence in Brief*, the IEE's e-newsletter published each fortnight, which goes to nearly 15,000 subscribers around the world. He is the IEE's lead on the Research Schools Network project, supporting 22 schools aiming to lead the way in evidence-based practice.

Georgeta Ion is an associate professor at the School of Education and researcher of the research group in Organizational Development (EDO) at the Universitat Autònoma de Barcelona. Her research is linked to the study of the research culture in universities and research utilization in policy and practice. She also conducts research in students' assessment and feedback. Since 2016 she has been Convener of the Network 22 (Research in Higher Education) of the European Educational Research Association. She has a Ph.D. in Education by the University of Barcelona with a study about the university organizational culture. The most recent publications are: Ion, G. & Castro, D. (2017) Transitions in the manifestations of the research culture of Spanish Universities. *Higher Education Research & Development*, 36 (2), 311–324 and Ion. G & Iucu, R. (2016) The impact of postgraduate studies on the teachers' practice. *European Journal of Teacher Education*, 39 (5), 602–615.

Ruth Kane (Professor at the Faculty of Education, University of Ottawa) is Director of Graduate Studies and Director of the Centre for Research on Educational and Community Services (CRECS), a bi-faculty center that collaborates with educational, social service, and community sectors to improve the well-being of children, adolescents and adults, including those who are vulnerable or who have special needs. She is Co-Director the Réseau de Savoir sur l'Équité / Equity

Knowledge Network , an Ontario-wide Knowledge Network on Equity. She is principal investigator in a five-year study funded by a SSHRC insight grant, of how school boards, teachers, and students take up citizenship within urban schools that serve youth from indigenous and first-generation immigrant communities.

Donna Kotsopoulos is the Provost and Dean, Faculty of Arts and Social Science, at Huron University College, London, Canada. Her research explores mathematical learning and development across the lifespan. She is an Ontario Certified Teacher and she has taught mathematics education in elementary, secondary, and post-secondary settings. She is the Co-Director of the Ontario Mathematics Knowledge Network.

John Eric M. Lingat is a Lyman T. Johnson Fellow in the Educational Psychology doctoral program at the University of Kentucky. He previously served as a dual-language elementary teacher and administrator in Washington, DC public schools. His research interest includes measurement, assessment, and evaluation related to cognition, performance, and achievement in a variety of learning environments. He was awarded a Graduate Student Research Award by the AERA Studying and Self-Regulated Learning special interest group for his research on calibration and metacognition.

Christopher Lubienski is a professor of education policy at Indiana University. His research focuses on the intersections of public and private interests in education in areas such as school choice, charter schools, voucher programs, and home-schooling, as well as in education policymaking. He was a post-doctoral Fellow with the National Academy of Education, and with the Advanced Studies Fellowship program at Brown University. More recently, he was named a Fulbright Senior Scholar for New Zealand, where he studies school policies and student enrollment patterns. His current research is on the equity effects of schools' organizational behavior in "local education markets," and policymakers' use of research evidence.

Stephen MacGregor is a doctoral student at the Faculty of Education, Queen's University. He is a project manager for several ongoing projects with the RIPPLE (Research Informing Policy, Practice and Leadership in Education) program of research. His doctoral research is focused on how the lessons learned from knowledge mobilization and research impact networks can be mobilized to support higher education institutions in Canada.

Veronika Manitius, (Dr. phil., TU Dortmund, is an advisor for science–practice cooperation at the Quality and Support Agency—Federal Agency for Schools, North Rhine Westphalia, Germany. Her work focuses on school and system development especially in disadvantaged communities, learning networks and social justice theory.

Doris McWhorter is the former Director of the Education Research and Evaluation Strategy Branch of the Ontario Ministry of Education. She has a longstanding commitment to research partnerships and the mobilization of quality evidence to improve school and system effectiveness. In her previous roles as educator, Research Officer and MISA (Managing Information for Student Achievement) Leader in a school district, Doris was instrumental in building capacity for data management and evidence use among classroom teachers, school and system leaders. She has championed research capacity building, knowledge mobilization and collaborative research–practice partnerships in a variety of roles and recently co-chaired the 2017 International Congress for School Effectiveness and Improvement.

Nicholas Ng-A-Fook is a Professor of Curriculum Studies, Past President of the Canadian Society of the Study of Education, and the Director of the Teacher Education at the University of Ottawa, Canada. He is also the Co-Director of the Equity Knowledge Network for the Province of Ontario. He has published several award winning edited collections such as, but not limited to *Provoking Curriculum Studies: Strong Poetry and Arts of the Possible in Education*, and *Oral History and Education: Theories, Dilemmas, and Practices*.

William R. Penuel is Professor of Learning Sciences and Human Development in the School of Education at the University of Colorado Boulder. His research sits at the intersection of learning sciences and policy. He studies the design, implementation, efficacy, and sustainability of efforts to improve science and mathematics education. He has explored how participatory design, professional development, curriculum, and teachers' collegial interactions support improvement efforts. Recent projects have examined the efficacy of project-based curricula in science, how teachers' assistance to colleagues can augment the effects of professional development, and how research–practice partnerships facilitate use of research among district leaders. He is co-principal investigator of the Research+Practice Collaboratory, which is developing and testing new approaches for relating research and practice more productively.

He is co-author (with Daniel Gallagher) of *Creating Research-Practice Partnerships in Education* (2017), co-editor of two recent volumes on educational research methodologies (*Learning Research as a Human Science*, 2010, with Kevin O'Connor; *Design-Based Implementation Research*, 2013, with Barry Fishman, Anna-Ruth Allen, and Britte Haugan Cheng), and author of numerous journal articles and book chapters.

Katina Pollock, Ph.D., is Associate Professor of Educational Leadership and Policy in the field of Critical Policy, Equity, and Leadership Studies at the Faculty of Education, Western University. A scholar in leadership and policy, Katina has been awarded several research grants and contracts with various funders. Two of these projects are funded by the Social Sciences and Humanities Research Council of Canada (SSHRC). The first, a SSHRC insight development grant, focuses on the contemporary work of secondary school principals (2013–2016) and the second, with Drs. Pinto and Winton, explores the complexities of policy layer enactment in Ontario secondary schools (2015–2020). Her most recent publication includes a co-edited book with Drs. Ken Leithwood and Jingping Sun entitled, *How School Leaders Contribute to Student Success*.

Jayson W. Richardson is an Associate Professor in the Department of Educational Leadership Studies at the University of Kentucky. He is a director of the Center for the Advanced Study of Technology Leadership in Education (CASTLE). He is passionate about the field of school technology leadership. Projects include tech-savvy superintendents, digital principals, virtual school principals, and school leaders' use of social media. Richardson is the co-editor of the *Journal of Educational Administration*.

Joelle Rodway is an assistant professor in Educational Leadership at the Memorial University of Newfoundland. Her primary research interests focus on the role of social capital in educational change in K-12 contexts. Specifically, she examines the ways educators' social networks mediate the ways in which they develop, understand, and implement educational policy and how these processes affect school improvement outcomes.

Davoud Sarfaraz is the Senior Knowledge Mobilization Coordinator at the Ontario Ministry of Education. He is the ministry lead for the Knowledge Network for Applied Education Research (KNAER) initiative and is responsible for facilitating the connection of policy with research and practice.

Nicholas J. Sauers is an assistant professor in the Education Policy Studies Department at Georgia State University. His scholarly interests include K-12 leadership and the role of technology in schools. More specifically, Nick has worked with many one-to-one school leaders nationally and internationally as they move to a more technology-rich environment. Nick is actively involved with research and training for school leaders across the country and internationally as they attempt to leverage technology as a tool for change. He also serves as an Associate Director for the Center for the Advanced Study of Technology Leadership in Education (CASTLE). Prior to his work in higher education, Nick served as a teacher and principal in Iowa.

Michelle Searle is an Assistant Professor of Program Evaluation at Queen's University. Her research focuses on increasing the usefulness of program evaluation through a focus on collaborative evaluation approaches and innovative forms of knowledge dissemination that enhance capacity within organizations.

Samantha Shewchuk, a doctoral candidate at Queen's University, is the program manager for RIPPLE (Research Informing Policy, Practice and Leadership in Education). She researches cross-collaboration in child welfare and education sectors. She wants to help children who experience maltreatment and the teachers and social workers that form a community around them.

Angela Şt. Trubceac is an international doctoral student from Moldova studying leadership, culture, and curriculum at Miami University. Her research interests include social studies teachers' knowledge, perceptions, and experiences of peace education and multiculturalism. Specific to this project, she is interested in understanding and strengthening knowledge exchange activities.

Erica van Roosmalen is the Director, Education Research & Evaluation Strategy Branch with the Ontario Ministry of Education and co-director of the Knowledge Network for Applied Education Research. She is an Adjunct Professor of Practice, Masters of International Education, Charles Sturt University. A dynamic educational leader and change agent with experience in elementary, secondary and post-secondary contexts, Erica works at the intersection of Research, Practice and Policy ensuring research evidence is meaningful, scalable and practical to a wide variety of stakeholders.

Vicky Ward is Reader in Management at the University of St Andrews. She has spent the last ten years researching aspects of knowledge mobilization and knowledge sharing across the health and social care sector, with a particular focus on how diverse groups of people (practitioners, academics, communities) create and share knowledge with each other. She has a particular interest in knowledge mobilization frameworks, knowledge brokering, knowledge co-production, and embedded research.

1

JOINING WORLDS

Knowledge mobilization and evidence-informed practice

Joel R. Malin and Chris Brown

Introduction

There are many ideas about what high quality education is and ought to be, and lively and crucial debates about how we might best bring about educational improvement. We do not claim through this book to fully resolve these vital debates. Nevertheless, we and contributors to this book **are unwaveringly committed** to a simple yet powerful idea that has been gaining purchase in various quarters around the world: that educational practice, as a general principle, should be *evidence-informed*. To the extent that we can help to make this aspiration a more consistent reality, we submit, educational practice will ever tend in the direction of progress and improvement.

Along these lines, in fact, **a broad and international push** is now underway to strengthen the connections between educational research and practice (e.g. Coldwell et al., 2017; Hammersley-Fletcher & Lewin, 2015). If educators are more research engaged and connected, we and others have reasoned, teaching and learning improvements are likely to follow. Indeed, evidence to support this assumption is emerging (Goldacre, 2013; Mincu, 2014; Supovitz, 2015; Wisby & Whitty, 2017; Rose et al., 2017). Such a focus, of course, is not exclusive to education—we can now see strong efforts across sectors to bring about evidence-informed policy and practice (e.g. Nutley et al., 2007).

So far, so good. However, plenty of evidence also discloses it is no small task to broadly strengthen research-practice connections, to consistently bring about evidence-informed policy or practice. What gives? A lot, actually. We are most certainly not dealing with a case of simple problem, simple solution. To the contrary, we are facing a 'wicked' or 'sticky' problem requiring understanding of and tending to different aspects of the educational ecosystem, and the undertaking of various efforts through which they might be brought into closer alignment.

Though *disconnects* between research and practice are multiply caused, at root are deep and thorny social, cultural, and structural divides: We can see longstanding and sizeable boundaries between the professionals who inhabit the realms of primarily 'research production' (e.g., universities) and those who inhabit primarily 'research use' (e.g., K-12 schools and districts) contexts (Caplan, 1979; Levin, 2013). Varied 'solutions' are possible, but at their center they do or should share an emphasis upon somehow spanning these unproductive boundaries for mutual benefit (i.e., better research, better practice, heightened sense of collective responsibility, enhanced infrastructure for educational improvement). Before we introduce and frame these various solutions, however, we believe a bit more problem analysis is in order.

On a practical level, research-practice gaps appear in several ways. Taking practitioners' perspectives, the most conspicuous difficulties concern the (in)accessibility, (ir)relevance, and (un)timeliness of much research (Hering, 2016). Regarding access, for instance, academic researchers often merely pursue publication via scholarly outlets (Cook, Cook, & Landrum, 2013; Goldacre, 2013) and do not further aim to promote or disseminate it—or, perhaps they make attempts, but to no or little avail. Meanwhile, K-12 educators do not typically read such work (for one, most of it is restricted access—part of the *accessibility* issue; Saunders, 2015). Compounding this, much research is viewed by educators as lacking clear relevance and actionability (Lysenko, Abrami, Bernard, Dagenais, & Janosz, 2014). Finally, concerning timeliness, even actionable information might be unfamiliar to would-be beneficiaries at the time it is needed (Sarewitz & Pielke, 2007).

Compounding these issues, educators tend to highly value information that is integrated in nature—for instance, evidence syntheses that can guide thinking and decision-making over and above more narrow sources (e.g., a single study addressing a narrow research question) (Hubers & Poortman, 2017; Malin & Paralkar, 2017). Yet, as a recent *Nature* editorial points out, the production of research syntheses is not incentivized in the academic sphere (Reward Synthesis, 2018, June 20). Thus, already we can see major issues, both at the level of individual studies and at the level of more holistic and broad-spanning evidence synthesis. And, it seems plain, the status quo will not solve such issues.

More deeply, there are social conflicts, tensions, and histories demanding consideration. First, in some contexts educational goals/standards and expectations have been churning so rapidly that educators have come to rely more heavily on their own beliefs than those of others (Lortie, 1975; Lysenko et al., 2014). Also, the implied intellectual superiority of academia over practice can deeply impair research-practice relationships (Lysenko et al., 2014) and, we contend, ultimately reduce both the quality and the influence of educational research production. Related to this, educators' tacit use of knowledge to support their professional judgments is commonly painted or internalized as being inferior to other knowledge sources (Hammersley, 2004), when actually it is often optimal (Leonard & Sensiper, 1998; Brown 2017). Accordingly, and as we will elaborate later in this chapter, we adopt a definition of research-informed practice that embraces and appreciates the integration of local and tacit knowledge alongside 'research knowledge.'

To summarize, what is demanded by practitioners is not typically being delivered by academics, and, related, academics' research programs are often not as well tuned to resolving clear 'problems of practice' than they could or should be. The issues we pointed out, and others as well (see Lysenko et al., 2014; Malin, 2016), are considerable and daunting indeed, however they are not insurmountable. We content that the most promising approaches involve via (1) some form of inter-mediation (i.e., a 3rd party, a mediator, a broker); and/or (2) boundary spanning, connective actions undertaken by members or research and practice communities. Within these broad categories, too (as you will see), is a good deal of variety. In fact, a variety of individuals and entities—operating variously but fundamentally as **knowledge mobilizers**—are in important ways doing such work right now.

To illustrate, let's return to the evidence synthesis issue—practitioners and policymakers desire such material, but academics (representing traditional 'knowledge producers'), other than a few notable exceptions (e.g. England's EPPI-centre), tend not to be producing them. Indeed, in some contexts, demand for such information may be at all-time highs—in the United States, for instance, federal policy includes "evidence-based" and "research-based" program selection requirements (Farley-Ripple, Tilley, & Tise, 2017). As a consequence, we have witnessed other individuals and entities stepping into the void to meet these demands—for instance, the *What Works Clearinghouse* and the *Best Evidence Encyclopedia* in the US and the Education Endowment Foundation in the UK. We also see prominent mediators like Kim Marshall (see Chapter 2), who in response to educators' demands specifically preferences "the pulled together stuff" (K. Marshall, personal communications, June 16, 2016) as each week he scours the literature for material to highlight for school principals and other educators.

Thus far what we are describing is happening primarily in the 'mediation' context, which plays a crucial—though not monopolistic—part in facilitating the mobilization of knowledge. Levin (2013) developed a framework representing the major dimensions of knowledge mobilization in education. In his view, educational knowledge mobilization occurs within three overlapping contexts— (1) the production of educational research ("production" context); (2) the settings in which the research is typically applied ("use" context); and (3) the "mediation" context—comprising all those who attempt in some way to better connect the production and use contexts (e.g., the aforementioned examples, plus think tanks and advocacy organizations, and some foundations). He also noted how the full process and all actors within are influenced by broader institutional, social, legal contexts, emergent technologies, and so on. Levin also emphasized overlaps between these contexts—for instance:

- some researchers can serve to repackage or otherwise mobilize their research and/or have reinvented their scholarship to occur in concert with educators
- some practitioners are producing and sharing important knowledge
- and some advocacy organizations are also producing 'knowledge' that fits their ideological proclivities.

This book takes up all of these possibilities (focusing specifically on the world of educational practice as opposed to the broader 'policy' world), attempting to make sense of and sharpen our thinking regarding knowledge mobilization in its various forms in varied educational contexts.

Though the key role of knowledge brokers in education (and other sectors; Davies, Powell, & Nutley, 2015) is increasingly noted, in education the lion's share of attention to date has been directed toward policy-focused think tanks and advocacy organizations. Lubienski, Scott, and Debray (2011), for example, have described a vast network of intermediary organizations in the US, many purportedly aiming to enhance decision makers' research use. Most such organizations, however, focus narrowly (e.g., promoting school choice reforms), strive to influence state and national policy more than teaching practice, and/or deliver messages that are driven more so by ideology than by rigorous, scientific evidence (Malin & Lubienski, 2015; Lubienski et al., 2011).

As a whole, we suspect such individuals and entities tend to add to, rather than subtract from, the complex and considerable issues that K-12 teachers and other educators face. A growing number of individuals and entities that serve brokerage functions, however, do focus directly on informing or improving educational practice and/or co-constructing useful, field-relevant knowledge. Because they have drawn less attention until now, in this book we have elected to focus intently on how they aspire to improve teaching and learning. We focus on those knowledge mobilizers (also referred as brokers, mediators, intermediaries, translators, and boundary spanners) who are key to connecting research and practice; in the process illustrating individuals and entities that primarily take up residence in each of the three major contexts Levin (2013) outlined. As such, we hope both to illuminate this 'brokerage' space (Farley-Ripple et al., 2017) as it currently exists, and to lay out some ideas regarding how it could be strengthened to more reliably and powerfully stimulate evidence-informed practice.

For this book we also adopt a broad and inclusive view of what it means to be research-informed, embracing the following definition of research-informed educational practice: "a combination of practitioner expertise and knowledge of the best external research, and evaluation-based evidence" (England Department for Education, 2014). Although not all will embrace such a definition or position the role of research in education in this way, we suggest doing so carries numerous benefits. Most importantly, it is *realistic:* Levin (2013, p. 16) points out that research is incapable of providing "recipes that can be blindly applied to practice. In many areas, there is simply not enough clear research knowledge to guide practice" (2013, p. 16). Likewise, Coldwell et al. (2017) argue, educators are unlikely to be persuaded to shift their practices by research evidence alone: such evidence must be reinforced by observed impacts and/or must be vetted by trusted colleagues discussing how it has improved practices/outcomes. Likewise, in our own research, we've noted that teachers' evidence use *in situ* is diverse and integrated (e.g., Brown, 2017; Brown and Flood, 2018; Malin, 2016; Malin, Brown, & Saultz, 2019).

The knowledge mobilization space too, as we will show, is diverse and dynamic. We take as our main task to examine knowledge brokers' diverse roles and functions and the ways in which their work strengthens, and/or could serve to further strengthen, the ties between research and practice communities and educators' abilities to function in evidence-informed ways. In doing so, we aim also to demonstrate the value and impact of those situated within this space, illustrating effective forms of brokerage while at the same time not shying away from legitimate challenges, conflicts, and tensions that can arise. This book's material, in turn, will benefit brokers themselves as well as those with whom they connect—thereby increasing/improving the use of research and other professional knowledge within education policy and practice.

In the remainder of this opening chapter, then, we do the following. First, we define key terms. Next, we introduce our conceptual framework, which serves both to organize the contents of the book and supports our analyses. We then preview the book's contents, and foreshadow intended contributions for readers from various vantage points.

Definitions

The following definitions guide us:

> **Evidence-informed practice** is "a combination of practitioner expertise and knowledge of the best external research, and evaluation based evidence" (www.education.gov.uk, 2014).

> **Diffusion** represents a process through which "an innovation is communicated through certain channels over time among the members of a social system" (Rogers, 1995, p. 5). It is rare, however, that innovations automatically spread like "ripples in a pond" (Hubers, 2018); likewise that knowledge will automatically flow through a school (ibid.). Rather, effort is required to encourage engagement and take up of new educational strategies and interventions.

> **Boundary Crossing**. Hubers (2016, p. 73) notes that schools are made up of multiple, overlapping, communities of practice . . . When individuals are not involved in a certain community, it is difficult for them to pick up the talk or tasks of an unfamiliar community, because the meanings that are invested in them are rooted in unspoken, tacit understandings that have developed over a long period of co-participation.

> As a result, discontinuities can often occur between the behaviors of those who participate in a community (and so have a shared history in relation to its specific tasks and knowledge-requirements or even a shared language or understanding of meanings) and those who do not. These discontinuities are referred to as boundaries. To cross these boundaries requires acts of brokerage. Hence

Brokerage is "a dynamic and complex set of actors, activities, motivations within which research is exchanged, transformed, and otherwise communicated" (Farley-Ripple et al., 2017, p. 13). This study focuses upon brokerage (vs. individual brokers).

Knowledge mobilization is one of several terms related to knowledge creation, movement, and sharing. We follow Davies, Powell, and Nutley (2015), who favored this term, applying it as "a shorthand for the range of active approaches deployed to encourage the creation and sharing of research-informed knowledge" (p. 2). We use knowledge mobilization to encapsulate a myriad of terms. In this sense our use is synonymous with the notion of the term K*, which was coined to reflect the myriad of terms associated with the concept of knowledge mobilization (Overseas Development Institute [ODI], 2012). Here the * represents an acceptance of the plurality of terminology and provides an umbrella for notions such as knowledge transfer, knowledge utilization, knowledge dissemination etc.

Networks in education can be thought of as "groups or systems of interconnected people and organizations (including schools) whose aims and purposes include the improvement of learning and aspects of well-being known to affect learning" (Hadfield et al., 2006, p. 5). Finally

Boundary objects are 'artifacts' that can be used to create and maintain common meaning across different communities of practice. Examples of boundary objects include documents, tools and manuals (Wenger, 1998).

Conceptual framework for this book

The conceptual framework, which serves to organize this book's content and supports our analyses, is essentially an integration of two main sources, Bush (2017) and Ward (2017).

Bush (2017) offers a typology of three main ways in which knowledge has been mobilized (i.e., *how*) in the educational landscape. He suggests, when we look at the various knowledge mobilizers in the educational space, they fit into three main 'roles.' These roles encompass those who:

1. create resources that distill and communicate evidence from research;
2. convene partnerships between researchers and practitioners; and/or
3. support practitioners to engage with evidence and test its impact locally.

We concur, and accordingly the three main sections of this book are organized in this manner.

Meanwhile, Ward (2017) developed a framework within which one can analyze and understand *why, what, whose*, and *how* knowledge is mobilized. Ward's framework developed from her cross-disciplinary analysis of 47 existing knowledge mobilization models. Here, asking and answering four questions (e.g., "What type of knowledge is being mobilized?", p. 1) results in the formation of several subcategories. Relative to *what* knowledge, for example, Ward identified three categories (scientific/factual knowledge, technical knowledge, and practical wisdom) while noting that some models emphasize one type whereas others rely on a mixture. Relative to *whose* knowledge, Ward identified five categories while noting sometimes multiple groups are featured: professional knowledge producers, frontline practitioners, members of the public/service users, decision makers, and product/program developers. Table 1.1 provides a more detailed accounting of Ward's framework.

The analytic categories Ward arrived upon provide a powerful means of better understanding and drawing out distinctions among different knowledge mobilizers and mobilization approaches. Fundamentally, educational knowledge mobilizers are making various choices (sometimes reflexively, and thus far almost entirely without theoretical or empirical guidance), which ultimately will hold major implications (e.g., their appeal, audience, effectiveness). For example, we suggest knowledge featured by multiple groups (who) and presented in an integrative and two-way manner (what and how: e.g., setting out both empirical evidence as well as practical, how- and why-to knowledge; telling compelling stories; generating dialogue) is more likely to be perceived as socially robust and to move action. Accordingly, we

TABLE 1.1 Summary of Ward's 2017 knowledge mobilization framework, by question

Why is knowledge being mobilized?

- Develop solutions to practical problems
- Develop policies/programs or recommendations
- Implement defined policies and practices
- Change practices and behaviors
- Produce useful research/scientific knowledge

Whose knowledge is being mobilized?

- Professional knowledge producers
- Frontline practitioners
- Members of the public/service users
- Decision makers
- Product/program developers

What type of knowledge is being mobilized?

- Scientific/factual knowledge
- Technical knowledge/skills
- Practical wisdom

How is knowledge being mobilized?

- Making connections/brokering relationships
- Disseminating and synthesizing knowledge
- Interactive learning and co-production

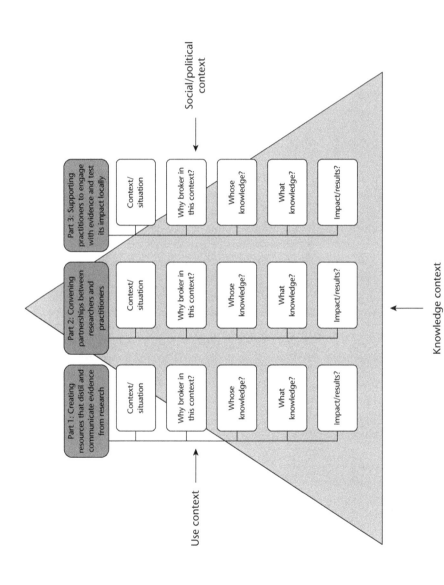

FIGURE 1.1 Depiction of conceptual framework and organization of book

Social/political context

Knowledge context

Use context

Part 1: Creating resources that distil and communicate evidence from research

Part 2: Convening partnerships between researchers and practitioners

Part 3: Supporting practitioners to engage with evidence and test its impact locally

Context/situation

Why broker in this context?

Whose knowledge?

What knowledge?

Impact/results?

are also interested in an element that sits outside Ward's (2017) and Bush's (2017) framework but that is, or ought to be, a consideration of all knowledge mobilizers—*impact*). The framework thus guiding us and contributors is shown in Figure 1.1.

Contributing authors have been asked, as is relevant to their topics, to apply the framework to assist them in considering and explicating the how, what and whose elements of the framework, and to more deeply describe their particular motivations—or, to describe the problem(s) that they are setting out to solve. They also have been asked to describe any evidence they have acquired regarding the impact of their activities. This aspect sits outside Ward's (2017) and Bush's (2017) frameworks but is represented in ours as an additional two-part question: Is knowledge actually being mobilized, and—if yes—to what effects?

The organization of this book

This book's first section addresses those who focus primarily upon "creating resources that distill and communicate evidence from research" (n. p.). These can include efforts to make research (and/or other knowledge sources) more accessible and practice-relevant for educational practitioners. Examples here include the George Lucas Education Foundation's Edutopia, Mr. Kim Marshall and his widely circulated Marshall Memo (Malin & Paralkar, 2017), and Harvard Graduate School of Education's Usable Knowledge. Likewise, some knowledge brokers have focused predominately on synthesizing existing (research) knowledge (see also Ward, 2017). For instance: England's EEF Toolkit, Australia's Evidence for Learning Toolkit, and Robert Slavin and colleagues' new Evidence for ESSA (USA). Likewise, educators and educational leaders can and do function as knowledge brokers within and beyond their organizations (Daly, Finnigan, Moolenaar, & Che, 2014; Datnow & Park, 2009), especially with the advent and acceleration of social media; these are topics of focus we also reserve for this portion of the book. This section includes chapter contributions reflecting knowledge dissemination/communication in two nations (USA and England) that have been highly active with respect to their policy pursuit of evidence-informed practice, as well as a chapter that addresses the burgeoning influence of social media on educational practice.

Our second section addresses those who primarily seek to "convene partnerships between researchers and practitioners" (n.p.). We consider partnerships to ideally represent learning networks. Here, drawing on the work of Poortman and Brown (2017), we consider the nature of such learning networks as comprising teachers and research brokers who come together with the intention of improving teaching and learning through their engagement with research. As such partnerships involve facilitated processes that encourage interactive and collaborative engagement with research. We view certain research-brokering organizations (Cooper, 2014) and interventions/initiatives (e.g., the Knowledge Network for Applied Education Research initiative [KNAER] in Canada) as exemplifying these efforts and focus accordingly in this section. This section includes chapters that will collectively enable readers to more deeply understand the nature and potential of productive, boundary-spanning partnerships and professional learning networks.

Our third section addresses those who are principally concerned with "supporting practitioners to engage with evidence and test its impact locally" (n. p.). In our view, these include various efforts to strengthen educators' ability to identify, interpret, and conduct or co-conduct research. In education, a growing set of research-practice partnerships (Coburn & Penuel, 2016) and networked improvement communities (Bryk, Gomez, Grunow, & LeMahieu, 2015) appear to exemplify this broad 'type,' as do certain disciplined approaches to action or design-based research. This section includes contributions and invaluable insights from internationally recognized leaders of three different forms of research-practice partnerships which also place school leadership front and center. This section also includes a chapter which will help readers to see how pre-service educators could be prepared to thrive within such partnerships, and/or to independently and effectively engage with research while on site. This third section highlights what some might consider the most ambitious efforts, those aiming to empower and equip educations to be able to successfully conduct locally meaningful research.

In the final chapter, Christopher Lubienski analyzes the book's content and presents thoughts and comments regarding the future of research use.

References

Brown, C. (2017). Further exploring the rationality of evidence-informed practice: a semiotic analysis of the perspectives of a school federation. *International Journal of Education Research*, *82*, 8–39.

Brown, C., & Flood, J. (2018). Lost in translation? Can the use of theories of action be effective in helping teachers develop and scale up research-informed practices?. *Teaching and Teacher Education*, *72*, 144–154.

Bryk, A. S., Gomez, L. M., Grunow, A., & LeMahieu, P. G. (2015). *Learning to improve: How America's schools can get better at getting better*. Cambridge, MA: Harvard Education Press.

Bush, J. (2017). Am I an evidence broker? Reflections on a trip to North America. [blog post]. Retrieved from http://www.evidenceforlearning.org.au/news/am-i-an-evidence-broker-reflections-on-a-trip-to-north-america/

Caplan, N. (1979). The two-communities theory and knowledge utilization. *American Behavioral Scientist*, *22*(3), 459–470.

Coburn, C. E., & Penuel, W. R. (2016). Research–practice partnerships in education: Outcomes, dynamics, and open questions. *Educational Researcher*, *45*(1), 48–54.

Coldwell, M., Greany, T., Higgins, S., Brown, C., Maxwell, B., Stiell, B., Stoll, L, Willis, B., & Burns, H. (2017). Evidence-informed teaching: an evaluation of progress in England. London: Department for Education.

Cook, B. G., Cook, L., & Landrum, T. J. (2013). Moving research into practice: Can we make dissemination stick? *Exceptional Children*, *79*, 163–180.

Cooper, A. (2014). Knowledge mobilisation in education across Canada: A cross-case analysis of 44 research brokering organizations. *Evidence and Policy*, *10* (1), 29–59.

Daly, A. J., Finnigan, K. S., Moolenaar, N. K., & Che, J. (2014). The critical role of brokers in the access and use of evidence at the school and district level. In K. S. Finnigan &

A. J. Daly (Eds.), *Using research evidence in education: From the schoolhouse door to Capitol Hill* (pp. 13–32). New York, NY: Springer.

Datnow, A., & Park, V. (2009). Conceptualizing policy implementation: Large-scale reform in an era of complexity. In D. Plank, B. Schneider, & G. Sykes (Eds.), *Handbook of education policy research* (pp. 348–361). New York: Routledge.

Davies, H. T., Powell, A. E., & Nutley, S. M. (2015). Mobilising knowledge to improve UK health care: Learning from other countries and other sectors: A multimethod mapping study. *Health Services and Delivery Research 2015, 3*, 27.

England Department for Education (2014). Online information. Retrieved from www.education.gov.uk. Accessed on December 16, 2015.

Farley-Ripple, E., Tilley, K., & Tise, J. (2017). Brokerage and the research-practice gap: A theoretical and empirical examination. Paper presented at the 2017 annual meeting of the American Educational Research Association.

Goldacre, B. (2013) *Building evidence into education*. Retrieved from https://www.gov.uk/government/news/buildingevidence-into-education

Hadfield, M., Jopling, M., Noden, C., O'Leary, D. & Stott, A. (2006). *What does the existing knowledge base tell us about the impact of networking and collaboration? A review of network-based innovations in education in the UK*. Nottingham, UK: National College for School Leadership.

Hammersley, M. (2004). Some questions about evidence-based practice in education. In G. Thomas & P. Pring (Eds.), *Evidence-based practice in education* (pp. 132–149). Maidenhead, UK: Open University Press.

Hammersley-Fletcher, L., & Lewin, C. (2015). *Evidence-based teaching: Advancing capability and capacity for enquiry in schools: Interim report*. Manchester, UK: National College for Teaching and Leadership. Retrieved from http://dera.ioe.ac.uk/24429/1/EBT_Interim_report_FINAL.pdf

Hering, J. G. (2016). Do we need "more research" or better implementation through knowledge brokering? *Sustainability Science, 11*, 363–369.

Hubers, M. (2016) *Capacity building by data team members to sustain schools' data use*. Enschede, NL, University of Twente.

Hubers, M. (2018). Lead the change series Q & A with Mireille D. Hubers. *AERA Educational Change Special Interest Group, 82*, 1–6.

Hubers, M. D., & Poortman, C.L. (2017). Establishing sustainable school improvement through Professional Learning Networks. In C. Brown C. and C Poortman (Eds.), *Networks for learning: Effective collaboration for teacher, school and system improvement* (pp. 194–204). London: Routledge.

Levin, B. (2013). To know is not enough: research knowledge and its use. *Review of Education, 1*, 2–31.

Leonard, D., & Sensiper, S. (1998). The role of knowledge in an uncertain world. *Sloan Management Review, 40*, 112–132.

Lortie, D. C. (1975). *Schoolteacher*. Chicago, IL: University of Chicago Press.

Lubienski, C., Scott, J., & DeBray, E. (2011). The rise of intermediary organizations in knowledge production, advocacy, and educational policy (ID No. 16487). *Teachers College Record*. Retrieved from http://www.tcrecord.org

Lysenko, L. V., Abrami, P. C., Bernard, R. M., Dagenais, C., & Janosz, M. (2014). Educational research in educational practice: Predictors of use. *Canadian Journal of Education / Revue canadienne de l'education, 37*(2), 1–26.

Malin, J. R. (2016). Educators' use of research and other evidence within local grant foundation applications. *Planning and Changing, 47*, 82–100.

Malin, J. R., & Lubienski, C. (2015). Educational expertise, advocacy, and media influence. *Education Policy Analysis Archives*, *23*(6), 6.

Malin, J. R., Brown, C., & Saultz, A. (2019). What we want, why we want it: K-12 educators' evidence use to support their grant proposals. *International Journal of Education Policy and Leadership*, *15*(3), 1–19.

Malin, J. R., & Paralkar, V. (2017). Educational knowledge brokerage and mobilization: The Marshall Memo case. *International Journal of Education Policy and Leadership*, *12*(7), 1–20.

Mincu, M. (2014). *Inquiry paper 6: What is the role of research?* Retrieved from https://www.bera.ac.uk/wp-content/uploads/2014/02/BERA-RSA-Interim-Report.pdf

Nutley, S. M., Walter, I., & Davies, H. T. (2007). *Using evidence: How research can inform public services*. Bristol, UK: The Policy Press.

Overseas Development Institute (2012). *K*: knowledge management and mobilization*. Retrieved from https://www.odi.org/projects/2650-k-knowledge-management-and-mobilisation

Poortman, C. & Brown, C. (2017). The importance of professional learning networks. In C. Brown & C. Poortman (Eds.), *Networks for learning: effective collaboration for teacher, school and system improvement*. London: Routledge.

Reward synthesis: Enlarge and incentivize efforts that examine past discoveries [Editorial]. (2018). *Nature, 558*, 344.

Rogers, E. (1995). *Diffusion of innovations* (4th Ed.). New York, NY: The Free Press.

Rose, J., Thomas, S., Zhang, L., Edwards, A., Augero, A., & Rooney, P. (2017). *Research learning communities: Evaluation report and executive summary*. Retrieved from https://educationendowmentfoundation.org.uk/

Sarewitz, D., & Pielke, R. A., Jr. (2007). The neglected heart of science policy: Reconciling supply of and demand for science. *Environmental Science & Policy*, *10*(1), 5–16.

Saunders, L. (2015). "Evidence" and teaching: A question of trust? In C. Brown (Ed.), *Leading the use of research and evidence in schools* (pp. 39–52). London, UK: IOE Press.

Supovitz, J. (2015). Teacher data use for improving teaching and learning. In C. Brown (Ed.), *Leading the use of research & evidence in schools*. London: IOE Press.

Ward, V. (2017). Why, whose, what and how? A framework for knowledge mobilisers. *Evidence & Policy*, *13*(3), 477–497.

Wenger, E. (1998). Communities of practice: Learning as a social system. *Systems thinker*, *9*(5), 2–3.

Wisby E. & Whitty, G. (2017). Is evidence-informed practice any more feasible than evidence-informed policy, presented at the *British Educational Research Association* annual conference, Sussex, 5–7 September, 2017.

2

EDUCATIONAL BROKERAGE AND KNOWLEDGE MOBILIZATION IN THE UNITED STATES[1]

Who, what, why, how?

Joel R. Malin, Chris Brown, and Angela Șt. Trubceac

Chapter overview

The research described in this chapter was conducted based on our understanding that: (1) educational intermediaries that can connect research to practice are of vital importance; but also (2) these entities are at present inadequately understood. To address this knowledge gap, this chapter compares/contrasts three particularly prominent US-based intermediaries—*Edutopia*, Kim Marshall's *Marshall Memo*, and the Harvard Graduate School of Education's (HGSE) *Usable Knowledge* (2017). We have aspired to understand the ways in which their activities and processes overlap and vary. In particular, in conducting this research, we have explored:

1. Why are these entities mobilizing knowledge?
2. What and whose knowledge are they mobilizing?
3. What are the features of their knowledge mobilization (KMb) approaches?

As expected, these entities varied widely both in terms of content and process features of their approaches. Moving past our expectations, we point to two distinctive types of brokerage and we reconnect with literature within and beyond the education sector as we consider implications. In particular, in the discussion we attend to ways in which interactive research engagement might be fostered and expanded in education.

R-P disconnects, and possible roles/functions for brokers

This volume's introductory chapter has provided an overview of some significant and persistent barriers to research-practice (R⇔P; hereafter denoted as R-P) connections, and has positioned intermediaries as offering one promising means of overcoming these barriers and bridging stakeholders operating in separate contexts.

In fact, US-based efforts to bridge R-P gaps in education via intermediaries are not new, perhaps beginning with the 1960s launch of federally funded Research Educational Laboratories. A more recent, governmentally funded example is the *What Works Clearinghouse*, which began in 2002 (Farley-Ripple, Tilley, & Tice, 2017). Government support for such efforts, however, has fluctuated across time (for reflections from a 40-year history of involvement and observation of such work, see Louis, 2016).

In the US, we have also seen R-P intermediaries arising from educators' demands—the Marshall Memo (*Case #2 for this study*) provides one such example, as does the online newspaper *EdNC*—indeed, some now argue educators' demands for research-based information is at historical highs (Farley-Ripple et al., 2017). We have also seen intermediaries' R-P bridging efforts arising from particular visions—e.g., entities such as the Carnegie Foundation for the Advancement of Teaching has assumed an R-P connecting position, as has Edutopia (*Case #3*), and we can also include a wide array of advocacy organizations and think tanks in this category—though we believe these organizations have focused more so on influencing practice secondarily, by way of influencing policy. In any case, we concur with Anderson, De La Cruz, and Lopez (2017) that these trends have also coaxed researchers, universities, and colleges (i.e., *knowledge producers* as traditionally viewed: Campbell & Levin, 2012) to consider whether/how to mobilize knowledge as well. Universities' activities and knowledge claims have become more complicated in recent years, and accordingly we are seeing intensified efforts by universities to extend their organizations' research influence (Dudo, 2015; Yettick, 2015), as is the case with HGSE's Usable Knowledge (*Case #1*).

To summarize, then, it appears educational knowledge brokering by intermediaries in the US is presently crowded, complex, and varied, which we also argue has not commanded sufficient attention. This chapter thus is aimed at least to get us started in addressing this issue, in particular by closely examining three prominent entities which, while operating in different 'fields,' are aiming explicitly to mobilize research and other knowledge within educational practice.

Background: definitions

The key terms/definitions we adopt for this chapter—related to *knowledge mobilization (KMb), brokerage*, and *boundary objects*—align with those as presented in this book's opening chapter.

How do knowledge brokering intermediaries mobilize knowledge?

Recent scholarship regarding R-P brokering in education has provided initial insights into their structure and function, organizational features, roles and activities, and favorable attributes (see Farley-Ripple et al., 2017). Relative to structure, for instance, attention is drawn toward the way in which some individuals/entities can serve to cross R-P boundaries by filling *structural holes* (Burt, 2004) between them. Research has begun to clarify brokers' activities and attributes. Ward, House, and Hamer (2009) differentiate brokers relative to whether their activities emphasize knowledge management, linkage/exchange, and/or capacity building. Neal et al. (2015) drew from Gould and Fernandez's (1989) broker typology and identified all five types (e.g., gate- keeper, liaison) in US education. Finally, research within and beyond education has sought to identify effective brokers' attributes. Trustworthiness has been identified across multiple studies (see Farley-Ripple et al., 2017).

Perhaps most fundamental—but underexamined—is to consider how knowledge mobilizers can vary regarding what and whose knowledge they feature (Ward, 2017). This study thus follows Ward and colleagues (Ward, 2017; Ward et al., 2009), who stress that brokerage might include multiple types of evidence, generated by multiple groups. We also draw from Hubers and Poortman (2017), who suggest specific content shared should flow from the broker's unique vision. Both views cohere with Gibbons et al.'s (1994) and Nowotny, Scott, and Gibbons' (2003) concept of "Mode 2," used to highlight changing trends in knowledge production. In particular, Mode 2 suggests a shift from the traditional academic disciplinary–based linear modes of production (Mode 1) to one where knowledge is generated in an application context. Related to Mode 2 knowledge is the concept of socially robust knowledge. Gibbons (1999) suggests "socially robust" knowledge is that which has not simply originated from quality research but is also likely to be understood and socially accepted. Altogether, we expect that intermediaries' variations on what and whose knowledge stem from unique premises and visions. We further expect these differences will hold implications relative to brokers' reach, popularity, and ultimate success in moving knowledge to action.

Conceptual framework

For this study, we relied primarily upon Ward's (2017) KMb framework, and also analyzed selected study data in relation to Hubers and Poortman's (2017) three suggested principles for effective boundary crossing in education.

Ward's (2017) framework, developed from a cross-disciplinary analysis of existing KMb models, is organized around four questions: "Why is knowledge being mobilised? Whose knowledge is being mobilised? What type of knowledge is being mobilised? How is knowledge being mobilised?" (p. 1). Answers to these questions form 16 subcategories (see Table 1.1, presented in this book's opening chapter). Relative to what knowledge, for example, Ward identified three categories and found some models exclusively mobilize one type and others address a mixture: scientific/factual knowledge, technical knowledge, and practical wisdom (a mixture, we argue, means brokerage efforts are more likely to result in applicable knowledge). Regarding whose knowledge is mobilized, Ward discerned five categories and here as well noted that sometimes multiple groups are featured: professional knowledge producers, frontline practitioners, members of the public/service users, decision makers, and product/program developers. We argue knowledge is more likely to become socially robust when/if various stakeholders are drawn upon. Ward's analytic categories were anticipated to support understanding these entities, and any detected differences were anticipated to hold meaning (e.g., whom does x highlight as expert, and what type(s) of knowledge does x preference?).

To further address questions regarding *what* and *how* knowledge is mobilized, we drew from Hubers and Poortman (2017). Describing effective professional learning networks in education, these authors identified boundary crossing as essential and advanced three principles, framed as questions, for effective knowledge mobilization. They are summarized below:

1. Given the vision for boundary crossing, what content should be shared? For instance, should the knowledge pertain to a specific subject, programs or new approaches, policy, background information, and so on?
2. At what level of detail should knowledge be shared? Specifically, these authors note brokers often remain stuck at the level of informing teachers about certain activities or describing these activities' outcomes. The next level of mobilization, however, involves creating 'how-to' schemas and/or explaining underlying principles behind certain strategies (Why should you do it? Why should it work?). Ultimately, they argue, addressing both levels is superior.
3. What knowledge-sharing activities could be used? It is most effective to share knowledge via active personal engagement (and ideally the engagement of others in a risk free trial where the knowledge in question can be experimented with in a safe way). This type of activity is preferred because it gives educators a concrete idea about what is expected. However, it is scarcely employed because of the level of resources required to achieve change at scale. Besides providing active personal engagement, personal communication can be used (e.g., formal presentations, updates during a meeting, even lunch conversations). However, the most-often-chosen activity, yet least likely to be effective, is written communication (e.g., an e-mail or a staff newsletter item). Written text offers a relatively fast way to reach all colleagues, but colleagues will not always read it and/or may not understand it as intended.

We read behind this discussion an implicit acknowledgment that boundary objects (e.g., flexible artifacts functioning instead of or in addition to personal connections; Star & Griesemer, 1989) are fundamental to knowledge mobilization. Professionals need time to come to understand new knowledge being brokered, and artifacts can enable knowledge to move across temporal and spatial boundaries, providing them with opportunities to visit/revisit it.

Methods

A full description of the methods we used can be found in Malin et al. (2018). In summary, we treated the Marshall Memo, Edutopia, and Usable Knowledge as 'cases' of educational KMb, and therefore pursued a multiple case study design. In particular, this design enabled us to investigate the compare/contrast three entities representing theoretically diverse positions/fields. We selected 'prominent' cases that included explicit aims directed toward educational *practice* (vs. policy) and core activities including dissemination and/or exchange of at least some research and/or research-based knowledge. We strived to develop a robust and trustworthy chain of evidence regarding these entities' features in relation to our main research questions. As such, we drew from multiple sources of evidence and underwent processes of reflection, interpretation and challenge as a research team until we were comfortable with our findings and claims.

We proceeded as follows. First, we developed broad, shared understandings of each entities' features and activities (e.g., origins, missions/visions, staffing, social media presence/activity; Cooper, 2014; see Table 2.1). We did so primarily by reviewing publicly available information. We then built and analyzed a data set containing at least three consecutive months' material (e.g., press releases, summaries, Facebook posts, videos) that each entity created and/or hosted and shared, via social media or their products or newsletters. For Edutopia, which was distinctly active across multiple platforms, we focused on content shared via Facebook and YouTube. Identified materials were classified beginning with Ward's questions and categories. We also drew from Hubers and Poortman (2017) to evaluate entities' characteristic depth of content (e.g., informational vs. how-to schemas). To address how knowledge was shared first entailed classifying the entities' dominant approach relative to Ward's three analytic categories. We also drew from, then extended beyond, Hubers and Poortman (e.g., their distinction between written material and personal connections), noting distinguishing process features for each entity. Further analyzing the how question required further research (e.g., we globally appraised Edutopia's presence on Pinterest and studied Usable Knowledge's Twitter activities and following). Finally, we compared our findings against the entities' explicit vision/purpose statements to discern *why* they were mobilizing knowledge.

TABLE 2.1 The entities categorized according to five dimensions

Entity	Type	Origin	Target Audience	Size (Staff)	Social Media Presence
The Marshall Memo	For profit	2003	A,T	1	No
Edutopia	Non-profit	1991	T,P,A,S, Pub	25	Yes (High)
Usable Knowledge	Non-profit	2014	T,P,A,HE, Pol	2	Yes

Note. T=Teacher; P=Parent, A=Administrator, S=Student, Pub=Public, HE=Higher Education Professionals, Pol=Policy

Educational KMb: the cases

Usable Knowledge describes itself as "a trusted source of insight into what works in education—translating new research into easy-to-use stories and strategies for teachers, parents, K–12 leaders, higher ed professionals, and policy-makers" (President and Fellows of Harvard College, 2017). Its listed staff at HGSE are Bari Walsh, senior editor, and Leah Shafer, staff writer. All content, including written posts and short videos, are hosted at https://www.gse.harvard.edu/uk. Usable Knowledge also disseminates a free monthly e-newsletter to subscribers. It has a Twitter presence (@UKnowHGSE) with 9,042 followers as of September 7, 2017. Its Twitter profile indicates its affiliation and focus: "From Harvard University, connecting @HGSE research to practice." HGSE has a large social media presence (e.g., 150,000 Facebook and 123,000 Twitter followers) and frequently highlights Usable Knowledge and its contents. For instance, on July 14, 2017, HGSE retweeted Usable Knowledge and added, "Follow @UKnowHGSE for strategies on how to improve the school experience for students and teachers alike" (HGSE, 2017). In terms of the credibility of the case, the US News and World Report (2017) appraises HGSE as the nation's top-ranked education school. HGSE is part of Harvard University, an elite private higher education institution.

The **Marshall Memo** (2017a, n.p.), "A Weekly Round-Up of Important Ideas and Research in K–12 Education," has been owned/published since 2003 by Kim Marshall. He claims it is the third most circulated US educational publication, behind only *Educational Leadership* and *American Educator*. It is designed to "to keep principals, teachers, superintendents, and other educators very well-informed on current research and best practices" (The Marshall Memo, 2017a). Initially aimed at school principals, its readership and focus has grown (Malin & Paralkar, 2017). Marshall subscribes to 60+ publications and scans many articles to select "5–10 that have the greatest potential to improve teaching, leadership, and learning" (The Marshall Memo, 2017a). He develops summaries, providing e-links to original articles when possible. He also highlights a few quotes and usually concludes with some "short items." It is concise, intended to be readable within 20 minutes. It is delivered by email to subscribers. Marshall also now produces a podcast version. Subscribers also have access to a website member's only area that includes access to past articles and a searchable archive, which also allows subscribers to see items/articles Marshall has identified as 'classics.' An individual subscription costs $50 per year, and Marshall offers organizational pricing. There is currently no social media presence.

Marshall works semi-independently, with a part-time assistant and informal support by his spouse. He worked for decades in Boston (Massachusetts) Public Schools, including 15 years as principal. Now, he also operates as an educational consultant. He holds undergraduate, masters, and honorary doctorate degrees from Harvard.

Edutopia is "a comprehensive website and online community that increases knowledge, sharing, and adoption of what works in K–12 education" (George Lucas Educational Foundation [GLEF], 2017a). Six core educational principles/ strategies are emphasized: "project-based learning, comprehensive assessment, integrated studies, social and emotional learning, educational leadership and teacher development, and technology integration" (GLEF, 2017a). Edutopia initially focused on the use/application of technology within education, and although this remains a priority, the organization's foci have expanded (Edutopia, 2016). It is part of GLEF, a nonprofit foundation established in 1991 by filmmaker George Lucas (GLEF, 2017a). Lucas Education Research (LER), the other division of GLEF, is "dedicated to building evidence for what works in K–12 education" (GLEF, 2017a). GLEF funds research through LER. GLEF is governed by a ten-member board of directors, and its executive director (since 2010) is Cindy Johanson. Twenty core staff members make up the Edutopia team.

Since spring 2010, Edutopia has taken an online-only approach. Content can be accessed free of cost (Manzo, 2010) from its website (edutopia.org, initiated in 1994). Previously, it published a subscription-based magazine, *Edutopia* (2004–2010), and it developed and distributed instructional/pedagogical videos. The website contains abundant and organized material. From the site, one can also access YouTube videos it has created and could, until recently, participate in community forum discussions (Edutopia recently retired this online community, noticing comments/community were increasingly occurring on social media platforms; C. Johanson, personal communication, March 21, 2018). The website also describes how someone might write (e.g., a blog post) or provide multimedia that Edutopia would consider hosting. Edutopia's social media presence is large and broad, including on Facebook (over 1.1 million followers on September 6, 2017), Twitter (971,000 followers), Instagram (85,300 followers), Pinterest (104,000 followers), and YouTube (67,300 subscribers).

Mobilizing knowledge: types, sources, features, and reasons

Study findings are detailed feature by feature in Malin et al. (2018), whereas in this chapter they are presented holistically by entity. The aim here is to give readers an opportunity to grasp the processes, products, and activities of these different entities. It is not our intention to 'endorse' or 'critique'—in fact, we believe each entity has successful identified an informational and structural niche—though in discussion we do re-connect with the literature so as to draw out some implications and recommendations.

A principal unstated motivation for **Usable Knowledge**, it appeared, was to enhance the stature/reach of HGSE; this could be gleaned particularly from noting *whose* knowledge was being featured (primarily HGSE faculty/staff). Consequently, it emerged as having the most traditional orientation, insofar as the knowledge being shared (*what* knowledge) had primarily been produced through university-based research. Their activities were primarily focused on getting research—most often converted into brief, actionable 'research stories'—into the hands of front-line practitioners and others, like policymakers. The guiding logic appeared to be that good research (*what*), emanating from traditional knowledge producers (who), exists but does not frequently/naturally enough reach those positioned to apply it. For example, as stated HGSE dean James Ryan:

> After a day of managing a classroom, grading assignments, and preparing a. . .lesson plan, a teacher probably isn't going to have time to read a full academic paper. But he or she may have time to watch a brief video on assessments and discover a better approach to prepare his or her students for a test.
>
> *(Gilbert, 2014)*

Thus Usable Knowledge were aiming to fill a structural gap/hole between communities. Largely, then, their activities were tilted toward one-way dissemination methods, from research to practice.

We did, however, note some exceptions to this pattern. For example, through their attachment to HGSE's One and All project, which related to bullying prevention and the promotion of prosocial communities. Using a particular 'tag' on social media, HGSE and Usable Knowledge shared some strategies and guidance that originated outside Harvard. We believe this occurrence might illustrate the ways in which focusing on particular topics/strategies can serve to transform and deepen the content being developed or shared. Usable Knowledge is fairly active via Twitter (more than 2,800 tweets appear to have been made since 2014) and benefits from its attachment to HGSE, which has a large, multiplatform social media presence.

The Marshall Memo appeared to have been shaped by practitioner demands. Marshall focuses on getting (the best new) *research and other ideas* into educators' hands, assuming educators crave such information but have insufficient time and access to otherwise attain it. Important to the memo's success, then, is subscribers' sense that he is comprehensively searching and selecting useful materials (Malin & Paralkar, 2017). Also, he has organized accumulated memo material into a searchable archive, a feature many subscribers appreciate (Malin & Paralkar, 2017). Marshall's activities accordingly also gear toward one-way dissemination (how) but with distinctly broad search/selection, relative to both whose and what knowledge aspects.

The Marshall Memo featured a mix of knowledge 'donors,' with about 50% of highlighted/summarized material having been authored/co-authored by academics or other researchers, and nearly 25% by current or former frontline practitioners. Marshall also featured the work of journalists or editors relatively frequently (12.9% education-specific, 7.8% non-specific). Related, in terms of *what* knowledge, Marshall liberally addressed all types, with none being clearly dominant and with much of his selected material itself being 'integrated' in nature (e.g., the original material contained scientific/factual knowledge, technical knowledge, *and* practical wisdom). He is especially partial to integrative, broad-spanning (vs. narrowly focused) articles—that is, he favors "the pulled together stuff" while being less taken by empirical articles, which "tend to be too narrow" (as quoted in Malin & Paralkar, 2017, p. 9). These decisions, we interpret, relate to his desire to select and share socially robust knowledge. Malin and Paralkar (2017) provide further information and insights about Mr. Marshall's selection and translation processes and overall reasoning, and provides an indication of the meaning of the memo to subscribing educators, should readers wish to learn more.

Edutopia, in marked contrast, is predominately user driven—although centrally curated—with most content developed by (articles) or heavily featuring (videos) frontline practitioners and routinely sparking substantial social media activity. Edutopia primarily shared knowledge produced by educators (e.g., 80% of reviewed YouTube videos featured educators demonstrating and describing particular practices/processes). Likewise, more than 50% of the written works (e.g., blog posts) that we analyzed were written by educators, with the next two largest categories being represented by Edutopia staff or contractors (about 17%) and traditional knowledge producers (e.g., professors; about 15%). We viewed these results as underscoring educators' key roles within the Edutopia community in terms of knowledge and meaning construction. Edutopia's material tended to preference technical knowledge but also frequently highlighted practical wisdom. For example, their videos included first-person accounts regarding *why* (rationale: from front-line practitioners) and *how* (implementation/process) to engage in particular practices. Scientific/factual knowledge was present but in secondary position. For example, "Metrics of Success" are presented at the end of "Schools That Work" YouTube videos. Likewise, research summaries related to each core strategy are housed on the Edutopia website for interested parties to review, but they are not promoted as extensively as are other materials posted there.

Although educators predominated, we also saw Edutopia as providing a platform that could serve to increase connection-making across stakeholder groups (Ward, 2017). For instance, university-based researchers, such as Maurice Elias, have utilized the Edutopia platform to share their research-based ideas. A post Elias (2016) wrote titled "How Do We Measure Social and Emotional Learning?" has been shared via social media nearly 8,000 times, which vastly exceeds the attention researchers typically enjoy when writing solely in traditional scholarly outlets. As another example, professor Nell Duke (2016) wrote, "What Doesn't Work: Literacy Practices We Should Abandon," a blog post that has been shared more than 57,000 times and was featured in Marshall Memo 642. Edutopia's social media reach shrouds the others', as noted. Also, its embrace of nonwritten materials (e.g., videos, imagery) shows some entities have moved beyond written communication and its pitfalls (Hubers & Poortman, 2017). Their ability to do so relates partially to their elevated human resource capacity (e.g., video/production specialists on staff).

We believe Edutopia's user-driven nature substantially explains both its popularity and its abilities to continually evolve. Edutopia, we concluded, ultimately aims to inspire educators to pursue particular strategies and to spread relevant examples and inspiration (e.g., how and why to do x; Hubers & Poortman, 2017). It is thus focused on addressing a different structural hole, related to the spread of ideas and strategies especially, although not exclusively, from educator to educator. It has accordingly embraced a model in which educators are positioned as experts in their own right, and its platforms are used to mobilize knowledge educators create. Edutopia appears to embrace the idea that education must continue to evolve and progress, which also means certain educators with new ideas and ways of doing are at a premium. They can be knowledge creators, producing evidence from implementation and demonstrating new and potentially promising areas of inquiry.

Discussion

In this chapter, we have described an analysis of three US-based KMb intermediaries relative to why and how they mobilized knowledge and what and whose knowledge they featured. We found these entities to vary substantially, and we also now suggest they reveal two distinctive types of brokerage. In this discussion, we reflect further on these types, and we suggest implications and future directions.

First, we offer that this study underscores the importance of understanding mobilizers' driving purposes (e.g., see Davies et al., 2015). While each of these entities aspired roughly toward common ends—to change educators' practices and behaviors (Ward, 2017)—we also identified distinct background motivations and distinct R-P connection problems (or structural holes) each sought to address. These nuances were somewhat predictable based on these entities' different social field positions (Anderson et al., 2017) and were key to understanding their overall KMb programs, as Farley-Ripple and colleagues (2017) had suggested.

As noted previously, we take the position that each of these entities has accurately identified specific informational niches, as the 'problem' of connecting research and practice is a complex and many-sided one. We also now suggest Edutopia's model is worthy of some further reflection here, as it may serve as a stimulus to push our thinking regarding R-P connections. Research–practice partnerships (RPPs; see Coburn & Penuel, 2016, and Chapter 11 of this volume), for instance, are proliferating, and they are forward-looking and can be powerful. However, too often embedded even within contemporary discussions about RPPs may be assumptions that they are primarily a means to help educators more readily access and use evidence produced by researchers (e.g., a one-way road; see Farrell, 2017). By contrast, two-way partnerships (as with Edutopia when at its best, we offer) can emerge, in which educators are not mere consumers of research (Anderson, Herr, & Nihlen, 1994; Brown, 2014) but rather are active knowledge creators, leading thinkers, expert identifiers of problems (and productive, energizing trends) of practice, and so on. In such partnerships, traditional knowledge producers presumably need to assume a different stance or position—one that recognizes and honors the creative potential of such arrangements and seeks to participate and add value within them. For instance, researchers could partner with educators to design and test promising new strategies, write compelling articles regarding how their theories or approaches might usefully fine-tune educators' thoughts or actions and vice versa (and so on). In such arrangements, though, they would no longer occupy privileged positions and might instead need to compete with various others for attention, credibility, and so on. However, insofar as they were able to secure productive entry into the conversation, they would be serving to strengthen R-P connections. For one, by participating in these conversations, researchers presumably would become more in touch with contemporary problems and trends, and could consider tuning their subsequent research activities accordingly.

This study supports and adds to Farley-Ripple and colleagues' (2017) conceptualization of brokerage in education as dynamic, complex, and diverse. This study tentatively identifies two distinctive types of brokerage: One that is primarily one-way in nature, enabling the communication of research (and/or other) knowledge to practice communities, and another is two-way, enabling its user community to document challenges and describe emerging trends in education practice. As Davies et al. (2015) summarized, relational and interactive exchanges are increasingly understood as required for knowledge to flow and influence practice. Edutopia thus demonstrates a vast menu of innovative approaches and products that might be emulated by others. At the same time, we concur with Ward (2017) that various KMb approaches can be justifiable depending on one's specific purposes, resources, and so on.

It is also important to note that knowledge brokering (like research production) is not neutral. Brokers must make choices relative to what to feature, and they cannot have full knowledge of all that exists. This study yielded insights into these choices, including how they flow from distinct motivations and how they affect both brokered products and processes. Notwithstanding, recipients of brokered knowledge are not passive consumers. If brokered knowledge is not practically applicable (i.e., Mode 2) and/or does not cohere with professional realities (i.e., lacking socially robustness), it will likely be ignored. Moreover, even trustworthy Mode 2 knowledge will not necessarily be adopted carte blanche. Since the late Carol Weiss's seminal work in the 1970s, approaches to using research to inform educational practice have broadly been categorized as having either instrumental or conceptual goals (see Weiss, 1980, 1982). The former suggests a direct link can occur between research findings and action, and the latter suggests research typically guides thinking and will be considered alongside other evidence. Grounded in the argument that conceptual research use is more likely and realistic than instrumental research use (e.g., see Brown et al., 2017), it seems likely that brokered knowledge will only ever inform the decisions of educators rather than steer them directly. As such, brokered knowledge will necessarily be combined by educators with practical and contextual knowledge as it is used.

This study's findings hold implications for educators, intermediaries, and scholars. For educators, this study provides a comparative examination of three intermediaries with large followings and may provide insights into how such entities can be leveraged to expand one's connections to ideas and to enhance practice. Meanwhile, it may be helpful to reflect on the different approaches that are under way and upon the distinct ways practicing educators are being positioned. For existing or prospective mobilizers, this study provides a clear view of the choices that are made and includes description of several innovative practices that might be adopted or adjusted. For scholars, this study provides further insight into intermediaries' vital and varied functions in education. Especially, it is hoped that scholars will continue to investigate the ways in which intermediaries are aiming to fill structural holes and, especially, how, why, and to what effect they are creating boundary objects to join people—spanning both research and practice—and their professionally relevant ideas.

Note

1 This chapter provides a condensed summary of the following article, which is available open-access via *AERA Open*: Malin, J. R., Brown, C., & Trubceac, A. S. (2018). Going for broke: A multiple-case study of brokerage in education. *AERA Open, 4*(2), 2333858418769297.

References

Anderson, G., De La Cruz, P., & López, A. (2017). New governance and new knowledge brokers: Think tanks and universities as boundary organizations. *Peabody Journal of Education, 92*(1), 4–15.

Anderson, G. L., Herr, K., & Nihlen, A. S. (1994). *Studying your own school*. Thousand Oaks, CA: Corwin.

Brown, C. (2014). *Evidence informed policy and practice in education: a sociological grounding*. London: Bloomsbury.

Brown, C., Schildkamp, K. & Hubers, M. (2017). Combining the best of two worlds: A conceptual proposal for evidence-informed school improvement. *Educational Research, 59*(2), 154–172.

Burt, R. (2004). Structural holes and good ideas. *American Journal of Sociology, 110*(2), 349–399.

Campbell, C., & Levin, B. (2012). Developing knowledge mobilisation to challenge educational disadvantage and inform effective practices in England (Discussion Paper).

Coburn, C. E., & Penuel, W. R. (2016). Research–practice partnerships in education: Outcomes, dynamics, and open questions. *Educational Researcher, 45*(1), 48–54.

Cooper, A. (2014). Knowledge mobilisation in education across Canada: A cross-case analysis of 44 research brokering organisations. *Evidence & Policy, 10*(1), 29–59. https://doi.org/10.1332/174426413X662806

Davies, H. T., Powell, A. E., & Nutley, S. M. (2015). Mobilising knowledge to improve UK health care: Learning from other countries and other sectors—a multimethod mapping study. *Health Services and Delivery Research 2015, 3*(27).

Dudo, A. (2015). Scientists, the media, and the public communication of science. *Sociology Compass, 9*(9), 761–775.

Duke, N. K. (2016). What doesn't work: Literacy practices we should abandon [Blog post]. Retrieved from https://www.edutopia.org/blog/literacy-practices-we-should-abandon-nell-k-duke

Edutopia. (2016). Celebrating 25 years of what works in education [Video file]. Retrieved from https://www.youtube.com/watch?v=8vDuGyToRoQ

Elias, M. J. (2016). How do we measure social and emotional learning? [Blog post]. Retrieved from https://www.edutopia.org/blogs/how-do-we-measure-sel-maurice-elias

Farley-Ripple, E., Tilley, K., & Tise, J. (2017). Brokerage and the research–practice gap: A theoretical and empirical examination. Paper presented at the 2017 annual meeting of the American Educational Research Association.

Farrell, C. (2017, September 4). Moving beyond building practitioner capacity to mutual learning in research–practice partnerships. *Education Week*. Retrieved from http://blogs.edweek.org/

George Lucas Educational Foundation (GLEF) (2017a). *About us*. Retrieved from https://www.edutopia.org/about

George Lucas Educational Foundation (GLEF) (2017b). *Meet the team*. Retrieved from Goldacre, B. (2013) *Building evidence into education*. Retrieved from https://www.gov.uk/government/news/buildingevidence-into-education

Gibbons, M., Limoges, C., Nowotny, H., Schwartzman, S., Scott, P., & Trow, M. (1994). *The new production of knowledge: The dynamics of science and research in contemporary societies*. Thousand Oaks, CA: Sage.

Gibbons, M. (1999). Science's new social contract with society. *Nature, 402*, C81–C84.

Gilbert, C. H. (2014, September 12). Ed school launches Usable Knowledge project. *The Harvard Crimson*. Retrieved from http://www.thecrimson.com/article/2014/9/12/GSE-usable-knowledge-launch/

Gould, R. V., & Fernandez, R. M. (1989). Structures of mediation: A formal approach to brokerage in transaction networks. *Sociological Methodology, 19*, 89–126.

Harvard Graduate School of Education [HGSE]. (2017, July 14). Follow @UKnowHGSE for strategies on how to improve the school experience for students and teachers alike. Retrieved from twitter.com/hgse

Hubers, M. D., & Poortman, C. L. (2017). Establishing sustainable school improvement through Professional Learning Networks. In C. Brown & C. Poortman (Eds.), *Networks for learning: Effective collaboration for teacher, school and system improvement* (pp. 194–204). London, UK: Routledge.

Louis, K. S. (2016). Research use? Knowledge use? School improvement? Personal reflections on the last 40 years . . . [blog post]. Retrieved from http://www.research4schools.org/blog-post/research-use-knowledge-use-school-improvement-personal-reflections-last-40-years/

Malin, J. R., Brown, C., & Trubceac, A. S. (2018). Going for broke: A multiple-case study of brokerage in education. *AERA Open, 4*(2), 2332858418769297.

Malin, J. R., & Paralkar, V. (2017). Educational knowledge brokerage and mobilization: The Marshall Memo case. *International Journal of Education Policy and Leadership, 12*(7), 1–20.

Manzo, K. K. (2010). Edutopia to go online-only: Chen steps down as foundation head. *Education Week, 29*(21), 4–5.

Marshall Memo LLC (2017a). *The Marshall Memo*. Retrieved from https://marshallmemo.com

Marshall Memo LLC (2017b). *Why the Marshall Memo?* Retrieved from https://marshallmemo.com/why.php

Neal, J. W., Neal, Z. P., Kornbluh, M., Mills, K. J., & Lawlor, J. A. (2015). Brokering the research–practice gap: A typology. *American Journal of Community Psychology, 56*, 422–435.

Nowotny, H., Scott, P., & Gibbons, M. (2003). Introduction. 'Mode 2' revisited: The new production of knowledge. *Minerva, 41*(3), 179–194.

Star, S. L., & Griesemer, J. R. (1989). Institutional ecology, "translations" and boundary objects: Amateurs and professionals in Berkeley's Museum of Vertebrate Zoology, 1907–39. *Social Studies of Science, 19*(3), 387–420.

US News and World Report . (2017). 2018 best education schools. Retrieved from https://www.usnews.com/best-graduate-schools/top-education-schools

Ward, V. (2017). Why, whose, what and how? A framework for knowledge mobilisers. *Evidence & Policy*, 13(3), 477–497.

Ward, V., House, A., & Hamer, S. (2009). Knowledge brokering: The missing link in the evidence to action chain? *Evidence & Policy*, 5(3), 267–279.

Weiss, C. (1980). Knowledge creep and decision accretion. *Knowledge: Creation, Diffusion, Utilisation*, 1(3), 381–404.

Weiss, C. (1982). Research in the context of diffuse decision making. *Journal of Higher Education*, 53(6), 619–639.

Yettick, H. (2015). One small droplet: News media coverage of peer-reviewed and university-based education research and academic expertise. *Educational Researcher*, 44(3), 173–184.

3

PUSH AND PULL ON TWITTER

How school leaders use Twitter for knowledge brokering

Jayson W. Richardson, Nicholas J. Sauers, Vincent Cho, and John Eric M. Lingat

Educational leaders often serve as knowledge brokers for the students, teachers, families, and communities they serve. For example, building and district leaders may communicate information via staff meetings, newsletters, emails, or other announcements. However, internet communications technologies generally, and social media specifically, have changed the landscape of this knowledge brokering. Today, K-12 school leaders often leverage new media platforms, such as Twitter, to communicate with various constituencies. Topics of discussion may include, but are not limited to, practices, policies, research, and personal reflections (Carpenter & Krutka, 2014; Cho, 2016; Sauers & Richardson, 2015). This information sharing may also span various social circles, locally, nationally, or even internationally.

This chapter synthesizes the empirical literature relating to K-12 school leaders' uses of Twitter, focusing especially on leaders' roles as knowledge brokers in online communities of practice (see Cho & Jimerson, 2017; Ricoy & Feliz, 2016; Sauers & Richardson, 2015). It is important to understand social media use among school leaders because social isolation may adversely affect their performance (see Dussault & Thibodeau, 1997) and because social media are intended to foster interpersonal connections and communication. Indeed, school leaders who have access to the wisdom of others may be better able to garner and organize school resources, embody professional values, and handle the stresses of their positions (Leana, 2011; Peterson, 2002; Tirozzi, 2002). As such, this chapter opens the dialogue about how K-12 leaders might leverage or benefit from social media. We do this by looking at the research through the lens of the Professional Standards for Educational Leaders (PSEL) (National Policy Board Educational Administration, 2015). The PSEL are school leadership standards that are broadly adopted by many preparatory programs within the United States. Although the PSEL do not focus explicitly on social media use, for us, they served as a useful framework for envisioning how Twitter might or might not benefit school leaders' who broker knowledge and often serve as boundary spanners (as detailed in the opening chapter of the book). The findings herein speak broadly to implications on practice and research in a variety of areas in which brokering and mobilizing knowledge may be important.

A snapshot of Twitter use

Pat Lee, recently promoted to principal, looks over his notes from an education leadership convention and is filled with both excitement and anxiety. Pat wants to share and talk more about the recent session. Without the instructional leadership team present, it's harder to evaluate ideas and to trace out what next steps might be needed at the school. During a short break, Pat passes the time by strolling through his feed on Twitter, seeing updates from some friends and family.

But Pat's eagerness to discuss takeaways from the conference increases and the convention hashtag comes to mind. After searching for #Convention2018, Pat sees an active online discussion about the very session that has sparked his imagination: issues of implementation, barriers to consider, and success stories each appear on his Twitter feed. Other attendees are already live-tweeting from the next session, connecting ideas throughout the day and suggesting resources that might inform future conversations. Pat responds by thanking some of those posting as well as retweeting his favorite contributions. Almost immediately, Pat sees that his followers, which include teachers from the school, parents from the school, families, and colleagues, are noticing and appreciating his knowledge-sharing. At the same time, Pat notices that other school leaders are seeing his contributions and joining his list of followers.

Walking into the next session, Pat realizes that one of these new followers is sitting nearby. They strike up a conversation and realize that both are first-year principals. They both push and pull knowledge by comparing notes about the conference as well as sharing their work experiences. Within the span of only a few minutes, Pat's sense of connection to a pool of shared knowledge and to colleagues, online and offline, has increased.

Although fictionalized, the preceding vignette has elements that may resonate with many school leaders today. For example, Twitter and other social media platforms have become woven into the personal and professional lives of many – sometimes in ways that blur the traditional boundaries among those spheres. Twitter, seemingly ubiquitous since its establishment in 2006, currently hosts over 69 million active users in the United States alone as of the first quarter of 2018 (Statista, 2018). To some, Twitter might seem to be a form of entertainment or a tool for distraction. For others, it is a vital way to connect with others around mutual interests. For example, Twitter helped to promote a campaign known as the Ice Bucket Challenge, raising $115 million in one summer while also increasing awareness about amyotrophic lateral sclerosis (ALS Association, 2018). Discussing Twitter's role in the Arab Spring, Richardson and Brantmeier (2012) reported that "the world came to learn how social networks could be used for more than chatting with friends; they could be used to initiate massive global, collaborative efforts" (p. 257). Other social and political movements (e.g., Black Lives Matter, the #MeToo movement, #MAGA) have further demonstrated the potential of Twitter to distribute information and mobilize activism. As educators come to engage with others on Twitter, the question thus becomes how Twitter use might lead to productive knowledge sharing, knowledge utilization, and collaboration.

The push and pull of Twitter

Reflecting on Principal Lee from our vignette above, Pat can be understood as a leader and a learner as well as a knowledge broker. Pat is charged with both *pushing* out ideas and information to teachers or other stakeholders, as well as *pulling* those ideas from various pools of knowledge. As such, Pat, like many technology curious educational leaders, recognized that social media tools such as Twitter are important for knowledge brokering (McLeod, Richardson, & Sauers, 2015; Richardson & Sterrett, 2018; Sauers, Richardson, & McLeod, 2015). But for Pat, it is also neither clear nor obvious how to best apply tools like Twitter toward such aims.

In everyday life, it is not unusual to turn toward internet resources for advice and recommendations—be that finding a dinner venue, finding a job, or devising a classroom lesson plan. Twitter's unique functionalities, however, may especially make it conducive to activities commonly associated with communities of practice. For example, educators like Principal Lee might find that Twitter's public nature makes it possible for colleagues from various contexts (even beyond the school and organizational boundaries) to connect to and follow one another. This *boundary crossing*, as defined in Chapter 1, may be based on affinity or interests. These realities allow leaders like Principal Lee to push and pull (i.e., mobilize) knowledge relevant to their goals and challenges relating to school improvement. School leaders are thus knowledge brokers who can use these push–pull features to create and distill resources, to convene partnerships, and support practitioners by exchanging, transforming, or combining information even across communities that may not regularly interact.

As Perines (2016) posited, the goal of knowledge mobilization is to inspire progress and inquiry. In this vein, Twitter has the potential to help users serve as knowledge brokers by promoting the rapid, broad distribution of ideas, including the creation of new ideas via discourse and debate. For example, Paskevicius, Veletsianos, and Kimmons (2018) studied discussions of openness (e.g., open educational resources, open pedagogy, and open source software) on Twitter. Their data consisted of 178,304 tweets and involved 23,061 users and covered an exchange of ideas and content on an international scale. Although most tweets analyzed were posted by users in the United States, they also included users from around the globe including the United Kingdom, Germany, Canada, and Spain. It is thus not uncommon for a multitude of voices, organizations, and disparate groups of stakeholders to engage in knowledge sharing and creation through Twitter (Sauers & Richardson, 2015). Via Twitter, one can not only lurk but also to push out ideas about what is and what could be, in ways that would not be possible solely through face-to-face exchanges (e.g., Twitter chats hosted by Edutopia, described in Chapter 2).

Twitter may also facilitate knowledge brokerage, both online and offline, within schools. As Meyer (2010) put forward, knowledge brokerage involves a range of activities which may include "the identification and localization of knowledge, the redistribution and dissemination of knowledge, and the rescaling and transformation of this knowledge" (p. 120). At a basic level, users can publish updates, query or follow particular topics, share ("retweet"), or comment on the posts of others (Gao, Luo, & Zhang, 2012). In this way, individuals who might not normally connect could be exposed to, and exchange, new ideas. For example, a principal who might be dissatisfied with her school's discipline practices might ask Twitter peers for advice, learn about hashtags devoted to restorative justice or positive behavioral interventions, and then engage in debates or organized chats about that topic. This is done all while reading, tweeting, and retweeting knowledge about the topic and finding new pools of experts or colleagues who might be knowledgeable about such matters. A major advantage of engaging in such activities via Twitter is that new connections with other users are easily forged. A principal could also choose to broker knowledge within their respective school. For example, principals who learn about effective classroom practices via Twitter have been found to share ideas and resources with their teachers, such as via email or other communication outlets (Cho, 2016). Twitter is hence the medium of brokerage as it facilitates knowledge mobilization.

Altogether, such activities harken to the notion of professional learning communities (DuFour, Eaker, & DuFour, 2005; Van Lare & Brazer, 2013). In professional learning communities, school leaders can improve their practice, troubleshoot issues, and gather (i.e., pull) knowledge from others. Such communities may benefit professional and school effectiveness (Rieckhoff & Larsen, 2012) as well as student learning (Leithwood & Riehl, 2003). On Twitter, educators can connect to each other in an ad hoc fashion, as well as engage in moderated, self-organized 'chats' with each other about problems of practice (Carpenter & Krutka, 2014). For example, #SATchat is organized and moderated by practicing educational leaders. Participants come together on Saturday mornings to discuss a variety of topics related to their work.

Even in face-to-face environments, there is still much research to be done on how best to design or organize professional learning communities. For example, Marsh, Bertrand, and Huguet (2015) described how effective professional learning communities are not simply about having educators grouped by subject. These learning communities facilitate learning by providing those groups with appropriate knowledge resources, including people who have direct and specific expertise about the matters at hand. Thus, although Twitter affords ad hoc and organized access to other leaders, it is yet unknown how to ensure that such interactions are both informed by the appropriate experts and leveraged into everyday practice (Cho, 2016). Until recently, educational researchers have only minimally addressed these school technology leadership topics, especially as it relates to the use of platforms such as Twitter (McLeod & Richardson, 2011; Richardson, Bathon, Flora,

& Lewis, 2012). Nevertheless, there has been a call for educational intermediaries (like school leaders who are active on Twitter) to serve as brokers to translate research into practice (Malin, Brown, & St. Trubceac, 2018).

Leveraging the professional educational leadership standards through Twitter

In the preceding pages, we provided a snapshot of some of the ways in which educators might distribute and engage in knowledge brokering via Twitter. In what follows, we juxtapose the use of Twitter with the ten Professional Standards for Education Leaders (PSEL) (National Policy Board Educational Administration, 2015). Again, these standards have been adopted by many leadership preparation programs in the United States. Doing so provides us with insight regarding how leaders' brokering practices on social media could contribute to effective schooling and administration.

Knowledge brokering for building community

On Twitter, educational leaders find ways to engage with each other and sometimes support or supplement their online interactions with get-togethers at conferences or local venues (Cho & Snodgrass Rangel, 2016). Analyses of leaders' tweets suggest that leaders may broker knowledge about various topics amongst diverse users and audiences. Those topics might range from technology use, to leadership, to resources or knowledge gained at conferences (Sauers & Richardson, 2015) [Standard 2; Standard 9]. At the same time, this knowledge sharing is interspersed with interpersonal exchanges or "chit chat," thus suggesting the importance of developing and maintaining social ties among those audiences. Indeed, Cho (2016) reported how leaders on Twitter felt that its use helped reduce their sense of isolation, providing them with a sense of community, both online and offline. Research detailing what school leaders share on Twitter aligns with the knowledge mobilization framework (Ward, 2017) of the book where one question asked is 'what type of knowledge is being shared?'

Educational leaders are also tasked with organizing people around shared goals. Standard 1 of PSEL holds that as part of their places in the community, school leaders must be able to "develop, advocate, and enact a shared mission, vision, and core values of high-quality education and academic success and well-being of each student" (National Policy Board for Educational Administration, 2015, p. 9). Additionally, Standard 8 places an importance on meaningfully engaging with families and the community. One way for leaders to build community and increase momentum toward shared goals is to disseminate pertinent information to local stakeholders and vice versa. This act aligns the framework of the book where Ward's (2017) notion of why knowledge is being shared. As an example, Cho (2016) found that administrators frequently tweeted announcements about school events, online activities, and community development initiatives. These kinds of tweets have the potential to develop coherent narratives within the local community about a school and what it finds important or inspiring.

Knowledge brokering for building professional capacity of others

Many educational leaders use Twitter to share information about educational practices and reforms (e.g., research, or instructional innovations). Specifically, an exchange of information through link sharing and direct requests may help educational leaders leverage Twitter to "provide opportunities for collaborative examination of practice, collegial feedback, and collective learning," as stated in Standard 7 of the PSEL (National Policy Board for Educational Administration, 2015, p. 15). These acts also foster professional norms (Standard 2). K-12 educational leaders are faced with the task of understanding a wide knowledge base associated with leadership, change, and instruction. Through Twitter, leaders have access to a broad pool of experts and expertise, all in real time (Cho, 2016) [Standard 1; Standard 6].

PSEL promotes the expectation that school leaders will "develop and support intellectually rigorous and coherent systems of curriculum, instruction, and assessment to promote each student's academic success and well-being" (National Policy Board for Educational Administration, 2015, p. 12). Recent research suggests that educators on Twitter consider it an important avenue for professional learning (Carpenter & Krutka, 2014) and that school leaders have especially embraced the opportunity to share and learn about effective instructional practices (Cho, 2016; Sauers & Richardson, 2015). The leaders in these studies were interested not only in the effective use and integration of educational technologies but also other issues relating to school improvements, such as educational policies and managing changes (see Carpenter & Krutka, 2014; Cho, 2016; Sauers & Richardson, 2015). Altogether, these actions speak directly to Standards 4, 7, and 10.

Within the practitioner community, resource sharing is robust. For example, Cho and Snodgrass Rangel (2016) interviewed school leaders, some of whom considered themselves "Twittervangelists." These are people who championed Twitter among their colleagues as a space to share resources and gather information. Some school leaders found the web-based exchange to have an energizing effect on real settings (i.e., classrooms, schools) and promoted collaborative conversations about professional content (i.e., engagement, grade-level content). As educational leaders become more comfortable in their roles as 21st century leaders, the next logical step is to broker knowledge amongst their online and offline communities, including knowledge about cutting edge practices [Standard 7].

Knowledge brokering for their own professional learning

Standard 6 of the PSEL emphasizes leaders' responsibility to "tend to their own learning and effectiveness through reflection, study, and improvement" (National Policy Board for Educational Administration, 2015, p. 14). As school leaders engage in the push and pull of knowledge brokering, ranging from integration to implementation, Twitter conversations can foster a sense of community and sense of capacity that educational leaders need. Hitchcock and Young (2016) found that school leaders "were able to see past the ephemeral nature of Twitter to uncover valuable insights and connect with others" (p. 465). This is important given that the authors also noted the need for leaders to develop a "professional identity in a connected learning environment" (p. 465).

Knowledge brokering through Twitter can expand one's position of being an educational leader while also growing the profession. The journey of developing as a leader is often isolating, sometimes assuaged via district meetings or professional conferences with like peers. But often, leaders do not have a peer colleague to engage with for support or demonstrate their vulnerability. With the capabilities of real-time interactions on Twitter, the push and pull of this tool are invaluable to school leaders. In their literature review of microblogging in education, Gao et al. (2012) found that using Twitter engaged community participation, expanded professional collaboration, and fostered reflective practices. More specific to educational leadership, Cho (2016) found that participating in Twitter increased educational leaders' sense of belonging, thus reducing isolation and fostering "a sense of specialness" (p. 346). These are each a components of strong leadership development that are in line with Standard 10 of the PSEL given that educational leaders can leverage these Twitter conversations. By being a broker of knowledge in this way, educational leaders can foster professional norms [Standard 2] while building the professional capacity of self and others [Standard 6].

Sauers and Richardson (2015) found that most tweets by educational leaders included a URL, @, #, or RT which are indicators of acts of knowledge brokering. In addition to pushing information to other leaders, Twitter is a prime place for educational leaders to pull knowledge to enhance their own practice. Veletsianos and Kimmons (2016) discussed the ways educational researchers share resources through Twitter and suggested that as partners in education, K–12 leaders should have academic researchers in their Twitter networks, so that the practice of translation between the two can be conveniently facilitated. Shah and Cox (2017) found that academics used Twitter to develop a learning community and to disseminate and monitor research. Participants in their qualitative study communicated that "Twitter was a valued source of information, both academic and relating to general news and personal interest" (p. 103). Understanding that they can be part of the push and pull that researchers engage in, leaders can take advantage of the fact that they are inhabiting the same virtual space as their academic colleagues.

Knowledge mobilization for collaboration

In addition, communication through Twitter can enhance collaboration between local organizations that would otherwise function in isolation such as discussions around scheduling, transportation, or finance. Standard 8 of the PSEL states that effective leaders engage in regular and open discussions with families and the community. By using Twitter, not only do educational leaders maintain their presence, they act as an advocate for the needs of the community, as well as a bullhorn for the public celebration of the community's accomplishments. Through this social media platform, knowledge can be brokered through two-way communication, helping educational leaders maintain the mission, vision, and values of the community they serve, as well as engage the community in a meaningful way. This push and pull of community engagement through Twitter, knowledge is brokered in a way that builds partnerships between the schools and their wide social network. This boundary crossing can help eliminate the void in communication that often happens between different communities.

Cho (2016) found that school leaders use Twitter to interact with others through greetings (e.g., thank you, congratulations, you're welcome) and sharing their personal interests (e.g., sports teams, music, family). Likewise, Sauers and Richardson (2015) found that thoughts, opinions, and solutions were shared between colleagues serving in leadership roles. Leaders did this through the encouragement of others, resource sharing, and developing a sense of community.

Considering the benefits, drawbacks, and implications of Twitter

The research highlighted in this chapter captures many of the benefits that Twitter offers school leaders. Table 3.1 provides a crosswalk between the PSEL and prior research. It is clear that K-12 school leaders are using Twitter to build community, increase professional capacity, foster their own professional learning, and learn collaboratively.

As much as Table 3.1 highlights how school leaders' actions on Twitter might align with professional standards, it also reveals glaring gaps. Yet to be evidenced in research are the standards relating to cultural responsiveness [Standard 3] and promoting a community of care and support for students [Standard 5]. There may be several possible reasons for this. First, and most simplistically, it may be that researchers have not kept pace with leaders' online practices. For example, although it is striking that leaders have not been commonly found to promote issues of equity and social justice online, that is not to say that some leaders, perhaps operating in pockets or using hashtags focused more explicitly on such topics, are not doing so. A second potential explanation is that leaders might not feel that Twitter is best suited for engaging in conversations that speak to these standards. Returning to the example of communicating about equity and social justice, it is possible that such tweets could touch upon local hot-button topics. As such, some leaders might find themselves self-censoring their activities to conform to the expectations of audiences (Cho & Jimerson, 2017). If such silence does exist, then it may be necessary for the district and other local leaders to foreground the importance of equity (Rorrer, Skrla, & Scheurich, 2008), thus making it safe for leaders to communicate about reforms vital to the well-being of students and schools.

TABLE 3.1 Leadership standards, Twitter practices, and supporting research

PSEL Standard	Practice	Research on Educational Leaders
Standard 1: Mission, Vision, and Core Values	• Usually monologic • Communicate details about the school • Announce community development initiatives	Cho (2016) Tang and Hew (2016)
Standard 2: Ethics and Professional Norms	• Develop a digital social identity • Image management • Influence the local and greater communities	Cho (2016) Cho & Snodgrass Rangle (2016) Sauers & Richardson (2015) Wang, Sauers, & Richardson (2016)
Standard 3: Equity and Cultural Responsiveness	• Advocate for equity and fairness • Promote diversity and cultural responsiveness	
Standard 4: Curriculum, Instruction and Assessment	• Discuss instructional uses instead of troubleshooting technology • Use hashtags to categorize by topic • Integrate Twitter to engage students	Carpenter & Krutka (2014) Manca & Ranieri (2017) Sauers & Richardson (2015) Tang and Hew (2016)
Standard 5: Community of Care and Support for Students	• Celebrate student engagement • Post information about systems of support for students • Promote stakeholder relationships	
Standard 6: Professional Capacity of School Personnel	• Engage in canonical and non-canonical exchanges • Create a sense of community and expertise • Use as a backchannel for conference discussion	Carpenter & Krutka (2014) Cho (2016)
Standard 7: Professional Standard Community for Teachers and Staff	• Share information about educational practices and reforms (e.g., new policies, research, instructional innovations) • Foster and engage in team collaboration • Develop a sense of capacity • Reduce isolation	Carpenter & Krutka (2014) Cho (2016) Cho & Snodgrass Rangle (2016) Kimmons, Carpenter, Veletsianos, & Krutka (2018) Sauers & Richardson (2015)

(continued)

TABLE 3.1 *(continued)*

PSEL Standard	Practice	Research on Educational Leaders
Standard 8: Meaningful Engagement of Families and Community	• Most likely dialogic • Engage communities in conversations • Enhance collaborations between local agencies • Develop relationships through sharing personal interest • Allow advocacy regarding needs and problems • Promote public celebration of accomplishments	Cho (2016)
Standard 9: Operations and Management	• Share operational innovations and successes • Engage others in management and processes	Wang, Sauers, & Richardson (2016)
Standard 10: School Improvement	• Innovate and improve on P-12 practices, specifically professional development, communication, and classroom activities • Develop a sense of continuous improvement	Carpenter & Krutka (2014) Cho (2016) Manca & Ranieri (2017) Sauers & Richardson (2015)

Our analysis of research on Twitter use and school leaders, through the lens of the PSEL standards, shed valuable light into the field of knowledge brokering. Currently, the body of research tends to focus on what type of knowledge is being shared as well as why that knowledge is being shared. What is missing, however, is research on how knowledge is mobilized and whose knowledge is being mobilized. These are both pillars of Ward's (2017) framework that guides this book. Thus, these are areas of research that need to be further explored. By juxtaposing the how and who of knowledge mobilization as it relates to school leaders' use of Twitter, the field might be better informed about how these leaders can use this brokering tool to meet the standards of the profession.

In many ways, standards like PSEL are aspirational in nature. As such, we hope that school leaders will continue to innovate and find ways to meet or surpass them. For example, cultural responsiveness could be fostered via Twitter in several ways. Leaders could celebrate their students and their communities, use Twitter to develop ties with local organizations and parents, or learn lessons about such activities from other colleagues. In addition, a community of care could be fostered by posting tips on restorative justice, posting links to academic and social supports in the community, or celebrating the cultural diversity within the school. Some of these efforts might best be displayed visually in pictures and through videos.

Although there may be some gaps between current practices and PSEL standards, our sense is that Twitter may facilitate both formal and informal learning around a variety of matters relevant to educational improvement. As practitioners experiment and come to terms with what may be best for their particular needs, they pave the way for new insights about what it means to be a leader in the digital age. It is now a fruitful time, therefore, for the field to better understand how mobilizing knowledge via Twitter—or indeed other social media platforms—can result in positive outcomes for teachers and for students.

References

ALS Association (2018). Impact of the ALS ice bucket challenge. Retrieved from http://www.alsa.org/fight-als/edau/ibc-progress-infographic.html

Carpenter, J. P., & Krutka, D. G. (2014). How and why educators use Twitter: A survey of the field. *Journal of Research on Technology in Education*, *46*, 414–434. doi:10.1080/15391523.2014.925701

Cho, V. (2016). Administrators' professional learning via Twitter: The dissonance between beliefs and actions. *Journal of Educational Administration*, *54*, 340–356. doi: 10.1108/JEA-03-2015-0024

Cho, V., & Jimerson, J. B. (2017). Managing digital identity on Twitter: The case of school administrators. *Educational Management Administration & Leadership*, *45*, 1–17. doi: 10.1177/1741143216659295

Cho, V., & Snodgrass Rangel, V. (2016). Twitter through the lens of structuration: The social and technological dimensions to school leaders' practices online. *Journal of School Leadership*, *26*, 837–863.

DuFour, R., Eaker, R., & DuFour, R. (2005). *On common ground: The power of professional learning communities*. Bloomington, IN: Solution Tree.

Dussault, M., & Thibodeau, S. (1997). Professional isolation and performance at work of school principals. *Journal of School Leadership*, *7*(5), 521–535.

Gao, F., Luo, T., & Zhang, K. (2012). Tweeting for learning: A critical analysis of research on microblogging in education published in 2008–2011. *British Journal of Educational Technology*, *43*, 783–801. doi: j.1467-8535.2012.01357.x

Hitchcock, L. I., & Young, J. A. (2016). Tweet, tweet!: Using live Twitter chats in social work education. *Social Work Education*, *35*, 457–468. doi: 10.1080/02615479.2015.1136273

Kimmons, R., Carpenter, J., Veletsianos, G., & Krutka, D. G. (2018). Mining social media divides: An analysis of K-12 U.S. school uses of Twitter. *Learning, Media and Technology*, *43*, 1–19. 10.1080/17439884.2018.1504791.

Leana, C. R. (2011). The missing link in school reform. *Stanford Social Innovation Review*, (Fall). Retrieved from http://www.ssireview.org/articles/entry/the_missing_link_in_school_reform/

Leithwood, K., & Riehl, C. (2003). *What we know about successful school leadership*. Retrieved from http://www.principals.in/uploads/pdf/leadership/1_NCLP.pdf

Malin, J. R., Brown, C., & St. Trubceac, A. (2018). Going for broke: A multiple-case study of brokering in education. *AERA Open*, *4*(2), 1–14. doi: 10.1177/2332858418769297

Manca, S., & Ranieri, S. (2017). Implications of social network sites for teaching and learning: Where we are and where we want to go. *Education and Information Technologies*, *22*, 605–622. doi: 10.1007/s10639-015-9429-x

Marsh, J. A., Bertrand, M., & Huguet, A. (2015). Using data to alter instructional practice: the mediating role of coaches and professional learning communities. *Teachers College Record, 117*(4), 1–40.

McLeod, S., & Richardson, J. W. (2011). The dearth of technology coverage. *Journal of School Leadership, 21*, 216–240.

McLeod, S., Richardson, J. W., & Sauers, N. J. (2015). Leading technology-rich school districts: Advice from tech-savvy administrators. *Journal of Research on Leadership Education, 10*(2), 104–126. doi: 10.1177/1942775115584013

Meyer, M. (2010). The rise of knowledge broker. *Science Communication, 32*, 118–127. doi: 10.1177/2F1075547009359797

Paskevicius, M., Veletsianos, G., & Kimmons, R. (2018). Content is king: An analysis of how Twitter discourse surrounding open education unfolded from 2009 to 2016. *International Review of Research in Open and Distributed Learning, 19*.

Perines, H. (2016). Knowledge mobilization in education. Connection between the research the policy and practice: a theoretical approach. *Revista Páginas de Educación, 10*, 137–150. doi: 10.22235/pe.v10i1.1362

Peterson, K. (2002). The professional development of principals: Innovations and opportunities. *Educational Administration Quarterly, 38*(2), 213–232. https://doi.org/10.1177/0013161X02382006

National Policy Board Educational Administration. (2015). *Professional standards for education leaders*. Reston, VA. Retrieved from http://npbea.org/wp-content/uploads/2017/06/Professional-Standards-for-Educational-Leaders_2015.pdf

Richardson, J. W., Bathon, J., Flora, K., & Lewis, W. D. (2012). NETS-A scholarship: A review of published literature. *Journal of Research on Technology in Education, 45*, 131–152.

Richardson, J. W., & Brantmeier, E. (2012). The role of ICTs in catalyzing conflict transformation in Egypt. *Education, Business and Society: Contemporary Middle Eastern Issues, 5*, 254–266. doi: 10.1108/17537981211284434

Richardson, J. W., & Sterrett, W. (2018). District technology leadership then and now: A comparative study of district technology leadership from 2001–2014. *Educational Administration Quarterly*. doi: 10.1177/0013161X18769046

Ricoy, M-C., & Feliz, T. (2016). Twitter as a learning community in higher education. *Educational Technology & Society, 19*, 237–248.

Rieckhoff, B. S., & Larsen, C. (2012). The impact of a professional development network on leadership development and school improvement goals. *School-University Partnerships, 5*, 57–73.

Rorrer, A. K., Skrla, L., & Scheurich, J. J. (2008). Districts as institutional actors in educational reform. *Educational Administration Quarterly, 44*(3), 307–357. https://doi.org/10.1177/0013161X08318962

Sauers, N. J., & Richardson, J. W. (2015). Leading by following: An analysis of how K-12 school leaders use Twitter. *NASSP Bulletin, 99*, 127–146. doi: 10.1177/0192636515583869

Sauers, N. J., Richardson, J. W., & McLeod, S. (2015). Technology-savvy superintendents: Successes and challenges. *Journal of School Leadership, 24*(6), 1177–1201.

Shah, N. A. K., & Cox, A. M. (2017). Uncovering the scholarly use of Twitter in the academia: Experiences in a British university. *Malaysian Journal of Library & Information Science, 22*, 93–108. doi: 10.22452/mjlis.vol22no3.6

Statista. (2018). Number of monthly active Twitter users in the United States from 1st quarter 2010 to 2nd quarter 2018. Retrieved from https://www.statista.com/statistics/274564/monthly-active-twitter-users-in-the-united-states/

Tang, Y., & Hew, K. F. (2016). Using Twitter for education: Beneficial or simply a waste of time? *Computers and Education, 106*, 97–118. doi: 10.1016/j.compedu.2016.12.004

Tirozzi, G. N. (2002). Associations and the principalship: A history of advocacy, a horizon of opportunity. In M. Tucker & J. Codding (Eds.), *The Principal challenge: Leading and managing schools in an era of accountability* (pp. 347–392). San Francisco, CA: Jossey-Bass.

Van Lare, M. D., & Brazer, S. D. (2013). Analyzing learning in professional learning communities: A conceptual framework. *Leadership and Policy in Schools, 12*(4), 374–396.

Veletsianos, G., & Kimmons, R. (2016). Scholars in an increasingly open and digital world: How do education professors and students use Twitter? *The Internet and Higher Education, 30*, 1–10. doi: 10.1016/j.iheduc.2016.02.002

Wang, Y., Sauers, N., & Richardson, J. (2016). A social network approach to examine K-12 educational leaders' influence on information diffusion on Twitter. *Journal of School Leadership, 26*, 495–522.

Ward, V. (2017). Why, whose, what and how? A framework for knowledge mobilisers. *Evidence & Policy, 13*(3), 477–497.

4

EVIDENCE FOR THE FRONTLINE

More questions than answers

Caroline Creaby and Jonathan Haslam

Introduction

A substantial amount of education research is undertaken each year by universities, charities, independent research organizations, and others. There is a natural hope that somewhere within this body of knowledge lies useful information for improving all aspects of school life, and outcomes for children. The principle of turning this research into improvement in the classroom is appealing, yet there are many barriers that prevent it from happening. They are not placed there intentionally, in fact quite the opposite. Throughout the education sector, individuals are keen, and working hard, to make the most of education research.

Though there had been efforts before then, in the early 2000s, interest in this issue began to grow. Simplistically, there were two groups with an interest in education research—policy makers and practitioners. Policy makers could see the benefit of having policies that were evidence-based. It gave independent authority to the ideas that they were proposing. It offered too, perhaps, a way to retreat from the over-politicization of the classroom. Previously, it was more common to see policy-based evidence than evidence-based policy. But there were signs this was changing.

In 2001, the No Child Left Behind Act was introduced in the US. It aimed to set, and hold schools to, higher standards for elementary and high school students. These standards were assumed to materialize as a result of using good quality research. Such was the enthusiasm for evidence-informed practice that No Child Left Behind recommended the use of programs and practices 'based on scientifically based research' more than 100 times (Slavin, 2008). A year later, the Institute for Education Science was founded, with a remit to carry out this kind of research and, through the What Works Clearinghouse, to evaluate and synthesize existing research in a way that provided useable advice for practitioners.

In England, in a speech to the National College in 2010, Michael Gove, the then Secretary of State for Education, said that he wanted:

> to see more data generated by the profession to show what works, clearer information about teaching techniques that get results, more rigorous, scientifically-robust research about pedagogies which succeed and proper independent evaluations of interventions which have run their course. We need more evidence-based policy making, and for that to work we need more evidence.
>
> *(GOV.UK, 2010, online)*

At this time, the government was establishing a network of What Works Centres across the fields of social policy. This included The National Institute for Health and Care Excellence (NICE) for healthcare, and the College of Policing for crime. In education, spurred on by the sentiments expressed by the then Secretary of State for Education above, the main What Works Centre was the Education Endowment Foundation (EEF), set up in 2011. Their approach is based on a cycle of four strands of activity: summarizing the existing evidence; making grants; evaluating projects; sharing and promoting the use of evidence. As more evaluations have been carried out, so the last of these has become more important.

At the same time a number of initiatives arose across the education sector, aimed at supporting and encouraging this agenda. For example, researchED, a series of national and local conferences for teachers, is a grassroots reaction to the uncertainty about what research can usefully tell us and a desire from teachers to own and shape how research is used, rather than leave this to national and local government. The Coalition for Evidence-based Education (CEBE) was formed with the intention of providing a space where those who were interested in putting research into practice could come together and share their ideas. Crucially, CEBE's aim was to incubate these ideas into specific projects – identifying where there were gaps in the current system and trying to develop projects that addressed these gaps. In 2010, work on Evidence for the Frontline (E4F) project began. At its simplest, the project aimed to connect teachers with researchers, acting as a brokerage service in helping to answer the questions that arise in schools with the best information available from research, resulting in actionable solutions in the classroom.

The research on research-use

Using research in policy and practice is not as straightforward as it sounds. As articulated in Chapter 1 (Malin & Brown, this volume), there are several reasons behind the 'research-practice gaps' that exist and explain why teachers are not using research evidence in practice; these include issues of accessibility, relevance and timeliness. Helpfully, however, the issue of research-use has spawned its own field of research, with researchers keen to identify the mechanisms that lead to success. A recent review by the EPPI-Centre in London has looked at the existing research across the social sciences (Langer, Tripney, & Gough, 2016). They posited a number of possible routes and mechanisms for research-use, and looked at what the current research has to say about the effectiveness of these mechanisms. Where teachers were supported to use research evidence in practice, there was reliable evidence that interventions that facilitated access to research evidence and interventions that helped teachers make sense of evidence were effective.

In education, this raises interesting questions about effective mechanisms for research-use. In particular, the idea that research-use requires building teachers' skills to access and make sense of evidence before it becomes effective. For educators at all levels, one problem here is time. Time is at a premium in schools and having the time to engage in research at the depth that is required is a major issue. This also affects the quality of the teachers' engagement with the research. Often, the ideal is to be provided with an immediate answer that can be implemented. Relating this to Ward's (2017) knowledge mobilization framework (set out in Table 1.1 in Chapter 1), the knowledge being sought to be mobilized is often technical or practical in nature. While this might satisfy the needs of the teacher, it is often unrealistic. Research evidence is rarely actionable (Lysenko et al., 2014); it is unable to guide one directly to the best answer that can be implemented immediately in the classroom as knowledge is often in the form of implications or recommendations. In any case, providing such an answer doesn't necessarily deepen the teachers' knowledge and understanding of research which is important for a thoughtful and purposeful approach in practice.

These findings influenced the design of the E4F brokerage service. As Nutley and colleagues said:

> Interpersonal and social interactions are often key to the use of research, whether among policy and practice colleagues, or more directly with researchers themselves. This begins to suggest that research-use means more than simple application, and may involve instead the complex social processing of research-based knowledge.
>
> *(Nutley, Walter, & Davies, 2007, 302)*

The design of E4F aimed to build on this, creating an approach that encouraged dialogue and interaction between teachers and researchers. The team leading and administering the service (a team led by the authors, a school and university practitioner respectively) were essentially playing the two roles advocated in Chapter 1, both spanning boundaries between researchers and teachers and also acting as intermediaries between them. Teachers would ask questions of researchers through the online platform. Before these were directed to researchers, the administrators would clarify any details not clear from the wording of the question. Having had questions directed to them, the researchers might give an initial answer, but as important would be the activity that took place beyond that. This might be further online dialogue between the teacher and the researcher, a visit to the school or university, a call—activity that took the discussion further and supported the 'complex social processing of research-based knowledge'. Supporting this social interaction was a key element of the E4F brokerage service from the start—the service should allow users to interact with each other, to draw out the significance of the research—challenge, shape, and own it—to facilitate its use in practice. It was also important, though, that the design of this social interaction should be left to the users, particularly teachers. What did they need? How did they want it to work?

Developing evidence for the frontline

After several years of development, the E4F project received funding from the Education Endowment Foundation. Importantly, the project was school-based, situated at Sandringham School in Hertfordshire, England. School staff would take the role of broker, mediating between teachers and researchers by ensuring that questions were framed in a clear way that researchers could respond to. Staff at the Institute for Effective Education (IEE) at the University of York supported the project by sourcing researchers and research for the project. Between them, the school and university staff leading the project were able to effectively and authentically span the boundaries of research and practice. The project began in 2015 with two phases of activity—a development phase, where 12 schools came together to design the E4F brokerage system, and a pilot phase, where an additional 20 schools joined to use the new system.

Development phase

In the development phase, 12 schools from across England, and a mix of primary, secondary, and special schools, signed up to participate. For each school there was support from the head teacher, and the school appointed a 'research champion,' a senior member of school staff who would be the lead for the project within school, and in contact with the team at Sandringham School and the IEE. The concept that there should be a relatively senior member of school staff responsible for seeking out useful research information and incorporating it back into school or individual practitioner priorities has taken root over the last few years, whether described as a research champion or a research lead (Brown, 2017). Although encouraging research champions to make the most of being involved in the project, and providing resources to help them to do so, they were offered no particular direction as to how information from E4F might fit into wider school processes and priorities.

The project was designed through three meetings in the summer term of 2015. The original concept of the project had been that communication might take place in a number of ways. Questions might come in by post, phone, email, website, Twitter, app, etc. However, the schools were clear that the most important medium was the website. Time pressures experienced by teachers meant that they wanted to be able to access information at a time that suited them: a 24/7 service where they could drop off questions when they had a moment, and then look up the answers at a later date.

The design of the website then focused on making it as simple to use as possible. Again, many of the ideas came from the perceived importance of reducing the time demands on busy teachers. Registration should be straightforward, but there was clearly a necessity to make the site secure. Research champions were therefore provided with notifications when school staff had registered. Teachers could only register with an email address from the school's own domain, so the opportunities for inappropriate registration were limited. The schools spent time considering the way that information on the site might be classified, so that teachers could easily find the information that they were looking for, whether that be a question and answer, or schools, staff, researchers or resources that were within their area of interest. This led to a search system on the site that looked across all these domains, but then categorized the information into Question, Staff, Researchers, Resources, and Schools, so that it was easy to navigate around these categories.

The question submission and answering process was also much discussed. The approach taken was to submit questions (mostly) privately. Any member of staff could submit a question, but this would only be visible to the administrators of the site (staff from Sandringham School and the IEE), and the teacher's research champion. The purpose was to encourage openness and, by making this fairly private, give staff the confidence to ask questions. However, the research champion would be able to see the kinds of questions that were being asked by colleagues and the way that these fitted in with the wider school agenda.

Comments could be added to the question to allow the administrators to clarify the question or the type of answer required. This facility was designed to enable the 'social interaction' that Nutley and colleagues (2007) identified as an important part of the research-use process and help build relationships between the E4F broker and the teachers. Importantly, these comments could help direct the administrators' next steps as they were able to clarify the specific nature of the question and therefore the type of research or a researcher that might help answer the question. After using this comment function early in the pilot phase, the administration team decided to include more guidance about asking a good question on the site itself.

Comments could also be added to the answers once they were published publicly on the site. This function was designed to allow dialogue between the teacher and the researcher. For example, it was envisaged that a teacher might provide feedback to the researcher about the usefulness of the answer provided and their next steps in school. It was decided that all users on the site could add comments to published answers. For example, a teacher in another school, interested in the same topic, could add comments to the answer with their thoughts or reflections. It was hoped that this would lead to school-to-school dialogue and interaction on and off the site. The ability to connect and interact with others on the site was also enabled by a 'request further dialogue' function. When a teacher asked a question or a researcher answered one, their name was highlighted on the site and adjacent to their name was a clickable link to request dialogue through email, telephone, or other means.

The pilot phase

Following the development of the site, the service was launched in September 2015. In addition to the 12 developer schools already involved, 20 additional schools joined the pilot phase. All schools in the pilot phase committed to the project by nominating a research champion for their school and attendance at two development days at Sandringham School, one day at the launch of the service in the autumn term and one at the start of the spring term. Together, the 32 schools represented a range of schools in England; they were geographically spread over 15 counties, included infant, junior, primary, secondary, and all-through schools, included mainstream and special schools, included schools in different socio-economic areas and also varied according to school examination performance.

The launch involved providing research champions with very practical support. For example, research champions were provided with time to log in to the site, create accounts for themselves and their schools and build up familiarity by spending some time navigating the site and looking at a couple of 'trial' questions that had been placed on the site. The E4F team also created resources for research champions to use when they returned to their schools. Such support was important to enable research champions to support their teachers to engage with evidence through the site. This launch event also served to provide an opportunity for the E4F team to build relationships with each of the research champions, a key aspect of our role. In terms of the theoretical model presented in Chapter 1, this event was an essential step in our subsequent work which involved convening partnerships between the research champions and the teachers in their schools and researchers and through enabling champions to support teachers' engagement with research.

After the launch date, the administrators were poised and ready for questions to be posed on the site. Within just one month, over 80 questions had been asked and there were more than 180 users on the site—teachers had clearly been able to use the site and began posing a whole range of questions to researchers. Even at this early stage, it was evident that the service's design was facilitating teachers to engage with evidence, part 3 of the theoretical model presented in Figure 1.1 in Chapter 1. Some schools posed a flurry of questions, while there was a more consistent, but smaller stream of questions from others. This reflected the different ways in which research champions were encouraging use in their schools, something reflected on in more detail later in this chapter.

The nature of the questions varied. Topics ranged from the teaching of spelling to how to tackle poor behavior. Over time, it was clear that some topics were gaining more interest than others, with the most popular topics emerging as behavior, motivation, memory and feedback. The design of the service enabled questions to be connected—when questions were asked that were similar to those asked previously, the questions and answers could be linked.

The nature of the questions also varied with respect to what was being sought. Some teachers asked about the evidence relating to a particular approach or strategy, for example the question below:

> *What evidence, either for or against, is there in the benefit of setting pupils by ability levels or gender in KS4?*

While other teachers asked about the recommended approaches emerging from research exemplified in this question:

> *Are there any evidence based resources for teachers developing their behavior management / classroom climate strategies?*

In the main, most of the questions asked for the implications for practice arising from research. As already identified, research evidence rarely identifies actionable strategies that can be implemented immediately in schools. However, the answers provided by the researchers pointed to the implications for practice arising from the research and offered suggestions.

Behind the scenes, the administrators were beginning to hypothesize about the role of the champion in each school and the priorities of each school, given the pattern and nature of questions asked. A second day with research champions in the spring term was very illuminating in this respect. Each of the champions reflected on their experiences so far, and each shared a short case study of a teacher from their school who had used the site. This exercise generated a lot of valuable feedback and five common themes emerged:

1. Answers to questions should be provided more quickly,
2. Teachers should be able to access all research that was referenced in answers,
3. More teachers in schools should use the service,
4. More time was needed in school for teachers to use the service,
5. Teachers and researchers should engage in more dialogue on the site.

This feedback related to two broad categories: the nature of the service itself and the leadership of this service in schools. For example, our champions discussed points 1 and 2 at length. They felt that quicker responses would create more enthusiasm amongst users and generate more interaction with the site. Points 3 and 4, on the other hand, related to the ability of the research champion to reach and support teachers in their schools. Some champions were headteachers and were therefore able to provide time and direction for all or most of their staff to use the site. Other champions had positions in school, which meant that exposure to teachers was more limited. Point 5 related to the willingness of users to engage in dialogue. In particular, the administrators had observed that teachers rarely commented on the answers that were provided to their questions; this was an underused function and therefore didn't facilitate the social dynamic (Nutley, Walter, & Davies, 2007) that the site was designed to support.

Early lessons

The pilot phase of this project provided a valuable opportunity to learn about evidence use. In particular, much was learned about the nature of teachers' questions, the complexities of providing evidence-based answers and the actions that research champions could take in schools in order to support their colleagues to draw upon research to support their practice.

As already outlined, the nature of teachers' questions varied both by topic and by what teachers were looking for. Relating to the model outlined in Chapter 1, 'what knowledge' teachers were seeking often differed from that available from the research evidence (Ward, 2017). Teachers were commonly looking for practical strategies arising from the research, whereas research tends to only generate implications, it is unable to provide the 'recipes' that teachers may desire (Levin, 2013). This requires work for teachers and school leaders to consider how to bridge the gap between implications from research and what would be a sensible evidence-informed approach in the classroom. Embracing a broad and inclusive view of what it means to be research-informed, as advocated in Chapter 1, which comprises a combination of both teacher knowledge and that from the research community, is important here. Teachers are critical in the process of translating the implications arising from research; their knowledge of the 'cut and thrust' of classroom life is needed when designing research informed strategies to use with students. This distinction differs from a research-*based* view of research-use which suggests deference to the research evidence (Sharples, 2013).

When providing answers to teachers through the E4F brokerage service, the administrators and researchers couldn't categorically suggest specific approaches that would 'work'; this would require interpretation and planning on behalf of the teacher to develop the next steps. Anecdotal feedback from school champions suggested that some teachers expected that precise strategies should be outlined for their use. This illustrates that, potentially, there was more work to do in terms of supporting teachers' research literacy i.e. their understanding of the nature of research and its limitations. Furthermore, in terms of the support that is offered to teachers, research champions and school leaders engaging in evidence-informed practice, this suggests that they need help to bridge the gaps between research implications and practicable classroom strategies.

There were also lessons about the evidence base. As each question was submitted to the site, the administrative team would consider three main avenues to help answer the question:

1. Was there a researcher already engaged with the service with relevant expertise?
2. Was there an existing research resource on the site relevant to this question?
3. Could the administrative team find research or a researcher that was relevant?

Using these three avenues throughout the pilot, the administrative team were building relationships with researchers in order to encourage relationships between the researchers and teachers, part 2 of the theoretical model presented in Figure 1.1 in Chapter 1. In doing so, issues relating to the evidence base and to the accessibility of the evidence base were identified. There were gaps in the evidence base that made it more difficult to respond to teachers' questions. For example, research relating to the teaching of handwriting was limited and suggested that more might be undertaken in this area. As questions became more specific the evidence base was more limited. For example, the following question was submitted to the site:

What strategies are used to ensure clear differentiation in KS3 Drama lessons?

For this question, there is research evidence relating to differentiation. However, the evidence base relating to Key Stage 3 drama is non-existent.

In addition to there being limits in the evidence base, where there was promising research, the process of contacting and building relationships with researchers with expertise in these areas was time consuming. Some researchers responded positively to being approached and subsequently answered teachers' questions. However, despite positive initial responses, some researchers were less able to answer questions due to other commitments, while other researchers were unable to provide help to the service at all. The researchers were essentially being asked to carry out this work in addition to their own roles, free of charge. This assumes researchers will necessarily want to help support teachers and practice and be able to devote their own time to do so. Where the administrative team had existing relationships with researchers or where relationships could be built through more than just email communication, researchers would engage more. This points to the challenges of supporting relationships between teachers and researchers, highlighting the importance of building a sustainable network of researchers, alongside a network of school champions, to enable the success and scalability of a brokerage service like E4F.

Lessons were also learned about the leadership of evidence-informed practice in schools. At the launch of the E4F service, research champions were provided with resources (e.g. presentations) to help them promote the service and engage teachers in their schools. While suggestions were offered, it was left to the research champion to decide what was best for their context. In their research into teachers' use of research in schools, Leat, Reid, and Lofthouse (2015) identified that support from 'key individuals' in school, such as members of the school's leadership team, is an important supportive mechanism for research-use, something also identified by Bell, Cordingley, Isham and Davis (2010) and Brown (2015). All schools involved in the pilot had a research champion and hence at least one 'key individual' to support research engagement. However, from case studies provided by research champions, the position the champion held in school had a bearing. For example, one school champion was the school's headteacher and she was able to integrate E4F into teachers' allocated professional development time. This led to all teachers in that school using the service and being supported to act on answers provided. In other pilot schools, champions with senior positions were able to engage groups of teachers and even whole staff bodies. Generally, in schools where the research champion's role was less senior, they were less able to engage as many teachers in using the service. In their research, Leat, Reid and Lofthouse (2015) suggested that key individuals in schools may be members of the school's leadership team and this is echoed in research by Coldwell et al. (2017) who note that school leaders are often the gate keepers for school research. Experience of leading the pilot of E4F echoes these findings.

To a certain extent, we were also learning lessons about the role that the school's context was playing in the leadership of evidence-informed practice in schools. A range of schools were involved in the pilot and one of the ways they differed was their grading from Ofsted, England's national inspectorate of schools. In our experience, schools with lower Ofsted grades generally posed fewer questions to E4F. The nature of E4F puts teachers in the driving seat to ask their own questions, pertinent to their own practice. Implicit in this is the assumption that teachers themselves are trusted (Tschannen-Moran, 2004) and are able to adapt their own practice accordingly (Roberts, 2015). However, research has recognized that more authoritarian approaches to leadership are prevalent in schools in more challenging circumstances (Gray, 2000). This approach to leadership may not confer opportunities for teachers to independently engage with their practice and innovate.

Conclusion

The E4F service has demonstrated that teachers from some schools have an appetite for research. They want research that can help them understand the efficacy of different approaches used within schools and to identify practical strategies that can be used to enhance learning. This suggests that teachers themselves are interested in the body of knowledge generated by universities and research organizations to help improve school life and outcomes for children. It also demonstrates that a brokerage service like E4F has the potential to support teachers to engage with research in this way. This provides hope that there is a desire from the education sector to become more evidence informed.

The particular emphasis of the E4F brokerage service was that teachers could have their specific questions answered by researchers or by the administrative team drawing on available research relevant to the question. In the year of the pilot, of the 252 questions posed on the site, 174 had been answered. The unanswered questions reveal gaps in research and challenges in accessing research. For schools to move to a position where they can call upon evidence to support decision making on a regular basis, as envisaged by the DfE and the EEF, it will be important that the gaps in the research base are filled with new research studies into the areas that concern schools. This will be key for any brokerage service seeking to enable relationships between researchers and teachers and for those seeking to support teachers in becoming more evidence-informed.

This service has provided a bridge between schools and researchers, which is rare in the UK. There were some examples of some dialogue between teachers and researchers but, in the main, the communication was one-way, researcher to teacher. This could suggest a lack of time that teachers have to engage more fully, but could also suggest a lack of experience or confidence from teachers to comment on research implications. Yet researchers involved in the project respected the tacit knowledge and experience of school life that the teachers brought. Greater opportunities for teachers and researchers to interact on a more mutual basis could encourage teachers to engage more readily with researchers on the E4F site. This has implications for those seeking to broker relationships between teachers and researchers.

Overall, the early experience of piloting E4F has demonstrated that such a brokerage service can enable evidence informed practice to develop within schools. It played a key role in encouraging relationships between researchers and teachers and supported teachers to engage with evidence. As such, E4F served to mobilize research knowledge. However, it is only one piece in the educational ecosystem. Other pieces, such as leadership support within schools, improving teachers' research literacy, improving teachers' confidence in their own tacit knowledge, bridging the gap between theory and practice and research that addresses the needs of teachers and schools, lay beyond the scope of the E4F project. Yet all these, and more, must be in place before we can realize the full potential of knowledge mobilization approaches.

Acknowledgements

This work was supported by the EEF under Grant 1829. The authors would like to express their appreciation of the schools involved in developing and piloting Evidence for the Frontline.

References

Bell, M., Cordingley, P., Isham, C., & Davis, R. (2010). *Report of professional practitioner use of research review: Practitioner engagement in and/or with research.* Coventry: CUREE, GTCE, LSIS & NTRP.

Brown, C. (Ed.) (2015). *Leading the use of research and evidence in schools.* London: IOE Press.

Brown, C. (2017). How to establish Research Learning Communities. *Professional Development Today, 19*(2): 30–55.

Coldwell, M., Greany, T., Higgins, S., Brown, C., Maxwell, B., Stiell, B., Stoll, L, Willis, B. & Burns, H. (2017) *Evidence-informed teaching: An evaluation of progress in England.* London: Department for Education.

GOV.UK. (2010). Speech: Michael Gove to the National College Annual Conference, Birmingham. https://www.gov.uk/government/speeches/michael-gove-to-the-national-college-annual-conference-birmingham [Accessed: July 1st 2016]

Gray, J. (2000). *Causing concern but improving: A review of schools' experience.* London: DfEE.

HM Government. (2013). *What works: Evidence centres for social policy.* London: Cabinet Office.

Langer, L., Tripney, J., & Gough, D. (2016). *The science of using science: Researching the use of research evidence in decision-making.* London: EPPI-Centre, Social Science Research Unit, UCL Institute of Education, University College London.

Leat, D., Reid, A., & Lofthouse, R. (2015). Teachers' experiences of engagement with and in research: What can be learned from teachers' views? *Oxford Review of Education, 41*(2): 270–286.

Levin, B. (2013). To know is not enough: Research knowledge and its use. *Review of Education, 1,* 2–31.

Lysenko, L., Abrami, P., Bernard, R., Dagenais, C. and Janosz, M. (2014). Educational research in educational practice: Predictors of use. *Canadian Journal of Education, 37*(2), 1–26

Nutley, S., Walter, I., & Davies, H. (2007). *How research can inform public services: Using evidence.* Bristol: Policy Press.

Roberts, C. (2015). Impractical research: Overcoming the obstacles to becoming an evidence-informed school. In C. Brown (Ed.), *Leading the use of research & evidence in schools,* IOE Press: London, pp. 107–116.

Sharples, J. (2013). *Evidence for the frontline: A report for the alliance for useful evidence.* London: Nesta.

Slavin, R. (2008). What works? Issues in synthesizing educational program evaluations. *Educational Researcher, 37*(1): 5–14.

Tschannen-Moran, M. (2004). *Trust matters: Leadership for successful schools.* San Francisco, CA: Jossey-Bass.

Ward, V. (2017). Why, whose, what and how? A framework for knowledge mobilisers. *Evidence & Policy, 13*(3), 477–497.

5

FOSTERING IMPROVED CONNECTIONS BETWEEN RESEARCH, POLICY, AND PRACTICE

The knowledge network for applied education research

Doris McWhorter, Erica van Roosmalen, Donna Kotsopoulos, George Gadanidis, Ruth Kane, Nicholas Ng-A-Fook, Carol Campbell, Katina Pollock, and Davoud Sarfaraz

Introduction

Making meaningful connections between policy, research, and practice requires us to reflect on the priorities and problems of practice in schools as well as our individual and organizational readiness and commitment to work together in new ways to address them. In Ontario, Canada, current priorities for attention among educational researchers, policy makers, and practitioners include: improving children's mathematics achievement; addressing systemic barriers to children and youth from marginalized groups; supporting the physical, emotional, and mental health of all students; and improving Indigenous education and achievement. These priorities inspired the development and implementation of the collaborative networks of the Knowledge Network for Applied Education Research (KNAER), for which continuous improvement of teaching and learning in classrooms and schools is the ultimate goal.

The KNAER was established in 2010, funded by the Ontario Ministry of Education (Ministry), as a tripartite agreement between the Ministry, University of Toronto, and Western University. The Network's mission is to develop thematic networks and build system-wide capacity for knowledge mobilization and evidence use in order to implement evidence-informed education practices to support Ontario's vision for education (see also Campbell et al., 2014; Pollock et al., 2019). The KNAER includes four thematic knowledge networks that bring together multiple partners to form provincial networks and local communities of practice: Mathematics Knowledge Network (MKN), Knowledge Network for Student Well-Being, Réseau de Savoir sur l'Équité/Equity Knowledge Network

(RSEKN), and Indigenous Education Knowledge Network (IEKN). Each thematic network is closely aligned with one or more government education priorities and strategies, and each has a unique structure based on its desired outcomes, organizational partners, and problems of practice. Network Host organizations act as brokers to facilitate and connect the work of communities of practice, while the KNAER Secretariat and the Ministry act as intermediaries to broker knowledge across the four thematic networks and facilitate connections with multiple partners throughout the broader education system.

The KNAER takes a systems approach to enhancing knowledge mobilization, which we define as moving from linear processes of research-to-practice to a more complex process involving interaction, co-creation and implementation of evidence throughout all levels of a system (Best & Holmes, 2010; Campbell et al., 2014; Pollock et al., 2019). The KNAER model (see Figure 1.1) provides an interconnected infrastructure bringing together provincial partners and thematic networks to foster communication, coordination, and ongoing, reciprocal relationships among policy makers, researchers and practitioners. The overarching tri-partite partners (Ministry and two universities) provide overall strategic leadership for the development of KNAER as brokers and boundary spanners who act "in a 'third space' in between the research and practice" communities (Farley-Ripple et al., 2018, p. 241). The model intentionally provides focus and flexibility across its thematic networks and communities of practice, enabling partnerships to grow and evolve and creating opportunities to bridge gaps to deepen and align research production and use throughout the system.

Conceptual framework applied to the KNAER

Farley-Ripple et al. (2018) have developed a conceptual framework for understanding research use in schools "as a means of prompting conversations about the bidirectional nature of the problem and guiding inquiry around connections between research and practice" (p. 237). They identify five gaps in assumptions and perspectives between the research and practice communities. The first is the **usefulness of research products**, or the extent to which practitioners value, access and utilize the products created and valued by researchers. The second involves the **nature and quality of research** valued by the research and practice communities and the extent to which they overlap. The third is the **problems addressed by research** or the relevance of the research to problems of practice. The fourth involves the different **structures, processes and incentives** that influence both researchers and practitioners in the production and use of research. The fifth gap is influenced by **relationships between the communities**, including indirect relationships and the role of research brokers and boundary spanners. Moreover, the authors hypothesize that the magnitude of these gaps act as drivers of the depth of research use and production on six dimensions of practice (evidence, search/dissemination, interpretation, participation, frequency, and stage of decision-making).

The KNAER attempts to increase the depth of evidence informed decision-making in education by bringing together research communities and practice communities, as Farley-Ripple et al. (2018) conceptualize in their model. Yet, achieving the depth of evidence-informed decision making envisaged by Farley-Ripple et al. (2018), in our experience, goes beyond simply bringing together research communities and practice communities. Rather, it requires the development of an infrastructure and intermediaries to support evidence-informed decisions to inform policy and address problems of practice. As Farley-Ripple et al. (2018) identified, addressing gaps in structures, processes, and incentives between research and practice communities and developing relationships between these communities is essential.

In this chapter, we examine the KNAER approach to networks and partnerships and draw from the conceptual framework developed by Farley-Ripple et al. (2018) to illustrate strategies for navigating gaps between research and practice communities across two of KNAER's thematic networks (MKN and RSEKN). We also identify key challenges and lessons learned through this work. However, KNAER goes beyond the two communities of research and practice (Lavis et al., 2003) by emphasizing knowledge mobilization as a dynamic and interactive process of engagement and collaboration among all potential stakeholders (including policy makers and public community members beyond traditional research and practice communities) (Pollock et al., 2019). Consistent with the dimension of 'whose knowledge' in the framework for knowledge mobilisers developed by Ward (2016), KNAER facilitates multidirectional knowledge exchange among researchers, practitioners and service providers, members of the public, and policy makers. Finally, we summarize what we are learning about making productive use of research–policy–practice partnerships to improve professional practice and student outcomes.

The case of the Mathematics Knowledge Network (MKN)

Valuing the learning of mathematics from early childhood and throughout pre-post-secondary education is common across most cultures and education systems. Yet, mathematical experiences of children can vary from classroom to classroom, most notably due to the individual agency and readiness of the teacher to engage in meaningful mathematical learning. Many teachers report that while they view mathematical learning as important, they perceive themselves as lacking the requisite content or pedagogical knowledge necessary to provide optimal and individualized learning environments (McGarvey, Sternberg, & Long, 2013).

Some studies suggest that school and district leadership play an important role in advancing mathematical learning by providing resources, encouraging partnerships, and prioritizing mathematical learning (Dumay, Boonen, & Damme, 2013). Indeed, changing mathematical cultures to occasion student learning is complex and highly contextualized. Still, there are important and compelling reasons to do so. Children are particularly susceptible to developing a mathematical identity that may be inconsistent with their actual potential (Allen & Schnell, 2016).

Mathematics education lacks a tradition or expectation that the mathematics learned in school may be communicated or be of interest beyond the classroom. Making math "worth talking about" necessitates we create rich learning experiences that offer mathematical surprise and insight (Gadanidis, 2012). To move in this direction, Gadanidis, Borba, Hughes, and Lacerda (2016) suggest a targeted model of reform that empowers teachers, by starting with topics that they themselves identify as areas of interest or need:

> We are not seeking a revolution in mathematics education, but a strategic focus on mathematics worthy of attention, worthy of conversation, worthy of children's incredible minds, which thirst for knowledge and for opportunities to explore, question, flex their imagination, discover, discuss and share their learning.
>
> *(p. 225)*

The Mathematics Knowledge Network (MKN) is hosted at the Fields Institute for Research in the Mathematical Sciences. Within the MKN there are four communities of practice (CoP): (1) Critical Transitions, (2) Indigenous Knowledge, (3) Computational Thinking, and (4) Teacher Leadership. Each CoP consists of university faculty/faculties, teachers, principals, school district leaders (e.g., subject specialist consultants, supervisory officers), community partners (e.g., provincial television broadcaster, subject associations, professional associations, etc.), and parents. The MKN's approach from the outset has reflected a view that teachers have agency and are critical mediators and brokers of knowledge. Teachers are central in defining classroom-based needs and creating classroom cultures that promote the enjoyment of mathematics and supporting mathematical learning by all students. The MKN began with 14 partners including faculties of education, schools and school districts, professional organizations, and community partners. MKN partners in 2018 exceed 70 organizations.

The MKN focuses on connecting research to practice and facilitating collaboration across stakeholders. According to Lysenko and colleagues (2015), there are three ways to use research in the classroom: (1) instrumental (concrete practices applied in the classroom), (2) conceptual (change in thinking or understanding), and (3) symbolic (perception of using research to support decision-making). The MKN creates a strategic interconnected structure of collaboration across stakeholders—including those in schools, university faculty/faculties, and community partners. There is a continual bidirectional flow of knowledge. Sharing may also, for example, inform the ongoing research of university faculty. Accordingly, there is an unprecedented level of access to varying forms of mathematical expertise that help support evidence and research use in practice by creating a structure of cross-sector and cross-discipline relationships. In short, the MKN principles and structure provide a framework for transcending the cultural, professional and organizational boundaries (Penuel et al. 2015, p. 188) between research and practice and for addressing gaps in assumptions and perspectives identified by Farley-Ripple et al. (2018).

Readiness to engage in joint work

One key observation from our early efforts is the "readiness" of partners (e.g., school districts, researchers, community groups) to engage in joint work at the boundaries between research and practice (Akkerman & Bakker, 2011). From the outset, it was clear that some school districts demonstrated a high level of engagement with mathematics, and thus were keen to connect their communities with opportunities through the MKN. One illustrative example is that of Wellington Catholic District School Board (Wellington) where joint work has resulted in incredible opportunities in classrooms with and for teachers and students.

Wellington, located in a large urban setting, has engaged extensively with the Computational Thinking (CT) CoP to support teachers and students in integrating CT into mathematics classes and elementary classes. In 2016–2017, Wellington engaged in a district-wide initiative to use coding to model and investigate math concepts and relationships in elementary education, using the model of building rich learning experiences around teacher-identified needs. In 2017–2018, the initiative grew with the addition of an integrated grade 10 mathematics and grade 10 computer studies (Gadanidis & Cummings, 2018). The theme of computational modelling in mathematics education was also taken up by the Dr. Eric Jackman Institute of Child Study, in collaboration with educators from St. Andrews Public School (TDSB), to develop lesson studies in primary classrooms (Gadanidis & Caswell, 2018). Students, in particular, are self-reporting deeper engagement and understanding from this work, which sought to increase the usefulness and relevance of research and deepen its use in classrooms through strengthened and reciprocal relationships between educators and researchers.

Readiness of practitioners to engage in joint work

Five key features were evident in schools and school boards that exemplified readiness to engage in joint work with the research community to reduce gaps and increase the depth of use of research-based knowledge. First, these school boards had leadership teams that had already engaged in the heavy lifting of setting district-wide goals. The vision and the benchmarks were at the ready and these leaders were already champions of professional development. Research suggests that an education leader's prior experience predisposes them to supporting professional development and to aligning such development to strategic initiatives (Hardy, 2009). School leaders are also critical mediators and brokers of knowledge and are instrumental in supporting and creating contexts where this is possible for all learners.

Second, these institutions were prepared to invest resources (including teacher release) to support advancing the strategic direction. This is particularly important. Professional collaboration has been found to be very valuable in shifting teacher practices (Kennedy et al., 2011); for this to occur, school boards must be prepared to provide opportunities for such engagement and this requires an intentional commitment of resources. Third, district leadership teams had already identified internal champions of the mission who had both on the ground engagement and classroom-level experience. Hargreaves and Ainscow (2015) describe this as "leading from the middle" (p. 44). Fourth, these districts welcomed the collaboration of external partners (e.g., university colleagues or other district leaders) in supporting their advancement of understanding; more than just welcomed collaboration, they actively facilitated and sought out the collaborations. Finally, the status quo was not an option; that is, these school districts were prepared to venture into perhaps unfamiliar pedagogical spaces with the ultimate aim of advancing student learning.

Readiness of researchers and other partners to engage in joint work

Researchers and community partners must also show a readiness to engage in joint work and the key features relevant to these stakeholders differs from those of schools and school districts. Farley-Ripple et al.'s (2018) conceptual framework is particularly useful in outlining these key features—particularly the notions of "value" and "usefulness."

First, engagement with schools and school districts requires researchers and community partners to value and be open to a teacher/school-driven mandate rather than a researcher-based research program or a community-driven focus. This requires these stakeholders to remain open to evaluations of research relevance based on school-based needs, varying school contexts, and even differing values. Relevance of the research to authentic problems of practice may be subject to practical critique and this may be source of discomfort. Mathematics is replete with math-myths and is hindered by negative past experiences. Respect and values for these views are paramount. Again, openness and value for bidirectionality is key.

Second, the structures and the processes for valuing knowledge mobilization in universities or within community groups may vary and may have limited influence on processes such as tenure and promotion, or performance reviews. Consequently, a readiness to engage in joint work of this nature must be valued broadly by partner institutions (i.e., time provided to do the work outside of the institution, and value in performance evaluations, funding, etc.). The engagement must be seen by researchers and community partners as useful to advancing the production of scholarly knowledge.

The case of the equity knowledge network

The Réseau de Savoir sur l'Équité / Equity Knowledge Network (RSEKN) is a bilingual network hosted by the University of Ottawa Faculty of Education and the Center for Research on Educational and Community Services (CRECS) with a mandate to promote equity and diversity as a priority in schools and their wider communities. The work of RSEKN is guided by the Ministry of Education's

Ontario Equity Action Plan, which builds upon past equity policies and documents with the aim of "identifying and eliminating discriminatory practices, systemic barriers and biases from schools and classrooms" (Ontario Ministry of Education, 2017, p. 4).

A relational model of knowledge mobilization (Ng-A-Fook, et al., 2015) structures and informs how RSEKN seeks to facilitate opportunities to connect teacher candidates, teachers, administrators, researchers, parents, students and community groups who seek to challenge systemic barriers for marginalized and racialized children and youth within public education across Ontario. According to Ng-A-Fook et al. (2015), a relational model of knowledge mobilization is a "best practice" for developing partnerships among policy makers, educational researchers, community, and public-school educators. We argue that faculties of education are in a unique position to become secondary brokers for implementing policy reforms within public education systems through bringing together educators, community groups, researchers, parents and students.

The RSEKN aims to extend existing local, regional and provincial networks to address systemic barriers within our education system across six intersectional priority themes: (1) anti-racist education; (2) refugee and newcomer education; (3) gender and sexuality education; (4) education for students with disabilities; (5) minority language education in pluralist contexts; and (6) income inequality and poverty. The RSEKN's work is underpinned by a commitment to four key principles through which we understand and conduct our work:

- *Bilingualism*—in recognition of the range of linguistic varieties present and performed across the province in French, English, bilingual and plurilingual contexts;
- *Intersectionality*—in recognition that social categories of identity—including but not limited to—race, gender, socioeconomic status, sexuality, and religion are interlocking concepts;
- *Relationality*—grounded in a relational understanding of human beings and acknowledges connections and interdependence at all levels including individual, group, institutional, and systemic; and
- *Serving communities*—grounded in a place of mutuality that fosters the notion of working together in partnerships, and acknowledges the existence of multiple, localized communities and their respective contexts.

RSEKN is structured as four regional teams each comprising the team lead (a recognized equity innovator in their respective fields), a communications officer, and several representatives from French and English school boards, educational institutions, parent groups, and community organizations who share a commitment to working towards equity and inclusion. With attention to the relational model of knowledge mobilization (Ng-A-Fook et al., 2015), and mindful of the complexity of research-policy-practice multidirectional connections

(Farley-Ripple et al., 2018), the RSEKN has sought to reach beyond immediate university-school partners to embrace, and to be informed through, relationships with community-based groups doing innovative equity work.

In the first phase of implementation, RSEKN established infrastructure (including web site, social media, communication officers); sponsored and promoted school and community-based events and conferences; communicated through blog posts and Twitter to ignite discussion around issues of equity within education; created and shared educational resources related to equity and diversity; and synthesized research studies toward making them more accessible to different educational stakeholders. For example, the English education communities hosted a *Lead Associate Teacher Day* at a local Ottawa high school, attended by researchers, educators, teacher candidates, high school students and equity innovators such as spoken word poets, whereas the Francophone team featured a keynote conference on inclusion issues in French-speaking communities and held a series of workshops for different stakeholders at the University of Ottawa. In line with our commitment to reaching beyond historical partners to engage with community, the RSEKN supported a Black Youth Conference facilitated entirely by racialized youth from a number of local high schools.

Each regional team is evolving in unique ways to address education priorities based on their organizational and individual partnerships with the view to consolidating and extending these each year to embrace additional educational and community partners. For example, the Eastern Ontario region offered a weekly RSEKN Lecture Series in which invited speakers shared their ongoing equity work with a public audience in order to make connections with and among stakeholders across the broader community. The Southern Ontario regional team is working with four regional school boards to determine their needs and translate research knowledge into accessible formats that will be mobilized to assist in addressing systemic inequitable treatment of racialized, poor, and students with special educational needs with respect to suspensions and expulsions. In another example, the Greater Toronto Area region of RSEKN is focused on exploring identity-based data collection, integration and reporting as a systemic response to social and educational inequities. In partnership with the York University Faculty of Education Summer Institute, community partners, faculty, teacher candidates, and educators have been involved in the co-creation and mobilization of systemic, equity-minded knowledge, which will eventually be shared as monographs and an online database is under development.

Capacity to collaborate to address systemic barriers

As a province-wide bilingual network, the RSEKN has evolved in multiple ways and the UOttawa co-Directors and regional leads have faced a number of challenges in relation to both our own and our partners' capacity to collaborate to address systemic barriers within public schools. We present some of these here as lessons learned and, for some, as ongoing challenges that we continue to navigate in this complex and critical equity work. We examine our own challenges against the RSEKN guiding principles (see above) in an effort to be reflective and hold ourselves accountable and responsible to the communities we seek to serve.

Readiness to include multiple contexts and perspectives

First and foremost, a network is a system of people and groups connected through shared belief, commitment, context, or understanding. For a network to become established and to extend, members need to build trust and respect and create a context where members can question without fear of exclusion—particularly so when one is speaking of a network focused on equity and inclusion! We ourselves, as network co-directors and regional leads, have been called upon repeatedly to reflect on how we (as a leadership team) are working in equitable and inclusive ways and how we are living in ways that respect the RSEKN core principles of *relationality* and *intersectionality*. We speak to some of these challenges, both internal and external, in an effort to be open and transparent as to the difficult work we have each committed to.

Being inclusive of both French and English education communities is a challenge not just in terms of communication, but also in recognizing that different linguistic communities have different contextual and cultural needs. Rather than establishing a largely English network and merely translating our products into French, we need to take the time to understand the nuances of the different equity work being done in French and English communities, work in partnership to serve the many different bilingual and plurilingual communities across Ontario, and favor cross-pollination between communities. Living up to the RSEKN guiding principle of *bilingualism* is challenging and we continue to seek ways to work together more effectively.

Ensuring spaces to build trust and respect among the leadership team is another challenge. We have prioritized opportunities that foster mutually beneficial, multi-directional, and collaborative dialogue about how to improve all of our work. As the equity network, we recognize that we have a real opportunity to put equity practices into action—not just in our 'products' but in how we work as a leadership team and within regional teams. As a leadership team we have had to be open to internal critique and challenge and to find a path through our responsibilities as co-Directors and enabling regional leads the autonomy to identify their own priorities and activities, according to the relationships and priorities of their respective communities. The lessons learned in this respect is to perhaps step back as co-Directors and to listen and hear community. To trust community-based relationships to guide work at a regional level and to focus more on brokering, facilitating and supporting connections. Moving forward, we are seeking to use tension arising from different assumptions and perspectives as opportunities for learning and growth and we have committed to sharing openly and honestly with the intention of collaboration and inclusion.

Valuing practitioner and community knowledge

We continue to work with our partners to counter a traditional reluctance to examine our assumed positionalities. As university researchers and teacher educators, we all have established relationships with school communities and often these relationships are grounded in research activities that bring with them a certain real or imagined hierarchy. How can we successfully work towards *serving communities* if the ways in which we work are based on entrenched hierarchies? As teacher educators engage with the RSEKN work we are mindful of the need to create ". . . hybrid spaces in teacher education where academic and practitioner knowledge and knowledge that exists in communities come together in less hierarchical ways" (Zeichner, 2010, p. 89). Valuing different knowledges and experiences has led us to engage with community artists and equity innovators and to strive to attend to voices from the community that are so often marginalized—students, parents, artists, performers—in spite of their role as key activists in advancing goals of equity and inclusion. The RSEKN seeks to amplify the ways in which we actively seek direction from community-based partners, equity actors and innovators. During our establishment phase in Year One we have had to face the challenges of working across multiple cultural, professional, and organizational differences both within the leadership team and with our community partners in the regional teams. We bring our internal reflections and negotiations, alongside the voices of our community partners, into our day to day work as professors, teachers and researchers. As we look forward, we will further assess the usefulness of research products created for our website, and the nature and quality of our relationships with our partners as we work to challenge to the different systemic barriers that still exist for different teachers and students within the public schooling system.

Our goal is not necessarily to create new activities but rather to ensure that those people currently doing innovative and groundbreaking work that promises to challenge systemic barriers to equity and inclusion are supported in bringing their work to educators, practitioners, researchers and policy makers. Our role as equity relational knowledge brokers is to amplify the voices of equity innovators and actors across the province and to facilitate connections of community-based equity innovators with schools and teachers.

Conclusions

Globally we are learning more about the complexities of building capacity for effective research use in schools and evidence-informed practice in education more generally (Nutley et al., 2007; Tseng, 2012; Coburn & Penuel, 2016; Farley-Ripple et al., 2018). Our experience with KNAER supports the argument made by Nutley et al. (2007) that research use is "a dynamic and complex mediated set of interactions between policy makers and practitioners, and researchers" (p. 305). It also exemplifies research–practice partnerships based on shared ownership and reciprocity, in which knowledge moves from research to practice as well as from practice to research or what Tseng et al. (2017) call "building two-way streets of engagement" (p. 3). Partnerships "require participants to navigate multiple cultural, professional and organizational differences" and these differences "can become obstacles that close down collaboration, or boundaries to be understood and navigated" (Penuel et al. 2015, p. 188).

The KNAER, with its interconnected thematic knowledge networks, is a significant development in research–practice partnerships. First, the Network is explicitly structured, funded and supported as a research–policy–practice partnership designed to build capacity for evidence informed policy and practice across multiple and diverse stakeholders. The KNAER model, by design, is a systems approach (see Best & Holmes, 2010). It recognizes that, if genuine connections between and among research and practice are to be made, an infrastructure is required to address challenges, including the gaps between research and practice identified by Farley-Ripple et al. (2018). Second, KNAER is an example of the next generation of research-practice partnerships (RPP), building on previous collaborations guided by principles of mutualism, commitment to long term collaboration and trusting relationships (Tseng et al., 2017). By incorporating multiple, interconnected thematic knowledge networks connected to provincial, regional and local communities of practice, the Network model reflects a growing understanding of knowledge mobilization as the multidirectional exchange of knowledge among institutional decision makers, researchers, educators, community members and policy makers (Nichols, Phipps, & Johnstone, 2014). Third, knowledge brokers and intermediaries in the KNAER Secretariat, thematic networks and communities of practice, government, and community partners are working intentionally to navigate professional, organizational, role, and cultural boundaries to ensure the usefulness and relevance of research products to inform professional practice and support improved student outcomes.

Implications and recommendations

The evolution of the KNAER over time illustrates the value of engaging researchers, practitioners and policy makers in long-term collaborative research–policy–practice partnerships designed to support continuous improvement in education. It also promises to generate new learning about conditions that facilitate or inhibit knowledge brokering, as well as strategies for building individual, organizational, and system readiness to engage in joint work that deepens research use and production.

Navigating cultural, professional, and organizational differences in the research, policy and practice communities requires knowledge brokers in and between universities, government, and school districts to co-create and share knowledge to inform practice. This work is multidirectional and challenging, as exemplified by the thematic networks and their respective communities of practice. Building readiness for collaborative work and knowledge mobilization requires all network partners to examine their own assumptions and increase their understanding of other professional roles and organizational cultures, processes, and priorities. Building trusting, reciprocal relationships that support this joint work takes time.

We recognize that additional work is needed to identify the factors that enhance and inhibit deeper and more effective research production and utilization and we expect further evidence of the KNAER's impact to emerge as the networks evolve. While the conceptual framework developed by Farley-Ripple et al. (2018) is based on a bidirectional model, it may be useful to expand these concepts to research–policy–practice models in order to deepen our understanding of knowledge brokering, the capacities required of intermediaries and boundary spanners, and how research–policy–practice partnerships can reduce gaps to improve education outcomes over time.

Further research on individual, organizational, and system readiness to undertake joint work across professional, organizational, and cultural boundaries, including a review of the literature on organizational readiness from other fields, may also generate new insights into the importance of innovation and risk taking and the role of brokers in facilitating collaboration among network partners.

References

Akkerman, S. & Bakker, A. (2011). Boundary crossing and boundary objects. *Review of Educational Research*, 81(2), 132–169.

Allen, K. & Schnell, K. (2016). Developing mathematics identity. *Mathematics Teaching in Middle School*, 21(7), 398–405.

Best, A. & Holmes, B. (2010). Systems thinking, knowledge and action: Towards better models and methods. *Evidence & Policy*, 6(2), 145–159.

Campbell, C., Pollock, K., Carr-Harris, S. & Briscoe, P. with Bairos, K., & Malik, S. (2014). *Knowledge network for applied education research (KNAER): Final report*. Ontario Institute for Studies in Education, University of Toronto, and Western University.

Coburn, C. & Penuel, W. (2016) Research–practice partnerships in education: Outcomes, dynamics, and open questions. *AERA Open*, 45(1), 48–54.

Dumay, X., Boonen, T., & Damme, J. V. (2013). Principal leadership long-term indirect effects on learning growth in mathematics. *The Elementary School Journal*, 114(2), 225–251.

Farley-Ripple, E., May, H., Karpyn, A., & Tilley, K. (2018). Rethinking connections between research and practice in education: A conceptual framework. *Educational Researcher*, 47(4), 235–245.

Gadanidis, G. (2012). Why can't I be a mathematician? *For the Learning of Mathematics*, 32(2), 20–26.

Gadanidis, G., Borba, M., Hughes, J., & Lacerda, H. (2016). Designing aesthetic experiences for young mathematicians: A model for mathematics education reform. *International Journal for Research in Mathematics Education*, 6(2), 225–244.

Gadanidis, G. & Caswell, B. (2018). *Computational modelling in elementary mathematics education: Making sense of coding in elementary classrooms*. May 2018 White Paper from the KNAER Mathematics Knowledge Network. Retrieved June 18, 2018 from http://mkn-rcm.ca/wp-content/uploads/2018/05/MKN-white-paper2-May-2018.pdf

Gadanidis, G. & Cummings, J. (2018). *Integrated mathematics + computer studies (grade 10): Reforming secondary school mathematics education*. April 2018 White Paper from the KNAER

Mathematics Knowledge Network. Retrieved June 18, 2018 from http://mkn-rcm.ca/wp-content/uploads/2018/04/MKN-white-paper-April-2018.pdf

Hardy, I. (2009). Teacher professional development: A sociological study of senior educator's PD priorities in Ontario. *Canadian Journal of Education*, *32*(3), 509–532.

Hargreaves, A. & Ainscow, M. (2015). The top and bottom of leadership and change. *The Phi Delta Kappan*, *97*(2), 42–48.

Kennedy, A., Deuel, A., Nelson, T. H., & Slavit, D. (2011). Requiring collaboration or distributing leadership? *The Phi Delta Kappan*, *92*(8), 20–24.

Lavis, J. N., Robertson, D., Woodside, J. M., McLeod, C. B., & Abelson, J. (2003). How can research organizations more effectively transfer research knowledge to research organizations decision makers? *Milbank Quarterly*, *81*(2), 221–248.

Lysenko, L., Abrami, P., Bernard, R., & Dagenais, C. (2015). Research use in education: An online survey of Canadian teachers. *Brock Education Journal*, 35–54.

McGarvey, L. M., Sternberg, G. Y., & Long, J. S. (2013). An unplanned path. *Teaching Children Mathematics*, *20*(3), 182–189.

Nichols, N. Phipps, D., & Johnstone, W. (2014) A case study from York University's knowledge mobilisation graduate student internship program: Planting the seeds for change. *J. Community Engagement and Scholarship*, *7*(2), 72–81.

Ng-A-Fook, N., Kane, R. G., Butler, J. K., Glithero, L., & Forte, R. (2015). Brokering knowledge mobilization networks: Policy reforms, partnerships, and teacher education. *Education Policy Analysis Archives*, *23*(122). doi: 10.14507/epaa.v23.2090

Nutley, S., Walter, I., & Davies, H (2007). *Using evidence: How research can inform public services*. Bristol, UK: The Policy Press.

Ontario Ministry of Education. (2017). *Ontario's education equity action plan*. Toronto, ON: Queen's Printer for Ontario.

Penuel, W. R., Allen, A. R., Coburn, C. E., & Farrell, C. (2015). Conceptualizing research–practice partnerships as joint work at boundaries. *Journal of Education for Students Placed at Risk* (JESPAR), 20 (1–2), 182–197.

Pollock, K., Campbell, C., McWhorter, D., vanRoosmalen, E., & Bairos, K. (2019). Developing a system for knowledge mobilisation: The case of the Knowledge Network for Applied Education Research (KNAER) as a middle tier. In D. Godfrey & C. Brown (Eds.), *Reforming education through research*. London: Routledge.

Tseng, V. (2012) *Partnerships: Shifting the dynamics between research and practice*. New York, NY: William T. Grant Foundation.

Tseng, V., Easton, J., & Supplee, L. (2017). Research–practice partnerships: Building two-way streets of engagement. *Society for Research in Child Development*, *30*(4): 1–17.

Ward, V. (2016). Why, whose, what and how? A framework for knowledge mobilisers. *Evidence & Policy*, *13*(3), 477–497.

Zeichner, K. (2010). Rethinking the connections between campus courses and field experiences in college and university-based teacher education. *Journal of Teacher Education*, *61*(1–2), 89–99.

6

AVENUES OF INFLUENCE

An exploration of school-based practitioners as knowledge brokers and mobilizers

Elizabeth Farley-Ripple and Sara Grajeda

Introduction

Ships passing in the night. It's a metaphor we might use to describe the relationship between research and practice in education. Decades of research have documented a disconnect between these two communities, often attributed to the different cultures, structures, and purposes of each. Bogenschneider and Corbett (2010) describe this as *community dissonance*, and it permeates not only education but other sectors such as health, social work, and others. Efforts to understand and reconcile this dissonance trace back to as early as the 1960s, with significant efforts to better link research and practice through research and policy. In education in the US, specifically, federal investments were made to build an infrastructure to support research, dissemination, development and utilization. For example, the Educational Research Information Centers (ERIC) system was initiated in 1966, the Regional Educational Laboratories system was established in the early 1960s, and the National Diffusion Network began operations in 1974.

In spite of these and other efforts, many would regard the gaps between research and practice decades later as persistent, with continued concerns about relevance, accessibility, conflicting findings, the need for research translation, and few system-wide structures that promote engagement across communities (Broekkamp & van Hout-Wolters, 2007; Burkhardt & Schoenfeld, 2003). This issue has garnered significant attention in recent years, in part because of accountability policy in the US public education system. Beginning with No Child Left Behind in 2001, federal policy has set expectations for decisions at the school, district, and state levels to be informed by data and evidence. The need for evidence-based decision-making thus has become more salient than ever before, demanding a deeper knowledge of the relationship between research and practice but also of the levers that can enable stronger ties.

Two lines of work respond to this demand. First are efforts to create *direct* links between research and practice. Research–practice partnerships (RPPs) represent one promising strategy. Stemming from consistent findings that the use of research is a relational issue—that is, one in which shared interests, trust, transparency, and continuous engagement across communities are important (Harrison, Davidson, & Farrell, 2017; Huberman, 1990)—effective RPPs offer a structure that surmounts typical barriers to research use, including relevance, timeliness, access, and actionability (Creaby & Haslam, this volume; Henrick et al., 2017; Farrell et al., 2017). RPPs have been supported with federal funds as well as funds from local and foundation sources, and as they've become more widespread, some evidence suggests that research resulting from this work is useful and has had an impact on local decision-making, though significant additional research on outcomes of RPPs is needed (Coburn & Penuel, 2016).

A second set of efforts focuses on opportunities to leverage *indirect* links between research and practice. This includes knowledge brokerage (KB) and knowledge mobilization (KMb)—the foci of this book—widely recognized as potential levers for bridging the two communities (Cooper & Levin, 2010; Massell, Goertz, & Barnes, 2012; Malin et al., 2018). For example, individuals or organizations that engage in KB or KMb activities may serve as linkage agents (Louis, 1977; Hood, 1982), particularly when direct relationships between communities are difficult to establish or sustain, by engaging in translating, sharing, or otherwise communicating knowledge. In doing so, they may have the ability to draw from a broad range of research or researchers and can reach a broader set of practitioners, overcoming the challenges of scale that direct relationships might pose. In fact, recent research suggests that these indirect mechanisms are the primary means by which education leaders access research information (Penuel et al., 2017).

Such mechanisms, however, aren't well understood in the context of education. And as is suggested in the goals of this book, there is a need to unpack the roles Bush (2017) identifies for knowledge brokers, as well as the *who, what, how,* and *why* components Ward (2017) sets out, to deepen our understanding of linkages between education research and practice. In this chapter, we use these frames to explore the specific case of school-based practitioners as knowledge brokers. We do this by bringing three sets of ideas together: knowledge brokerage and mobilization, teacher networks, and the use of research evidence in education.

Conceptualizing school-based practitioners as knowledge brokers

Our interest in understanding the role of school-based practitioners as knowledge brokers positioned to bridge the gap between research and practice stems from work in the Center for Research Use in Education (CRUE). The CRUE conceptual framework (Farley-Ripple et al., 2018) draws on early theories of two communities (Caplan, 1979; Dunn, 1980) and expands on the idea of community dissonance (Bogenschneider & Corbett, 2010) in the context of education. Central to its work is the premise that the use of research evidence is not merely an issue of increasing practitioner uptake or improving researchers' production and dissemination of knowledge. Rather, we argue this problem is *bidirectional*, demanding attention to mechanisms that coordinate or link research and practice in ways not currently supported by neither the educational system nor the research enterprise.

Literature suggests that there are roles and functions that are not inherent in either the work of educators or researchers that may improve the use of research evidence—roles and functions that may be played by knowledge brokers. Early work on "linking agents" in school improvement provides insight into those functions, including coordinating and boundary spanning, finding resources, providing individual technical assistance, serving as curriculum expert, and providing problem-solving or implementation support (Hood, 1982; Louis, 1977; Louis & Kell, 1981). More recently, Kochanek, Scholz, and Garcia (2015) report important activities that brokers perform in addressing the gap, such as: identifying common goals, negotiating a research agenda, organizing alliance meetings, and facilitating alliance communication. Similar activities are reported by others (Lomas, 2000). Brokers also build and maintain relationships, provide "coaching" related to technical and administrative components of research use (Huberman, 1990), and translate research jargon into ordinary language that is more accessible to those who might put the research findings into action (Jackson-Bowers, Kalucy, & McIntyre, 2006).

Despite agreement about the potential value of knowledge brokers, in education, the concept has been understudied, undertheorized and often conceptualized narrowly. For example, Neal and colleagues (2015) find that the chain of brokerage between research and practice is more complex and much longer than prior theory suggests, and is likely to involve multiple kinds of participants with multiple kinds of roles. Further, literature to date has primarily focused on *brokers* as organizations or individuals, but prior work (Farley-Ripple et al., 2017) suggests that understanding *brokers* provides a limited perspective on the ways in which research and relationships between research and practice occur. Rather, we are concerned with a broader set of ideas which we refer to as *knowledge brokerage*—a dynamic and complex set of actors, activities, motivations within which research is exchanged, transformed, and otherwise communicated. Implicit in this definition are Bush's (2017) and Ward's (2017) perspectives, as well the framework around which this book is organized (Malin & Brown, this volume).

Figure 6.1 provides an illustration of the complexity that underlies knowledge brokerage, constructed from preliminary qualitative work of our Center. In it, we recognize that the traditional idea of brokerage—featured at left with an arrow leading from researcher (R) to an intermediary to practitioner (P)—does not capture the multiple combination of actors, nor the direction of relations (solid versus dotted lines), the motivations that lead to relations (yellow text) nor the activities that occur in each knowledge transaction (black text). Fortunately, the study of research brokerage and knowledge mobilization is growing exponentially, and as evidenced in this book, we are developing useful knowledge about many of the actors, relations, and activities described in this figure.

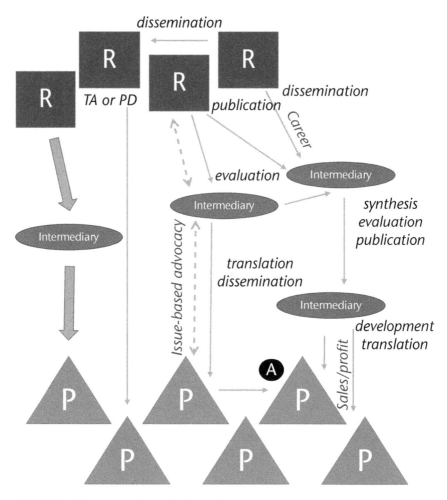

FIGURE 6.1 Illustration of knowledge brokerage

Of particular interest in this chapter is the arrow marked A. This arrow denotes the role of an educator as a knowledge broker and knowledge brokerage as a process that can happen within schools. This phenomenon has gone largely unrecognized in the study of research use in education, which tends to focus on intermediary organizations, though a few studies note its presence. The most direct observation of school-based knowledge brokerage comes from Finnigan, Daly, and Che (2013), who found that the spread of research-based ideas within schools tended to be attributed to the principal. Additionally, Neal et al. (2015) and Hopkins et al. (2018) draw on Gould and Fernandez's (1989) typology of brokers to explore research brokerage, two types of which involve members of the same group (gate-keepers and coordinators) sharing information with peers. Applied to the context of education, these are cases where a member of the education community serves as a broker between colleagues and another internal actor or an external actor—such as a researcher or research organization.

Although understudied in the literature on research use in education, the idea of educators as brokers is well documented in the study of teacher networks and school improvement. Extant literature has established the importance of teacher networks in a variety of educational processes and outcomes (Coburn & Russell, 2008; Cole & Weinbaum, 2010; Penuel et al., 2009; Daly & Finnigan, 2009; Daly & Finnigan, 2011; Spillane et al., 2009; Yoon & Baker-Doyle, 2018; Moolenaar, 2012; Penuel et al., 2012; Baker-Doyle, 2011; Frank et al., 2011).

These networks are powerful levers for social capital and organizational trust, but also for the flow of information and resources throughout the school community. Several studies have documented the role of advice networks in shaping teachers' instructional practice (Farley-Ripple & Buttram, 2015; Liou & Daly, 2018; Penuel et al., 2018; Hopkins et al., 2018; Daly, et al, 2010). Central actors—those to whom members of the school turn for advice or resources—may be highly influential in shaping the work of schools. Sometimes this influence is due to formal roles given to individuals. For example, a school might be organized to ensure instructional coaches are positioned to support (a form of influence) teachers at multiple grade levels (Farley-Ripple & Buttram, 2018). Other times this influence may be less formal or planned. Teachers may turn to someone based on trust, expertise, or even proximity.

Teachers also rely on sources external to their school or organization. For example, the growing literature on professional learning networks (Brown & Poortman, 2018) suggests that such networks help educators to develop new knowledge and skills which, in turn, can lead to improvement. Specific work on supporting teachers' engagement with research finds networks to be promising in developing research-based knowledge and building organizational capacity to use research informed practices (Brown, 2018).

Bringing together literature on the use of research evidence, the role of brokers in bridging the research-practice gap, and the power of teacher networks to shape school practice, we argue that school-based practitioners that engage in knowledge brokerage are positioned to influence the role of research in schools by mobilizing research-based information within school networks. In this chapter, we explore these ideas more deeply. Specifically, we seek to understand:

1. Who acts as knowledge brokers in schools?
2. Why do they engage in knowledge brokering?
3. What do they broker?
4. What activities do they engage in as brokers?

Our approach

The Center for Research Use in Education (CRUE) is charged with measuring and studying research use in schools as guided by our conceptual framework

(Farley-Ripple et al., 2018). As a preliminary step in research design, we interviewed educators, researchers, and organizational leaders positioned to serve as research brokers about their work. These data were collected as part of the instrument development process for a larger research project on research use in education conducted through the Institute of Education Sciences (IES) funded Center. The sample consisted of 15 researchers, 16 intermediary organizations and 15 practitioners at the district and school levels across three states. The objective of this phase of our work was to compare and contrast an emergent set of concepts related to brokerage against existing frameworks to identify areas in need of further theoretical and empirical examination. Therefore although we do not present these qualitative data here, the results of this inquiry were instrumental in building of a conceptual framework employed here, including Figure 6.1 and the definition of brokerage that guides our inquiry (see Farley-Ripple et al., 2017).

In order to understand the concepts we uncovered in more depth and on a broader scale, we developed a survey. The purposes of the survey were to be able to address some of the lingering questions from our qualitative results as well as to ask more about research use concepts from the perspectives of research, practice, and intermediary communities at scale. Here, we focus on our survey of practitioners. We built a blueprint from our framework that would capture these data through five separate sections of the survey intended to comprehensively measure research use. The survey has undergone two rounds of pilot data collection. After each pilot, the survey has undergone measurement analyses and many revisions to improve the clarity and validity of the findings.

For the purposes of this chapter, we focus on survey measures that address the elements of brokerage described earlier, including *what* gets brokered, brokerage *activities*, and *purposes and motivations*. Table 6.1 explains how our survey items map onto the brokerage framework, and the complete set of survey items is included in the appendix.

Data from the two pilots include 1,628 survey responses (54% response rate) from teachers and administrators in over 60 schools. Schools came from urban, suburban and rural areas and represented elementary, middle and high school grades. Across schools, the average proportion of students receiving free or reduced-price lunch was 48% and 15% of students were in special education programs. In total, 4% percent of students had limited English proficiency. Just over half (51%) of students belonged to racial minority groups with black students having the highest representation (31%). Of the practitioners who responded, most were classroom teachers (60%), or special education teachers (14%). A total of 6% of responses were from school or district administrators.

The full survey had around 400 questions and took between 30 and 45 minutes to complete. As such, not all respondents finished all sections of the survey, and 873 responses were able to be included in our analysis. Below we explain what we learned about each of our research questions from these data.

TABLE 6.1 Description of measures by dimension of conceptual framework

Element	Measures
Individual characteristics	School role Experience Education level Research experience and training
Purposes and motivation	Agreement with statements about attitudes towards education research and the value of research use, e.g. • whether researchers understand the evolving problems in schools, • whether educators in their school are expected to use research, • whether they believe student learning improves when they use research-based strategies.
What gets brokered?	Frequency of sharing research products and their format, frequency of sharing capacity-building strategies, sources of research-based information
Brokerage activities	Frequency of the following activities when sharing research, e.g.: • evaluating quality, • providing technical assistance, • developing products or programs, • facilitating discussion.

The who, what, and how of knowledge brokerage in schools

Who acts as knowledge brokers in schools?

Many people in schools engage in some form of knowledge brokering, though some are more active in that role than others. Brokerage items in our survey asked how frequently practitioners had shared certain types of research (e.g., articles, district evaluations, PD materials, expert opinions) in the past year. More than 85% of respondents reported sharing at least one of these types of materials with colleagues at least 1–2 times per year, suggesting that research, in its various forms, does move through schools through educator networks. However, other forms of knowledge brokering were less common. A second group of questions asked if practitioners shared strategies for accessing, understanding, or implementing research, or helped others connect to share or discuss research. In each category, approximately 50% of participants indicated that they never shared strategies or connected other people in the previous year and 35% reported never engaging in any of those activities.

In order to pull out the more active or potentially influential knowledge brokers in our sample, we combined questions about how often participants were sharing research or research related strategies in a latent class analysis (LCA). The results revealed a set of participants engaged in active brokering—sharing all types of research often, moderate brokering—sharing all types of research sometimes, or they were rarely sharing any research at all (Loglikelihood = -9806.97, AIC = 19705.97, BIC = 19925.46, Entropy = 0.92). We focus on the class of *active knowledge brokers* (heretofore, simply knowledge brokers) as they are likely to be more central in school-based networks and to be influential in the diffusion of research and research-based ideas.

We found 96 knowledge brokers in our sample. Of schools with at least one knowledge broker, there were, on average, 2.2 knowledge brokers per school. However, 16 of the 59 schools who answered brokering questions had no (active) knowledge brokers. Though differences were small, schools with brokers tended to believe more strongly that school personnel were generally expected to use research to inform decisions, and they more often agreed that research changed the way they thought about practice and continually expanded practitioners' knowledge about teaching and learning. Our data do not permit deeper inquiry into these differences but we note that this issue warrants further attention.

The distribution of knowledge brokers across school roles matches the distribution of roles across the larger sample, and they have similar levels of experience and education. This suggests that there is no typical professional profile for a knowledge broker. However, knowledge brokers have had many more different experiences than their peers. On nearly every measure of prior experience or training, knowledge brokers report greater exposure to and engagement with research as part of their professional learning opportunities, as indicated in Table 6.2. Across the board, knowledge brokers were more likely to have experience with research through undergraduate and graduate programs, PD around critically consuming

TABLE 6.2 Differences in research training and experience

Research training and experience	All educators	Knowledge brokers
Graduate program emphasized research use	32.3%	58.3%***
Conducted research in graduate program	33.3%	51.0%**
Participated in a research–practice partnership	5.4%	14.6%**
Participated in PD around critically consuming research	13.5%	33.3%***
Used research in PLCs	23.8%	42.7%***
Participated in a research conference	10.4%	21.9%**
Took an introductory statistics course	81.3%	78.9%
Took a course in research design	43.0%	60.5%**

Notes: Chi-square tests were conducted to determine whether differences were statistically significantly different. * indicates p<.05, ** indicates p<.01, and *** indicates p<.001.

research, engaging with research through PLCs, attending research conferences, and reviewing research and applying research to their own work.

Why do they broker research?

In order to get at purposes and motivations, we draw on questions about their role but also their beliefs about research and its utility in practice. Across the larger sample of practitioners, 43% said that sharing research was *not* expected as part of their role in their school or district, and only 3% said it was highly expected of them. However, among our knowledge brokers, 80% felt at least some expectation to share research as part of their professional responsibilities, with nearly half indicating moderate or greater expectations for their role. We note that 19% perceived no expectation at all and still shared research often. Higher expectations were reported across roles for knowledge brokers except for school administrators, who tended to polarize toward the two of extremes of no expectation and high expectation.

Knowledge brokers may engage in this work for different reasons as well. We asked participants to share some of their perspectives on education research including how they valued research and how they think research is used in their organization. We used a chi-square test for differences between knowledge brokers and the rest of the sample on 12 questions. In many aspects, knowledge brokers had similar perspectives to the rest of the sample—particularly in areas dealing with views on the research that is produced, research salience, and organizational support for incorporating research into practice.

Interestingly, knowledge brokers seemed more positive than their peers in the belief that using research translates into better practices. They also were more likely to report that there were general expectations across their organization to be using research in decisions. Finally, knowledge brokers are more likely to think that other teachers in their school are using research conceptually to refine their knowledge and perspectives of their practice. Knowledge brokers seem to have a more positive outlook on the potential of research to improve practice, even though they face some of the same challenges and frustrations as their peers with the state of research generally.

What do knowledge brokers share?

As described earlier, it is important to understand *what* knowledge brokers mobilize. We asked about two categories of brokerage—one in which research itself, in any number of forms, is shared and one in which research-related capacities were shared. Figure 6.2 indicates the frequency of those behaviors as reported by knowledge brokers. Evident in the image is the fact that capacities or strategies related to research use, including connecting people, strategies for reading/understanding, accessing, and implementing research, are among the most commonly brokered "items" in schools. External research (e.g. articles, reports) and materials

TABLE 6.3 Differences in perceptions related to purposes and motivation to broker knowledge

Purposes and motivation	All educators	Knowledge brokers
Researchers have a solid grasp on evolving problems in schools.	44.0%	52.2%
Researchers need to do more to make their work relevant for my school.	75.1%	75.8%
Research addresses the most important issues schools face.	45.4%	51.5%
Most education research suggests actionable steps to take in practice.	53.8%	65.2%
Research takes into consideration the varying levels of resources available to schools to implement research findings.	35.4%	44.1%
Practitioners often struggle to find research on issues in their classrooms.	42.9%	47.8%
In general, we are expected to use research to inform decisions.	68.2%	80.3%**
Our school/district prioritizes research in decision making.	59.7%	70.8%
When I use research-based strategies, student learning improves.	80.0%	92.3%***
We use research because a supervisor or administrator requires it.	53.2%	56.1%
Research has changed the way I think about my practice.	67.9%	87.7%**
I have used research to continually expand my knowledge about teaching and learning.	71.6%	87.9%**

Notes: Chi-square tests were conducted to determine whether differences were statistically significantly different. * indicates p<.05, ** indicates p<.01, and *** indicates p<.001.

from professional development rank highly as well. Less common but still note-worthy are formal analyses of data, school-generated research, and program or publisher materials. Opinions of national experts and central office research are least likely to be shared across a school.

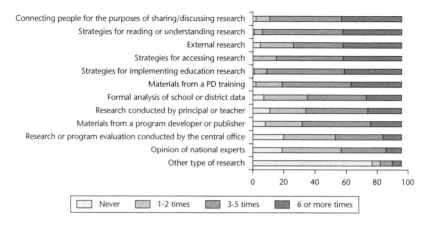

FIGURE 6.2   Types of knowledge shared in schools

As a follow up, we asked in what format knowledge brokers share research. Practitioners primarily share the original research product, an interpretation of the findings, or strategies that were developed based on the findings. On average, knowledge brokers share these formats equally frequently, with between a quarter and third indicating they share each format often, and about half indicating they share research in that format sometimes.

As important as *what* knowledge is brokered is *whose* knowledge is brokered, as Ward (2017) notes. The professional networks— including individuals, organizations, and media sources—knowledge brokers rely on for research are likely to indirectly influence school practice and decision-making. We asked respondents to identify up to ten of each type of source and to categorize them to facilitate comparing and contrasting networks. We entered these data into UCINet's E-net software to generate ego networks—that is, data that captures the size (number of sources) and composition (types of sources, operationalized as the proportion constituted by each source) of their professional networks for connecting to research. We compare means between knowledge brokers and their peers on these two dimensions, using ANOVA to test for statistically significant differences.

Knowledge brokers' networks were larger (mean=8.4) than other educators' networks (mean=6.1, p=.003) but had about the same proportion of individuals, organizations and media sources. Overall, about half of educators' networks for connecting to research is through individuals, with organizations and media equally constituting the other half. Many of the most frequently relied upon sources are considered "local" (Rosenkopf & Almeida, 2003), or within the practice community (e.g. colleagues, professional associations). Knowledge brokers reported connections with the same types of sources with roughly the same frequency as other educators, with some notable exceptions. On average, knowledge brokers were five times more likely to have connections to independent research organizations (average network proportion 2 versus .4, p<.001). Additionally, they were twice as likely to identify research databases as important sources more than their peers (5.8 versus 2.6, p=.002).

TABLE 6.4 Summary of networks by which knowledge brokers access research

Type	Category	Avg. proportion of network	Examples
Individual	Teacher	11.44	
	Principal	7.88	
	Instructional coach	6.37	
	District administration	4.76	
	Other school staff	4.22	
	External researcher	2.16	
	Program developer or professional developer	2.00	
Media	Research database	5.82	ERIC; Google Scholar; EBSCO Host
	Social media	3.59	Facebook; Pinterest; Twitter; or following specifically; US News Education; NatGeo Education; Edmodo
	Magazine	3.33	Education Leadership; Scholastic Teacher; Time; NASSP; ASCD Smart Brief; Philadelphia Public School Notebook
	News	2.45	Ed Week; New York Times; "reliable sources"
	Peer reviewed journal	1.97	The Reading Teacher; Journal of Applied Behavioral Analysis; Journal of Chemical Education
	Book	1.70	Driven by Data; Guided Math; I Wish my Teacher Knew; Teach Like a Champion
	Other databases	1.30	Google; Ed Reflect
	Blog	1.30	Edutopia; Cult of Pedagogy; George, Curious Principal of Change
	Curriculum	0.00	N/A
	Website	0.00	N/A

Organization	Professional association	8.50	ASCD; National Education Association; Delaware State Education Association; National Science Teachers Association;
	School district	3.98	
	Program developer or PD organization	3.34	Compass Math; Lexia; McGraw Hill; Pearson; ReadWriteThink
	University-based research organization	2.92	Penn GSE; University of Delaware; Harvard; Millersville University
	Independent research organization	1.97	Research for Action; CLASP
	Government agency	0.61	US Department of Education, Pennsylvania Department of Education, NASA
	Foundation	0.52	Wallace Foundation; the Cross Foundation; Howard Hughes Medical Institute
	Advocacy group	0.10	Art21 Educators; Autism Services, Education, Resources, and Training (ASERT); Delaware English Language Learners Teachers and Advocates (DELLTA)

Note: Examples for individual sources and districts as organizations are not provided as to protect the confidentiality of respondents.

What do knowledge brokers do when they share research?

Our early qualitative data suggested that brokers don't merely pass information, but engage in specific activities in order to mobilize that knowledge—leading us to ask further questions about *how* they broker. We asked about ten activities knowledge brokers might engage in, drawing on our preliminary qualitative data and

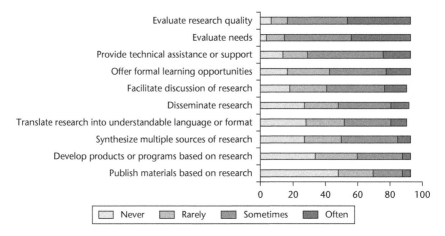

FIGURE 6.3 Activities knowledge brokers report engaging in when sharing research

prior literature to generate the list. In Figure 6.3, we present those results. Most often, knowledge brokers evaluate quality of research and the needs of the school or colleague when sharing research. They are also highly likely to provide technical assistance or support for using research as well as lead formal learning opportunities and facilitate discussion. Less common but still done at least "sometimes" by half the knowledge brokers are translation of research for practitioner audiences, synthesizing multiple sources of research, and simply disseminating research. The least common activities were to develop programs or publish products based on research.

Recognizing and supporting school-based knowledge brokerage

Literature to date has demonstrated the importance of teacher networks in a range of educational processes and outcomes, including the flow of information. Coupled with increased expectations for the role of research in educational decision-making, it is important to recognize and unpack the roles and activities of school-based knowledge brokers. Our data are an initial step toward this end. We find that research-based knowledge is, in fact, frequently shared in schools, but also through our LCA we find that a small percentage of educators are actively engaged in the work of knowledge brokering. An examination of this group through the data above provide important insights related to recognizing their contributions and supporting knowledge-brokering capacity at the school level

Recognizing contributions

The knowledge brokers identified in this study are positioned to help bridge the gap between research and practice and they may do so in a number of ways: by building skills, by expanding the types of research that flows through schools, and by strengthening a culture of research use.

First, knowledge brokers were more likely to broker research-based ideas and information as well as strategies for using research than their peers. We especially note the latter contribution, which bears important resemblance to early work on external linking agents (Louis, 1977; Hood, 1982). Sharing strategies for accessing, interpreting, and implementing research as well as connecting people around research are among the most common resources knowledge brokers share with colleagues. This finding is consistent with the types of research-related experiences that knowledge brokers have had and now bring to their school. Further, sharing these skills may help build research use capacity school-wide and may, as observed by Brown (2018), ultimately make a difference in whether and how education research shapes decision-making in their context.

Additionally, our examination of knowledge brokers' professional networks finds that their networks are both larger than others' and include research-specific resources. Practically speaking, larger networks may mean increased access to research-based information and in general greater access to information and expertise (Honig & Coburn, 2008; Finnigan, Daly, & Che, 2013). Further, they were much more likely to tap into research-specific resources such as research databases and research organizations, which may be tied to knowledge brokers' prior experiences. Ties to these types of resources may increase *direct* access to education research or researchers. Although beyond the scope of our work here, direct access, as opposed to access through an intermediary organization or media source, may change the type and quality of research information that schools access as part of their decision-making.

Lastly, knowledge brokers' work appears to be related to their beliefs about research and their experiences using research. Although not statistically significantly different, knowledge brokers have more positive attitudes about research in general. Additionally, they assign significantly different value to the use of research, as they are more likely to believe its use improves student learning and positively influences their work as an educator. These findings hint at their motivation for serving as knowledge brokers. They are also more likely to report an expectation to use research in their schools. Thus, there may be an association between knowledge brokering and a schools' culture of research use. As this is a cross sectional study, we cannot assign directionality to the relationships we found; however, coupled with other research with similar findings (Brown, et al, 2018; Brown, this volume; Coldwell et al., 2017) the potential influence of knowledge brokers on schools' decision-making cultures is promising and worthy of further study.

Supporting knowledge brokering capacity in schools

Results of our analyses suggest two sets of strategies for building and supporting capacity for knowledge brokerage at the school level. The first pertains to how we think about staffing schools, and the second pertains to how stakeholders in the educational system can support those that serve as knowledge brokers.

Staffing considerations. Evidence from our study suggests that knowledge brokers may make important contributions to the flow of information within schools, to the capacity of educators to engage with research, and to school culture. Given these potential contributions, two of our findings suggest that one way to support knowledge brokerage in schools is through staffing: the uneven distribution of knowledge brokers across schools and the notably different—and observable—experiences that knowledge brokers have had.

We noted earlier that 16 of 59 schools had no respondent classified as active brokers. This does not mean that no one shares research-based information in those schools or that there is no one whose job includes expectations for sharing research. Rather, it means that educators in these schools are less active in knowledge brokering, and, as a result, may miss out on some of the contributions identified above. Additional research is needed to understand the specific contexts in which knowledge brokers (as described here) work, in part to ensure access to their contributions is equitably distributed and available to benefit schools struggling to improve.

One way to address the distribution of knowledge brokers may be to explicitly seek out educators with the background or disposition to serve in such a capacity. Our data suggest that some of the differentiating characteristics of knowledge brokers are observable—that is, that they might be able to be captured during the hiring process, as opposed to soft attributes that are hard to evaluate without extensive interaction. For example, knowledge brokers were more likely to have been part of a research project or been in a program that emphasized research, as well as to have engaged with research in PLCs, professional development, or a research conference. They may also demonstrate different beliefs about the value and role of research. All of these may figure into hiring decisions, particularly for schools that lack active knowledge brokers or seek to build additional capacity.

Supporting knowledge brokers. Attending to knowledge brokering in the hiring process may depend on factors such as turnover, supply, and autonomy in staffing. However, capacity for knowledge brokerage in schools may be able to be built through intentional supports, whether from school leadership or from other stakeholders in the educational system. We emphasize *intentionality* here because we acknowledge that few knowledge brokers felt that this role was part of their formal expectations. We suspect that without formal recognition of this role or contribution, there are likely few supports explicitly targeting their needs. Relatedly, we suggest it may be important to have conversations within organizations to clarify, if not formalize, the work.

We found that basic background characteristics are not predictive of being a knowledge broker. It's not more likely with more education, and brokering doesn't come as you gain more teaching experience. Rather, brokering seems to be associated with increased exposure to research and research-related experiences through many venues. In fact, there was not just one experience that brokers were more likely to have; they were more likely to have all of the research-related experiences listed in the survey. Therefore, one way to bolster knowledge brokerage in schools is to make a concerted effort to give practitioners more direct experiences with research—a recommendation also issued by Drill and colleagues (2012) in one of the few studies of teachers' use of research in the US.

Relatedly, our findings related to *what* and *how* knowledge brokers share research also suggest opportunities for enhancing and supporting their work. Like others', knowledge brokers' networks tend to be "local"—i.e., be largely constituted by school or district colleagues and professional organizations related to their work. Knowledge brokers (and their schools) may benefit from opportunities that expand networks and remove constraints on the kinds of research that enter the school (Finnigan, Daly, & Che, 2013).

Both direct experience with research and opportunities to expand research networks might be supported by stakeholders within and outside of the education system. School leaders might consider giving financial support or release time to attend a research conference, providing professional learning opportunities to engage in research, or encouraging research use in PLCs. Outside of school, preservice and in-service preparation programs are well-positioned to support knowledge brokerage and could incorporate opportunities to engage *with* research, *in* research, and with *researchers*. Additionally, professional associations appear to be important resources for accessing research-based information. Mobilizing these organizations to increase exposure to research, to build research-related skills, and to expand the types and quality of resources accessed by knowledge brokers may help maximize and/or expand the research resources that highly utilized organizations.

Second, knowledge brokers also frequently engage in evaluation of needs and of research, interpretation of research, and development of strategies based on research—activities that demand particular skills and deep knowledge of their context. These are time consuming, resource intensive, and context specific—which means they are hard for researchers or intermediary organizations to enact at scale. In contrast, activities such as synthesizing research, dissemination, and developing programs were less likely to be part of knowledge brokers' activities. This may mean that researchers or intermediaries can support school-based knowledge brokers by engaging in this aspect of the work, enabling knowledge brokers to focus efforts on applications in their own schools. Although preliminary, this division of responsibilities may move us toward coordinated and complementary work across communities.

Conclusion

Our purpose, shared with the other authors in this volume, has been to shed light on this "third space" between research and practice with a focus on one particular, often overlooked, type of knowledge broker. Uniquely situated within their organizations, school-based knowledge brokers create avenues of influence by occupying important roles in school networks and possessing experiences, skills, and motivations that differ from their peers. Evidenced in our data, these individuals take on roles and activities not inherent in the work of researchers or practitioners and may make important contributions to the capacity for research use in school decision-making—in short, they engage in the roles and activities that Bush (2017) argues characterizes knowledge brokers. This is undoubtedly a first step in understanding the *who, what, how,* and *why* of knowledge broker-age in schools, but even these early findings suggest opportunities to recognize and support new roles for educators, and to harness their potential for generating meaningful change and improvement in education.

References

Baker-Doyle, K. J. (2011). *The networked teacher: How new teachers build social networks for professional support.* New York: Teachers College Press.

Bogenschneider, K., & Corbett, T.J. (2010). *Evidence-based policymaking: Insights from policy-minded researchers and research-minded policymakers.* New York, NY: Taylor and Francis Group.

Broekkamp, H., & van Hout-Wolters, B. (2007). The gap between educational research and practice: A literature review, symposium, and questionnaire. *Educational Research and Evaluation, 13*(3), 203–220.

Brown, C. (2018). Research Learning Networks: A case study in using networks to increase knowledge mobilization at scale. In *Networks for Learning* (pp. 38–55). New York: Routledge.

Brown, C., & Poortman, C. L. (Eds.). (2018). *Networks for learning: Effective collaboration for teacher, school and system improvement.* New York: Routledge.

Brown, C., Zhang, D., Xu, N. and Corbett, S. (2018). Exploring the impact of social rela-tionships on teachers' use of research: A regression analysis of 389 teachers in England. *International Journal of Education Research, 89,* 36–46.

Burkhardt, H., & Schoenfeld, A. H. (2003). Improving educational research: Toward a more useful, more influential, and better-funded enterprise. *Educational Researcher, 32*(9), 3–14.

Bush, J. (2017). Am I an evidence broker? Reflections on a trip to North America. [blog post]. Retrieved from http://www.evidenceforlearning.org.au/news/am-i-an-evi dence-broker-reflections-on-a-trip-to-north-america/

Caplan, N. (1979). The two-communities theory and knowledge utilization. *American Behavioral Scientist, 22*(3), 459–470.

Coburn, C. E., & Penuel, W. R. (2016). Research–practice partnerships in education: Outcomes, dynamics, and open questions. *Educational Researcher, 45*(1), 48–54.

Coburn, C. E., & Russell, J. L. (2008). District policy and teachers' social networks. *Education Evaluation and Policy Analysis, 30*(3), 203–235.

Coldwell, M., Greany, T., Higgins, S., Brown, C., Maxwell, B., Stiell, B., Stoll, L, Willis, B. and Burns, H. (2017). *Evidence-informed teaching: An evaluation of progress in England.* London: Department for Education.

Cole, R. P., & Weinbaum, E. H. (2010). Changes in attitude: Peer influence in high school reform. In A. J. Daly (Ed.), *Social network theory and educational change* (pp. 77–96). Cambridge, MA: Harvard University Press.

Cooper, A., & Levin, B. (2010). Theory, research and practice in mobilizing research knowledge in education. In *Knowledge Mobilization and Educational Research* (pp. 29–41). New York: Routledge.

Daly, A. J., & Finnigan, K. (2009). A bridge between worlds: Understanding network structure to understand change strategy. *Journal of Educational Change, 11*(2), 111–138.

Daly, A. J., & Finnigan, K. (2011). The ebb and flow of social network ties between dis-trict leaders under high stakes accountability. *American Education Research Journal, 48*(1), 39–79.

Daly, A. J., Moolenaar, N., Bolivar, J., & Burke, P. (2010). Relationships in reform: The role of teachers' social networks. *Journal of Educational Administration, 48*(3), 20–49.

Drill, K., Miller, S., & Behrstock-Sherratt, E. (2012). *Teachers' perspectives on educational research.* American Institute for Research. Retrieved from http://files.eric.ed.gov/full text/ED530742.pdf

Dunn, W.N. (1980). The two-communities metaphor and models of knowledge use. *Knowledge, 1,* 515–536.

Farley-Ripple, E.N., & Buttram, J. (2015). The development of capacity for data use: The role of teacher networks in an elementary school. *Teachers College Record, 117* (4), p. 1–34.

Farley-Ripple, E.N., & Buttram, J. (2018). Structuring for success. In Susan A. Yoon & Kira Baker-Doyle (Eds.), *Social capital, social networks, teachers, and educational change: Interventions and outcomes.* London: Taylor and Francis.

Farley-Ripple, E.N., Tilley, J., & Tise, J. (2017). Brokerage and the research–practice gap: A theoretical and empirical examination. Paper presented at the 2017 annual meeting of the American Educational Research Association.

Farley-Ripple, E.N., May, H., Karpyn, A., Tilley, K., & McDonough, K. (2018). Understanding educational research use in schools: A conceptual framework. *Educational Researcher, 47*(4), 235–245. doi.org/10.3102/0013189X18761042

Farrell, C., et al. (2017). *A descriptive study of the IES researcher–practitioner partnerships in education research program: Interim report.* Boulder, CO: University of Colorado, Boulder, National Center for Research, Policy, and Practice. Retrieved from www.ncrpp.org.

Finnigan, K. S., Daly, A. J., & Che, J. (2013). Systemwide reform in districts under pressure: The role of social networks in defining, acquiring, using, and diffusing research evidence. *Journal of Educational Administration, 51*(4), 476–497.

Frank, K. A., Zhao, Y., Penuel, W. R., Ellefson, N., & Porter, S. (2011). Focus, fiddle, and friends: Experiences that transform knowledge for the implementation of innovations. *Sociology of Education, 84*(2), 137–156.

Gould, R. V., & Fernandez, R. M. (1989). Structures of mediation: A formal approach to brokerage in transaction networks. *Sociological methodology,* 19, 89–126.

Harrison, C., Davidson, K., & Farrell, C. (2017). Building productive relationships: District leaders' advice to researchers. *International Journal of Education Policy and Leadership, 12*(4), 4.

Henrick, E. C., Cobb, P., Penuel, W. R., Jackson, K., & Clark, T. (2017). *Assessing research–practice partnerships: Five dimensions of effectiveness.* New York, NY: William T. Grant Foundation. Retrieved from http://wtgrantfoundation.org/

Honig, M. I., & Coburn, C. (2008). Evidence-based decision making in school district central offices: Toward a policy and research agenda. *Educational Policy, 22*(4), 578–608.

Hood, P. D. (1982). *The role of linking agents in school improvement: A review, analysis, and synthesis of recent major studies.* San Francisco, CA: Far West Laboratory for Educational Research.

Hopkins, M., Spillane, J. P., & Shirrell, M. (2018). Designing educational infrastructures for improvement: Instructional coaching and professional learning communities. In *Networked By Design* (pp. 192–213). New York: Routledge.

Huberman, M. (1990). Linkage between researchers and practitioners: A qualitative study. *American Educational Research Journal, 27*(2), 363–391.

Jackson-Bowers, E., Kalucy, L., & McIntyre, E. (2006). Towards better policy and practice in primary health care. *Primary Health Care Research & Information Service, 4,* 1–16.

Kochanek J.R., Scholz C., Garcia A.N. (2015). Mapping the collaborative research process. *Education Policy Analysis Archives, 23*(121).

Liou, Y. H., & Daly, A. J. (2018). Evolving relationships of pre-service teachers: A cohort-based model for growing instructional practice through networks. In *Networked by design* (pp. 103–128). New York: Routledge.

Lomas, J. (2000). Using linkage and exchange to move research into policy at a Canadian foundation. *Health Affairs, 19*(3), 236.

Louis, K. S. (1977). Dissemination of information from centralized bureaucracies to local schools: The role of the linking agent. *Human Relations*, *30*(1), 25–42.

Louis, K. S., & Kell, D. (1981). *The human factor in dissemination: Field agent roles in their organizational context. Linking R&D with schools*. Cambridge, MA: Abt Associates.

Malin, J. R., Brown, C., & Trubceac, A. S. (2018). Going for broke: A multiple-case study of brokerage in education. *AERA Open*, *4*(2), 1–14.

Massell, D., Goertz, M. E., & Barnes, C. A. (2012). State education agencies' acquisition and use of research knowledge for school improvement. *Peabody Journal of Education*, *87*(5), 609–626.

Moolenaar, N.M. (2012). A social network perspective on teacher collaboration in schools: Theory, methodology, and applications. *American Journal of Education*, *11*, 7–39.

Neal, J.W., Neal, Z.P., Kornbluh, M., Mills, K., & Lawler, J. (2015). Brokering the research–practice gap: A typology. *American Journal of Psychology*, *56*(3–4), 422–435.

Penuel, W. R. de los Santos, E., Lin, Q., Marshall, S., Anderson, C.W., & Frank, K.A. (2018). Building networks to support effective use of science curriculum materials in the carbon TIME project. In *Networked By Design* (pp. 192–213). New York: Routledge.

Penuel, W. R., Riel, M. R., Krause, A. & Frank, K. A. (2009). Analyzing teachers' professional interactions in a school as social capital: A social network approach. *Teachers College Record*, *111*(1), 124–163.

Penuel, W.R., Sun, M., Frank, K.A., & Gallagher, H.A. (2012). Using social network analysis to study how collegial interactions can augment teacher learning from external professional development. *American Journal of Education*, *119*, 103–136.

Penuel, W. R., Briggs, D. C., Davidson, K. L., Herlihy, C., Sherer, D., Hill, H. C., . . . & Allen, A. R. (2017). How school and district leaders access, perceive, and use research. *AERA Open*, *3*(2), 2332858417705370.

Rosenkopf, L., & Almeida, P. (2003). Overcoming local search through alliances and mobility. *Management science*, *49*(6), 751–766.

Spillane, J. P., Hunt, B., & Healey, K. (2009). Managing and leading elementary schools: Attending to the formal and informal organization. *International Studies in Educational Administration*, 37(1), 5–28.

Ward, V. (2017). Why, whose, what and how? A framework for knowledge mobilisers. *Evidence & Policy*, *13*(3), 477–497.

Yoon, S. A., & Baker-Doyle, K. J. (Eds.). (2018). *Networked by design: Interventions for teachers to develop social capital*. New York: Routledge.

Appendix: Survey items

Element	Survey item	Response scale
What gets brokered?	In the last year, have you shared any of the following types of research with others?	Never 1–2 times 3–5 times More than 5 times
	• Articles, reports, books, or summaries based on independent research or program evaluation (paper or web-based) • Research or program evaluation conducted by central office staff • Materials from a program developer or publisher • Research conducted by teacher(s) or principal(s) • Materials from a professional development training • Formal analysis of a school-wide or district-wide data • Opinion of national expert(s)	
	When you've shared these, how often have you shared. . .	
	• An actual product (e.g. the article, a link to the article, etc.) • Your interpretation or summary of the findings • Practices or strategies you developed based on the research	
Brokerage activities	When you've shared research, how often do you do any of the following?	Never 1–2 times 3–5 times More than 5 times
	• Evaluate the quality of research prior to sharing • Evaluate needs of schools, teachers or others so that you select the most relevant research	

(continued)

(continued)

Element	Survey item	Response scale
	• Deliver formal learning opportunities (e.g., professional development, training)	
	• Offer or provide support or technical assistance	
	• Publish (i.e., produce or release for distribution)	
	• Develop products or programs based on research	
	• Disseminate (i.e., actively distribute research)	
	• Synthesize multiple sources of research about a single topic, program, etc.	
	• Translate research into understandable language and/or format	
	• Facilitate discussion of research	
	To what extent is sharing research expected of you in your role in your organization?	Not at all Slightly Moderately Very
Purposes and motivation	Please rate your level of agreement with the following statements.	Strongly disagree Disagree Agree Strongly agree
	• Researchers have a solid grasp on evolving problems in schools.	
	• Researchers need to do more to make their work relevant for my school.	
	• Research addresses the most important issues schools face.	
	• Most education research suggests actionable steps to take in practice.	
	• Research takes into consideration the varying levels of resources available to schools to implement research findings.	
	• Practitioners often struggle to find research on issues in their classrooms.	

	• In general, we are expected to use research to inform decisions.	
	• Our school/district prioritizes research in decision-making.	
	• When I use research-based strategies, student learning improves.	
	• We use research because a supervisor or administrator requires it.	
	• Research has changed the way I think about my practice.	
	• I have used research to continually expand my knowledge about teaching and learning.	
Networks	Please list up to ten people whom you rely on for education research.	
	Please list up to ten organizations you rely on for education research.	
	Please list up to ten media sources you rely on for education research.	
Individual characteristics	Which best describes your current position?	Classroom teacher
		Special education teacher
		Instructional coach or specialist
		School administrator
		District administrator/ staff
		Other school instructional staff
	How many years of experience do you have working in a K-12 education setting, including district level positions?	Less than a year
		1 yr
		2–3 yrs
		4–6 yrs
		7–10 yrs
		11–15 yrs
		16–20 yrs
		21+ yrs

(continued)

(continued)

Element	Survey item	Response scale
	What's the highest degree you earned and when?	Associates Bachelor's Master's Doctorate (select year)
	What training and/or experiences have you had related to using research?	(Check all that apply)
	• I have conducted action research.	
	• I was in a graduate program that heavily emphasized research use.	
	• I was in a graduate program where I conducted research.	
	• I have been involved in a formal research-practice partnership.	
	• I have participated in other professional development around critically consuming research.	
	• I have engaged with research through a Professional Learning Community.	
	• I attend research conferences.	
	• I review research and apply it in my own work	
	I have participated in the following undergraduate/ graduate level courses. . .	
	• I have taken an Introduction to Statistics course.	
	• I have taken a Research Design course.	
	Please rate how confident you feel to determine whether. . .	Not at all confident Somewhat confident Mostly confident Very confident
	• a research study conducted appropriate statistical analyses.	
	• a research design was appropriate for the research questions posed.	
	• a research study had an adequate sample size.	

- results from a research study might be dismissed because they are actually attributable to something that the study missed.
- a program evaluation demonstrated real impacts versus improvement that would have happened even without the program.
- a comparison group is a good match to the treatment group.
- research supported (or not) inferences about the causal effects of a new program.
- the surveys and assessments used in a research study were reliable and valid.
- Please rate how confident you feel to determine whether—results from a research study are generalizable to different schools, districts, etc.
- results from a research synthesis (i.e., combining results across multiple research studies) are trustworthy.
- research evidence provided by a vendor is trustworthy, versus slanted to support their products.

7

KNOWLEDGE BROKERING

"Not a place for novices or new conscripts"

Amanda Cooper, Joelle Rodway, Stephen MacGregor, Samantha Shewchuk, and Michelle Searle

The resurgence of the evidence agenda

Interest in how large-scale education systems can (and should) be informed by evidence has seen a resurgence in the past few decades. While attention toward research utilization is by no means new (Carol Weiss's seminal work on *The many meanings of research utilization* was published more than three decades ago in 1979, followed by Knott and Wildavsky's famous piece in 1980 entitled "If dissemination is the solution, what is the problem?"), the requirements for governments, research funders, researchers, and practitioners in educational systems around research use have increased considerably. The rationale behind the momentum to use evidence to inform public service sectors is simple: better use of evidence should yield better decision-making at the policymaking level that, in turn, will yield better practices at the school level, ultimately resulting in better outcomes for students and communities. However, while the rationale is simple, the implementation of knowledge mobilization (KMb) across thousands of schools (and involving many professional groups and widely divergent contexts) is not.

Barriers to the use of evidence are well documented. Researchers often do not create practitioner-friendly versions of research or articulate implications for practice and policy. Busy practitioners are often not in a position to find, assess the quality, share or apply research findings even when they are so inclined, due in part to a lack of infrastructure in K-12 systems at organizational levels. Policymakers, similarly, are most often reacting to media and/or immediate crises rather than having the time and space to deeply engage with evidence that might inform decision-making. Recognizing the many barriers that exist for research producers and research users, many scholars have recognized the need for research brokering and skilled facilitation to bridge these divides (Cooper, 2014; Frost et al., 2012; Meyer, 2010; Ward, House, & Hamer, 2009). Brokering is often defined in terms of being in-between people, departments, processes, or organizations. As such, understanding and measuring brokering is a complex task; recently, this issue has been exacerbated by the global call to action for brokering without the requisite empirical work to theorize and define what brokering means, who does it, and to what effect. Perhaps a more important question is what is not brokering. The purpose of this chapter is, accordingly, to address the following questions: What kinds of brokering organizations exist in K-12 education systems? What research mobilization functions are brokers engaged in? How might we measure the impact of these efforts in order to better utilize brokering for school improvement?

This chapter arises from empirical work undertaken as part of the Research Informing Policy, Practice and Leadership in Education (RIPPLE) program—a program of research, training, and KMb aimed at learning more about how knowledge brokering (KB) can increase research use and its impact in education by facilitating multi-stakeholder collaboration (www.ripplenetwork.ca). Ultimately, RIPPLE aims to create a suite of evidence-informed resources and toolkits to increase KMb capacity for the major groups involved in KMb: researchers, knowledge brokers, policymakers and practitioners.

What gap does the evidence movement try to address?

Differing worldviews of researchers, practitioners and policymakers

Interrogating what might explain the gap between research and practice usually leads to a discussion of the different contexts of researchers, practitioners and policymakers. Labaree (2003), for instance, highlights that "differences in worldview between teachers and researchers cannot be eliminated easily because they arise from irreducible differences in the nature of the work that teachers and researchers do" (p. 13). Neumann, Pallas, and Peterson (1999) also outline three tensions between the roles of practitioners and researchers:

> One is the tension of agenda, which bears on whose questions get asked: researchers' or practitioners'. Another is the tension of perspective, which considers the ways in which the understanding of educational phenomena flows from the academic disciplines and from educators. The third is the tension of response (and responsibility) to primary stakeholders in the education enterprise, which examines the interplay of researchers' public and intellectual stakes in the study of educational phenomena.
>
> *(p. 251)*

These issues are incredibly important, especially that of responsibility. Whose job is it to improve education—teachers, politicians, researchers? We argue the responsibility should be shared among the many organizations and professionals that comprise the system. These tensions—agenda, perspective, and responsibility—ought to arise and be addressed within multidirectional and iterative, rather than linear/one-way, relationships. Too often we hear about evidence-informed practice, but what about practice-informed research? Our challenges in education are complex, and they will require diverse perspectives and alternatives simultaneously at multiple levels of the system for improvements to occur. Knowledge mobilization takes a whole system perspective to explore the relationships (or lack thereof) between diverse stakeholders at different areas of the system.

Conceptualizing knowledge mobilization

Knowledge mobilization is a contested concept (Cooper, Levin, & Campbell, 2009). There are many areas of debate including what counts as knowledge, what should be mobilized (and to who), what strategies should be used, as well as many issues related to measurement and accountability in a data-driven climate. One key concern is that collecting data and mobilizing both research from universities and data collected in school districts will be used punitively or to blame professionals. And, there have been initiatives and policies—such as No Child Left Behind in the United States—that have exemplified this concern. So before going on, it is important to define and conceptualize knowledge mobilization. The Social Sciences and Humanities Research Council of Canada (SSHRC) updated their definition of KMb in late 2018:

> Knowledge Mobilization: The reciprocal and complementary flow and uptake of research knowledge between researchers, knowledge brokers and knowledge users – both within and beyond academia – in such a way that may benefit users and create positive impacts within Canada and/or internationally, and, ultimately, has the potential to enhance the profile, reach and impact of social sciences and humanities research.

'Reciprocal' and 'complementary' are key concepts in a robust conceptualization of KMb because this type of definition values different kinds of expertise from across the system. Too often KMb is not thought of from a systems perspective— where alignment and coordination between universities, ministries and school districts are critical to achieving incremental success in a priority area.

Our conceptualization builds on and adapts Levin's model (2004) of KMb (see Figure 7.1).

This model shows KMb occurring through brokering mechanisms that integrate research, policy, and practice domains, all situated within a particular social context. The research domain includes funders, universities, researchers, and centers engaged in the production of empirical knowledge. The practice domain includes schools and districts where educational practitioners bring experiential knowledge to bear on teaching and learning. The policy domain includes governments and ministries of education or state education agencies, and other regulatory bodies that implement regional or national policies for public services. In this conceptualization, brokering is paramount and shown as the central domain of knowledge mobilization and impact, as it is the area where the other domains are debated,

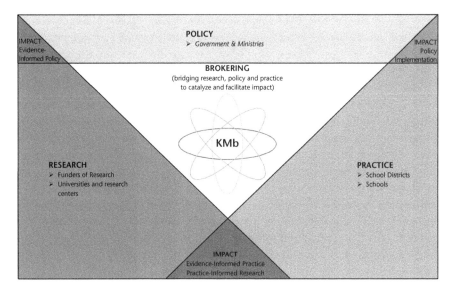

FIGURE 7.1   Knowledge mobilization at the interface of research, practice and policy—catalyzed and facilitated through brokering to create impact.

negotiated, facilitated, transformed, and, ultimately, integrated into the daily work of professionals. The results of successful brokering efforts are impacts (although not all KMb or brokering necessarily has impact). There are three areas of impact shown in the model: research-practice overlaps resulting in evidence-informed practice but also practice-informed research; policy-practice overlaps creating impact from policy implementation; and, research-policy overlaps creating impact through evidence-informed policies.

What is knowledge brokering?

One foot on the concrete shore, one foot in the human sea— Jackson Browne[1]

The KMb field is now burgeoning with different terms and definitions for intermediaries including knowledge brokers, research brokering organizations, innovation brokers, and mediators among others (for a detailed description of various definitions and conceptualizations of intermediaries, please see Cooper, 2013). These definitions sometimes refer to organizations, networks, or individuals embedded in the system, which can often muddy the waters about what constitutes knowledge brokering (KB). As Meyer (2010) highlights:

> Brokering involves a range of different practices: the identification and localization of knowledge, the redistribution and dissemination of knowledge, and the rescaling and transformation of this knowledge. Brokering knowledge

> thus means far more than simply *moving* knowledge – it also means transform-
> ing knowledge . . . knowledge brokering is likely to look very different in the
> various brokering spaces . . . not least because the needs and expectations of
> the knowledge users might differ substantially.
>
> *(p. 120)*

Meyer's definition is powerful due to the emphasis on transformation—knowledge
brokering is not the transfer of a static object or message, rather brokering is about
the complex ways in which research is understood, resisted, taken up and adapted
for local use to solve particular problems of practice. The quote from the song
Walking Town by Jackson Brown that opened this section provides a nuanced
analogy for brokering: the foot on the concrete shore is the focus on research
evidence, whereas the foot in the human sea represents the shifting nature of that
research (especially in relation to different actionable messages depending on the
target audience): it moves and changes with fluidity across the larger system as it is
interpreted by diverse stakeholder groups.

Because of the rising prominence of brokering as a mechanism to address
research–practice–policy gaps, there is an even greater need to articulate what brokering is, what it is not, and provide some clarity around who might be best suited
for the substantive role of brokering within complex education systems. Brokering
is not simply communications. Many people conflate strategic communication
with KMb and brokering. In fact Barwick, Phipps, Meyers, Johnny and Coriandoli
(2014) have recently contributed an article that delineates the important differences between the two concepts; namely, that communications is not necessarily
about research knowledge, nor does communications incorporate the challenging
and resource-intensive work of facilitating partnerships across diverse stakeholder
groups to translate research into policy or practice. The reason we bring this up, is
brokering has often been conflated with surface communication strategies—such
as using Twitter, creating a Facebook page, or sending out a research brief—which
devalues and obscures a more robust understanding of brokering. There is a big
difference between engaging in communication activities and being involved substantively in brokering in a public service sector.

The issue with conceptualizing brokering in a flimsy way (such as thinking that
tweeting is knowledge brokering) is that individuals without the requisite skills
or expertise have begun to be engaged in these processes. If simply communicating and using social media constituted brokering, everyone would be a broker.
Brokering almost always requires substantive expertise on one or more of the areas
outlined in Figure 7.1, of research and/or practice and policy worlds. And while
social media can be a mechanism for brokering, it is just that being a broker is far
more substantive than this front facing communications activity (see also Chapter 2
of this volume). Sandra Nutley, who is one of the prominent leaders in the field
of evidence-use, recently articulated that brokering is not a place for novices or
new conscripts. This is a very important point that cannot be overemphasized.
The work of transforming research knowledge alongside principals, teachers and

students for use in schools is incredibly demanding work. Brokers need to have both a proficient understanding of research as well as an accurate perception of the challenges that busy practitioners face when approaching their professional arenas. On top of those skills, effective brokers also need to have a systems perspective. It is not enough to understand the challenges one particular group in the system faces (such as teachers or researchers), rather these challenges need to be understood in the broader context of the large-scale education systems where budgets, resources, political pressure from the public and a myriad of other issues come into play. So, while strategic communication is a part of brokering, we argue that it is not the core—the core of brokering is building relationships to facilitate networks and partnerships. Similarly, in order to build those relationships, some level of credibility and expertise is needed—it could be experience in a classroom or particular community setting, years working in government and policymaking settings, or expertise in a particular area of research that builds this credibility in the eyes of different stakeholders. In fact, there is some evidence to suggest that having expertise in more than one of these areas actually makes for better brokers (Rodway, 2015), as the need to mediate between these very different contexts requires an understanding of the different vantage points.

Mallidou et al. (2018) in a recent scoping review of core competencies for knowledge translation (KT) in the health sector, identified three domains of competencies: Knowledge, Skills, and Attitudes (Table 7.1).

In addition to these three domains, Malidou included three other competencies: (4.1) Knowledge of quality improvement methods and tools, communication

TABLE 7.1 19 core competencies (adapted from Mallidou et al., 2018)

1. Knowledge	2. Skills	3. Attitudes
1.1 Understanding the context	2.1 Collaboration and teamwork	3.1 Confidence
1.2 Understanding the research process	2.2 Leadership	3.2 Having trust
1.3 Sharing knowledge	2.3 Sharing knowledge	3.3 Valuing research
1.4 Being aware of evidence resources	2.4 Knowledge synthesis	3.4 Self-directed lifelong commitment to learning
1.5 Understanding KT and EBP processes	2.5 Dissemination of research findings	3.5 Valuing teamwork
1.6 Understanding translation and dissemination activities	2.6 Use of research findings (or research use)	
	2.7 Fostering innovation	
	2.8 Knowledge brokering	

strategies, and health policy and systems; (4.2) Skills related to KT planning, project management, information technology, use, sound judgement, and discretion/ tact/ diplomacy, and resourcefulness; (4.3) Attitudes such as integrity, commitment to professional work ethic and behavior in interaction with contacts, commitment to high standards of professionalism, and interest in the latest developments in communication.

Many of the skills needed for KT—which is related, but not identical, to knowledge brokering—are also needed for brokering. After outlining knowledge, skills, and attitudes, we now explore the different types of brokering organizations that exist in K-12 education systems.

A typology of research brokering organizations

In other empirical work Cooper (2014) has conducted exploring 44 intermediaries across Canada. She uses the designation Research Brokering Organization (RBO) to describe third party intermediaries whose active role connecting research producers and users is a catalyst for KMb. Two inclusion criteria were used to decide which organizations 'counted' as RBOs. The first was audience—organizations had to connect both research producers and users in some way to be considered an RBO. This excluded organizations that were practitioner to practitioner or researcher to researcher; while these organizations undeniably provide support for target audiences, Cooper's conceptualization of brokering organizations explores how RBOs are mediating research use *across* the researcher-practitioner divide— from the ivory tower into the frontlines of practice and vice versa. A second criteria to be considered an RBO was a mission statement explicitly (or implicitly) related to KMb. This was meant to exclude organizations that do brokering as one of their many other activities. This study focused on organizations who considered KMb and research brokering their primary objective. Cooper's research was the first of its kind to attempt to map the types, organizational features, and functions of RBOs across Canada, or elsewhere for that matter (Figure 7.2).

The four major categories are distinguished by the location within the formal K-12 education system and where the RBOs get funding. Governmental organizations are funded provincially or federally and are within the K-12 system. Not for Profit RBOs are outside the formal K-12 system and usually funded by donations and sometimes by governmental funds (such as research centers). For profit RBOs are private companies that are funded by the free market. And membership organizations are funded by their members—so professional organizations might include teachers' unions and so on. Research brokering organizations have eight brokering functions (Figure 7.3).

Brokering involves a range of functions that improve KMb processes including: improving linkages and partnerships by facilitating collaboration among diverse stakeholders; increasing awareness of empirical evidence on an issue; increasing accessibility by tailoring research products for target audiences; increasing engagement through the use of interactive and multimedia products; capacity

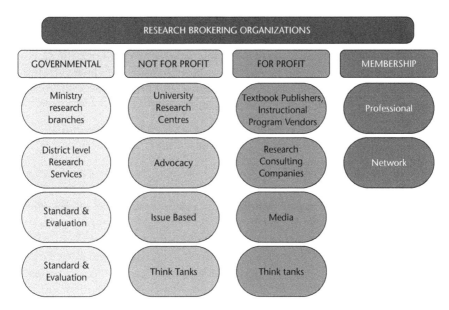

FIGURE 7.2 Typology of intermediary RBOs across Canada

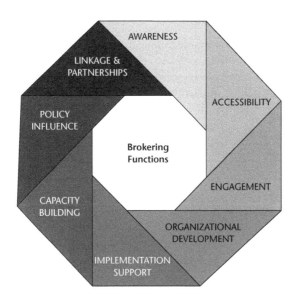

FIGURE 7.3 Brokering functions of Canadian RBOs

building for KMb with researchers, practitioners and policymakers; providing implementation support in practice and policy settings; organizational development through building KMb plans and requisite infrastructure to increase research use; and policy influence by using evidence to galvanize priorities or system change. Each function uses different KMb strategies that would require different impact metrics (to be explored more fully in subsequent section).

Exploring competencies, types of brokering organizations, and brokering functions provides a foundation to explore what evaluation frameworks might be useful in assessing multi-stakeholder networks and brokering in education.

What evaluation frameworks exist to measure brokering and partnerships?

Our team has recently completed a scoping review of research–practice–policy networks in education (Cooper et al., 2018). Coburn, Mata, and Choi (2013) defined research–practice partnerships as "long-term, mutualistic collaborations between practitioners and researchers that are intentionally organized to investigate problems of practice and solutions for improving district outcomes" (p. 2). One of the questions the scoping review addressed was: what methods and metrics are being used to evaluate the impact of KMb networks? This section explores three frameworks built from empirical work that propose indicators for measuring brokering and network activities.

1. Cooper: brokering functions

Cooper's (2014) eight brokering functions can provide fertile ground for thinking through both brokering strategies to accomplish specific goals, as well as what metrics might be needed to assess those efforts. Table 7.2 shows Cooper's brokering functions, including potential KMb strategies and indicators for each (from Barwick, 2011).

The strengths of using Cooper's functions is that the functions and strategies were empirically derived across a diverse sample of research brokering organizations; however, a potential weakness is that the indicators are taken from Barwick (2011) and as such may not (a) be fully transferrable from health sector to education, and (b) have not yet been empirically validated or tested in educational contexts. The second framework that could be usefully applied was developed in the United States for the purpose of measuring research–practice–partnerships in education. Unlike Cooper (whose framework focuses on brokering organizations), Henrick, Cobb, Penuel, Jackson, and Clark's (2017) framework focuses on assessing brokering networks.

2. Henrick et al. (2017): five dimensions of effectiveness

A new empirically derived framework, funded by the WT Grant foundation, has arisen from Henrick et al. (2017) outlining five dimensions of effectiveness for RPPs: (a) building and cultivating partnership relationships, (b) conducting rigorous research to inform action, (c) supporting the partner practice organization in achieving its goals, (d) producing knowledge that can inform educational improvement efforts more broadly, and (e) building the capacity of participating

TABLE 7.2 Brokering functions, KMb strategies, and potential impact metrics.

Eight brokering functions, KMB strategies, and impact indicators

1. **Linkage and partnerships:** facilitating collaboration among diverse stakeholders
KMb strategies: advisory committees, working groups, directories of researchers and brokering organizations, events, social media
Impact—collaboration indicators: # products/services developed or disseminated with partners, social network growth, # new partnerships formed

2. **Awareness:** increasing awareness of empirical evidence
KMb strategies: scoping review, annotated bibliography, research reports, conceptual papers
Impact—reach indicators: # distributed, # requested, # downloads/hits, media exposure

3. **Accessibility:** tailoring products to particular audiences
KMb strategies: research summaries, implication briefs for stakeholders, policy briefs, fact sheets
Impact—usefulness indicators: read/browsed, satisfied with, usefulness of, gained knowledge

4. **Engagement**: creating diverse research products
KMb strategies: multi-media products, YouTube, webinars, infographics, whiteboard animations, data visualization
Impact—use indicators: Google analytics, # intend to use, # adapting information

5. **Capacity building:** facilitating KMb skill development
KMb strategies: webinars, training sessions, workshops, cases studies of what worked and what did not, KMb planning templates
Impact—practice change indicators: # and type of capacity-building efforts, #trained, commitment to change, observed change, reported change

6. **Implementation support:** helping researchers implement KMb plans with end users
KMb strategies: toolkits, consultation requests, hotline support services for advice
Impact—program/service indicators: # consultations, calls to hotlines, toolkits downloaded, fidelity and uptake, process measures

7. **Organizational development:** assisting to build strategic KMb plans and processes for evaluating existing KMb practices within university research services
KMb strategies: meetings, awards, strategic plans, promotional materials, annual reports
Impact—system level indicators: provincial coordination, infrastructure, increased data sharing

8. **Policy influence:** using evidence to galvanize policy priorities or change
KMb strategies: policy briefs, media strategies (press, social media, podcasts, TV, radio)
Impact—multi-level indicators: # citations, # meetings with policymakers, invitations of researchers to meetings, involvement in policy process, media/social media coverage.

researchers, practitioners, practice organizations and research organizations to engage in partnership work. The framework was built from a review of the existing literature in conjunction with semi-structured interviews with two to three researchers from different RPPs (research alliances, design-research partnerships, and networked improvement communities). Henrick et al. asked about RPP goals and about indicators of these goals in addition to collecting metrics and documentation and tools that RPPs were using to assess their impact. Each of the five dimensions in the framework includes indicators (Table 7.3).

TABLE 7.3 Henrick et al.'s framework to measure effectiveness of RPPs

Dimension of effectiveness	Indicators
Building and cultivating partnerships	Researchers and practitioners routinely work together.
	The RPP establishes routines that promote collaborative decision-making and guard against power imbalances.
	RPP members establish norms of interaction that support collaborative decision-making and equitable participation in all phases of the work.
	RPP members recognize and respect one another's perspectives and diverse forms of expertise.
	Partnership goals take into account team members' work demands and roles in their respective organizations.
Conducting rigorous research to inform action	RPP conducts research that addresses problems of practice facing the practice organization.
	The RPP establishes systematic processes for collecting, organizing, analyzing, and synthesizing data.
	Decisions about research methods and designs balance rigor and feasibility.
	The RPP conducts research to clarify and further specify problems of practice prior to identifying and assessing strategies for addressing those problems.
	Findings are shared in ways that take account of the needs of the practice organization.
Supporting the partner practice organization in achieving its goals	The RPP provides research and evidence to support improvements in the partner organization.
	The RPP helps the practice organization identify productive strategies for addressing problems of practice.
	The RPP informs the practice organization's implementation and ongoing adjustments of improvement strategies.
Producing knowledge to inform educational improvement efforts more broadly	The RPP develops and shares knowledge and theory that contributes to the research base.
	The RPP develops and shares new tools and routines that can be adapted to support improvement work in other settings.
	The RPP develops two dissemination plans, one that supports partnership goals and a second plan for broader dissemination.
Building the capacity of participating researchers, practitioners, practice organizations and research organizations to engage in partnership work	Team members develop professional identities that value engaging in sustained collaborative inquiry with one another to address persistent problems of practice.
	Team members assume new roles and develop the capacity to conduct partnership activities.
	Participating research and educational organizations provide capacity-building opportunities to team members.
	The work of the RPP contributes to a change in the practice organization's norms, culture and routines around the use of research and evidence. Research and practice organizations allocate resources to support partnership work.

> There are shifts in professional expectations for education researchers and for practitioners that reward members from each organization for sustained participation in significant partnership work.
> The RPP establishes conditions in the practice organization that lead to sustained impact beyond the life of the partnership.
> Research and educational organizations allocate resources to support partnership work.

One of the strengths of Henrick et al.'s framework is its focus on indicators that relate specifically to practitioners. Similarly, issues of power between researchers and practitioners are explored; this framework attends to equity concerns that might arise from power imbalances that often exist in multi-stakeholder partnerships. The third framework, developed from projects that involved researchers and policymakers in Canada, distinguishes indicators based on the lifespan of a partnership and provides different expectations for early versus mature partnerships.

3. Kothari: indicators at the policymaker–researcher interface

Kothari, MacLean, Edwards, and Hobbs (2011) provided a set of practice-based indicators to measure collaborative knowledge creation and gauge the impact of partnerships between researchers and policymakers. The indicators arose from interviews with 16 health policymakers and researchers involved in eight research transfer partnerships in Ontario. Although they arose from work specifically with policymakers, they are relevant to other types of partnerships. Kothari et al. identified a set of, first, common partnership indicators: communication, collaborative research and dissemination of research. Each dimension includes success indicators (e.g., communication is clear, communication is relevant, communication is timely, communication is respectful). Recognizing that partnerships evolve as they mature, Kothari and her colleagues identified two further sets of indicators in relation to early partnership indicators (research findings, negotiations and partnership enhancement) and mature partnership indicators (meeting information needs, level of rapport and commitment). Each dimension includes further success indicators and potential sub indicators as well. This framework makes an important contribution to thinking through how partnerships with policymakers might differ from partnerships with practitioners (such as in the Henrick et al. [2017] model). There are few frameworks that exist to assess partnerships or brokering in education; we argue that these three frameworks (depending on the context and phenomenon of interest) provide fertile starting points to evaluate impact of complex multi-stakeholder configurations.

None of these frameworks, however, discuss explicitly the methods that might be best to use in order to study these indicators on the frontlines. In fact, a discussion of what research methods might be appropriate to study KMb in education, and brokering specifically, has been largely absent from the education literature. As such, we provide an overview of social network analysis, and argue it is one of the only approaches that might have the analytic power needed to substantively explore research brokering in education, especially across diverse stakeholders.

Methods to measure brokering: enter social network analysis

Getting at continually changing networks and KMb efforts, especially in relation to brokering that often occurs in-between organizations, departments, and stakeholder groups is challenging. So, what are some approaches that might allow us to capture network activity with more specificity? This section discusses social network analysis (SNA) as an approach to inquiry that may capture the complexity and fluidity of knowledge mobilization efforts in education.

Social network analysis

Networks are emerging as an effective knowledge mobilization strategy showing great potential in connecting research, policy, and practice across diverse stakeholder groups (Nutley, Walter, & Davies, 2007). Often, groups of people and organizations with common interests and shared goals are brought together and labelled as a network. While this may be true, without understanding how the actors within the network are interacting and what resources are being exchanged through those interactions, we cannot really understand the network (or even claim that it exists for that matter). Fortunately, advances in mathematics and computing have enabled greater access to SNA, providing tools useful for getting beneath the surface of the network to interrogate what is really happening within it (Rodway, 2018).

There is a nascent body of research in education that takes a social network perspective to connecting research and practice. This research highlights the importance of paying attention to the social dimensions of knowledge networks, which makes intuitive sense given that relationships within the network build awareness of and access to the knowledge and resources researchers and practitioners want to mobilize (Daly, 2010). When examining the social dimensions of knowledge networks, the essential units of measure are the *ties* that connect network members (Carolan, 2013). Taken together, ties of a specific kind identify the nature of a relationship and are labelled a *relation* (Borgatti, Everett, & Johnson, 2018). By quantifying the interactional qualities of a relation (e.g. frequency, strength), interpretations can be drawn about the flow of resources (e.g. knowledge, expertise) throughout a network. *Instrumental ties* (e.g. advice, information) represent those relationships that directly provide the resources necessary to carry out one's work whereas *expressive ties* (e.g. friendship and social support) are relations that provide the social conditions necessary to support that work (Wasserman & Faust, 1994). Education scholars have examined a range of instrumental and expressive relations to attempt to map and understand resource flow within and between school networks (Daly, 2010; Farley-Ripple & Buttram, 2015; Moolenaar, Sleegers, Karsten, & Daly, 2012).

Perhaps the most explored relationship within a social network is advice-seeking behavior (e.g. Coburn et al., 2013; Farley-Ripple & Buttram, 2013, 2015; Moolenaar, Sleegers, & Daly, 2012). By asking those in school networks to identify those from whom they seek work-related advice, insights about the flows of professional knowledge have been uncovered. For example, in their two studies of the advice-seeking behaviors for data use of elementary school teachers, Farley-Ripple and Buttram (2013, 2015) arrived at several key findings: (a) teachers relied on pre-existing, strong professional relationships, (b) teachers usually sought advice from those in formal leadership positions, (c) advice givers did not necessarily have more expertise than advice seekers, (d) both direct and indirect ties were important to consider and (e) teachers who interacted for data use were more similar in their data-use practices than those who did not interact. Cutting across these findings is an important conclusion: teachers' position in their school network has implications for their data-use opportunities and outcomes. Similar conclusions have been reached by scholars who examined the culture of innovation (Liou & Daly, 2016) and research-based knowledge exchange (Rodway, 2015). These studies focus on instrumental relations; however, researchers have begun to observe the substantive influence of expressive dimensions of knowledge networks.

In contrast to instrumental relations, expressive relations involve ties that extend beyond traditional school boundaries (e.g. friendship ties). While these informal ties remain understudied in educational contexts (Daly, Liou, & Brown, 2016), recent research has indicated that both teachers' and educational leaders' expressive networks hold implications for student learning and school climate. Moolenaar, Sleegers, and Daly (2012), for example, found that examining teachers' personal advice network in conjunction with their professional advice network enabled interpretations about teachers' perceptions of collective efficacy, which in turn provided clues about student achievement. A similar cascading influence of expressive networks was found by Daly, Liou, and Brown (2016) in their study of educational leaders' energy exchange relationships. By examining educational leaders at different levels of a school district, they observed that leaders' positions in their network influenced their perceptions about innovative school climate and thus their likelihood of sending or receiving energy ties.

Studying the relational dimensions of social networks can reveal previously undetectable flows of information and resources, and research in this area will likely continue to grow in the coming years.

Integrating SNA as a promising approach to assess brokering and impact

We argue that the integration of SNA to measure multi-stakeholder networks is needed to better understand the impact of brokering efforts. We close by proposing the strengths of this approach:

1. **SNA provides a suite of tools that can be used to establish base-line activity within a network and further trace the evolution of the network over time, providing robust statistical measures of impact.** Social network measures can provide insight into many different character-istics of the network including (but not limited to) overall activity levels, possible bottlenecks in resource flow, the existence of subgroups and untapped resources of network members who sit on the periphery of the network. The role of relationships in mobilizing knowledge is an area that, until recently, has been either completely ignored, or at the very least under-appreciated in the conversation about networks as an effective KMb strategy.

2. **SNA data can provide critical insights into the network that can then use to better support and improve the network.** Cultivating and sustaining research–practice partnerships and networks are challenges that require a nuanced understanding of who is and is not engaging in network learning. SNA insights help leaders target network-focused interventions with greater precision, an action empirically established in organizational research that will yield positive outcomes for the network more broadly (Cross & Parker, 2004).

3. **Network visualization (a key component of SNA) provides a powerful tool for summarizing complex concepts and helping one under-stand the patterns of activity within a network** (Moody, McFarland, & Bender-deMoll, 2005). Network maps offer a useful sense-making tool that instantly enables people to see how they are interacting with others in the net-work. Taken together with relevant network statistics, visualizations provide an x-ray of sorts, illustrating what is happening (or not) within a network. In this way, if applied appropriately, it has the potential to contribute to a new approach to developing evidence-informed networks.

4. **Social network theory provides a rich conceptual framework through which meaning can be attached to social network measures** (Wasserman & Faust, 1994). This is often a missing piece in studies that cur-rently employ SNA where people adopt the methods without the necessary theoretical understanding. Social network theory (and other related theories such as social capital theory) enable network organizers and members to plan and implement strategies to nurture network growth that enable the achieve-ment of the desired goals, such as by focusing on nurturing weak ties over strong ties (or vice versa) or distributing internal and external ties across a network depending on desired outcomes.

Knowledge networks that share empirical and practice-based knowledge pro-duce positive outcomes at the community, network and participant levels (Provan & Milward, 2001). However, no blueprint exists for successfully adapting and implementing networks across sectors and contexts (Conklin, Lusk, Harris, & Stolee, 2013). SNA permits us to actually measure network activity, something that has been missing in the discussion about networks as an effective knowledge mobilization strategy. Despite its challenges and limitations (see Carolan, 2013; Prell, 2012), SNA provides a multidimensional understanding of how brokering relationships within a network facilitate and constrain KMb efforts.

Note

1 From the song 'Walking Town' by Jackson Brown, cited in Bastow, Dunleavy and Tinkler, 2014

References

Barwick, M. (2011). *Knowledge translation planning template*. Toronto, Canada: SickKids Hospital.

Barwick, M., Phipps, D., Johnny, M., & Coriandoli, R. (2014). Knowledge translation and strategic communications: Unpacking differences and similarities for scholarly and research communications. *Scholarly and Research Communication*, *5*(3), 1–14. Retrieved from https://src-online.ca/index.php/src

Borgatti, S. P., Everett, M. G., & Johnson, J. C. (2018). *Analyzing social networks*. Thousand Oaks, CA: Sage.

Carolan, B. (2013). *Social network analysis and education*. Thousand Oaks, CA: Sage.

Coburn, C. E., Mata, W. S., & Choi, L. (2013). The embeddedness of teachers' social networks: Evidence from a study of mathematics reform. *Sociology of Education*, *86*(4), 311–342. https://doi.org/10.1177/0038040713501147

Conklin, J., Lusk, E., Harris, M., & Stolee, P. (2013). Knowledge brokers in a knowledge network: The case of seniors health research transfer network knowledge brokers. *Implementation Science*, *8*(1), 1–10. https://doi.org/10.1186/1748-5908-8-7

Cooper, A. (2013). Research mediation in education: A typology of research brokering organizations that exist across Canada. *Alberta Journal of Educational Research*, *59*(2), 181–207. Retrieved from http://www.ajer.ca/

Cooper, A. (2014). Knowledge mobilisation in education across Canada: A cross-case analysis of 44 research brokering organisations. *Evidence & Policy: A Journal of Research, Debate and Practice*, *10*(1), 29–59. https://doi.org/10.1332/174426413X662806

Cooper, A., Levin, B., & Campbell, C. (2009). The growing (but still limited) importance of evidence in education policy and practice. *Journal of Educational Change*, *10*, 159–171. https://doi.org/10.1007/s10833-009-9107-0

Cooper, A., Shewchuk, S., MacGregor, S., Mainhood, L., Beach, P., Shulha, L., & Klinger, D. (2018). *Knowledge mobilization networks in action: A scoping review of research practice partnerships in education*. Report prepared for the Ontario Ministry of Education. Kingston: Queen's University.

Cross, R. & Parker, A. (2004). *The hidden power of social networks: Understanding what really gets done in organizations*. Cambridge, MA: Harvard Business School.

Daly, A. J. (2010). *Social network theory and educational change*. Cambridge, MA: Harvard Education.

Daly, A. J., Liou, Y.-H., & Brown, C. (2016). Social Red Bull: Exploring energy relationships in a school district leadership team. *Harvard Educational Review*, *86*(3), 412–448. https://doi.org/10.17763/1943-5045-86.3.412

Farley-Ripple, E. N., & Buttram, J. L. (2013). Harnessing the power of teacher networks. *Phi Delta Kappan*, *95*(3), 12–15. https://doi.org/10.1177/003172171309500304

Farley-Ripple, E., & Buttram, J. (2015). The development of capacity for data use: The role of teacher networks in an elementary school. *Teachers College Record, 117*(4), 1–34. Retrieved from https://www.tcrecord.org/

Frost, H., Geddes, R., Haw, S., Jackson, C. A., Jepson, R., Mooney, J. D., & Frank, J. (2012). Experiences of knowledge brokering for evidence-informed public health policy and practice: Three years of the Scottish Collaboration for Public Health Research and Policy. *Evidence & Policy, 8*(3), 347–359. https://doi.org/10.1332/174426412X654068

Henrick, E. C., Cobb, P., Penuel, W. R., Jackson, K., & Clark, T. (2017). *Assessing research-practice partnerships: Five dimensions of effectiveness.* New York, NY: William T. Grant Foundation. Retrieved from http://wtgrantfoundation.org/

Knott, J., & Wildavsky, A. (1980). If dissemination is the solution, what is the problem? *Science Communication, 1*(4), 537–578. https://doi.org/10.1177/107554708000100404

Kothari, A., MacLean, L., Edwards, N., & Hobbs, A. (2011). Indicators at the interface: Managing policymaker-researcher collaboration. *Knowledge Management Research & Practice, 9*(3), 203–214. https://doi.org/10.1057/kmrp.2011.16

Labaree, D. (2003). The peculiar problems of preparing educational researchers. *Educational Researcher, 32*(4), 13–22. https://doi.org/10.3102/0013189X032004013

Levin, B. (2004). Making research matter more. *Education Policy Analysis Archives, 12*(56), 1–20. https://doi.org/10.14507/epaa.v12n56.2004

Liou, Y.-H., & Daly, A. J. (2016). Diffusion of innovation: A social network and organizational learning approach to governance of a districtwide leadership team. *Pedagogía Social: Revista Interuniversitaria, 28*, 41–55. https://doi.org/10.7179/PSRI_2016.28.04

Mallidou, A., Atherton, P., Chan, L., Frisch, N., Glegg, S., & Scarrow, G. (2018). Core knowledge translation competencies: A scoping review. *BMC Health Services Research, 18*(1), 502–515. https://doi.org/10.1186/s12913-018-3314-4

Meyer, M. (2010). The rise of the knowledge broker. *Science Communication, 32*(1), 118–127. https://doi.org/10.1177/1075547009359797

Moody, J., McFarland, D., & Bender-deMoll, S. (2005). Dynamic network visualization. *American Journal of Sociology, 110*(4), 1206–1241. https://doi.org/10.1086/421509

Moolenaar, N. M., Sleegers, P. J. C., & Daly, A. J. (2012). Teaming up: Linking collaboration networks, collective efficacy, and student achievement. *Teaching and Teacher Education, 28*(2), 251–262. https://doi.org/10.1016/j.tate.2011.10.001

Moolenaar, N. M., Sleegers, P. J. C., Karsten, S., & Daly, A. J. (2012). The social fabric of elementary schools: A network typology of social interaction among teachers. *Educational Studies, 38*(4), 355–371. https://doi.org/10.1080/03055698.2011.643101

Neumann, A., Pallas, A., & Peterson, P. (1999). Preparing education practitioners to practice education research. In E. C. Lagemann & S. Shulman (Eds.), *Issues in education research: Problems and possibilities* (pp. 247–288). San Francisco, CA: Jossey-Bass.

Nutley, S. M., Walter, I., & Davies, H. T. O. (2007). *Using evidence: How research can inform public services.* Bristol, UK: Policy Press.

Prell, C. (2012). *Social network analysis: History, theory, methodology.* Thousand Oaks, CA: Sage.

Provan, K. G., & Milward, H. B. (2001). Do networks really work? A framework for evaluating public-sector organizational networks. *Public Administration Review, 61*, 414–423. https://doi.org/10.1111/0033-3352.00045.

Rodway, J. (2015). Connecting the dots: Understanding the flow of research knowledge within a research brokering network. *Education Policy Analysis Archives, 23*. https://doi.org/10.14507/epaa.v23.2180

Rodway, J. (2018). Getting beneath the surface: Examining the social side of professional learning networks. In C. Brown and C. Poortman (Eds.), *Networks for learning: Effective collaboration for teacher, school and system improvement* (pp. 172–193). New York, NY: Routledge.

Social Sciences and Humanities Research Council of Canada. (2018, November 2). *Definitions of terms.* Retrieved from http://www.sshrc-crsh.gc.ca/funding-financement/programs-programmes/definitions-eng.aspx?pedisable=true#km-mc

Ward, V. L., House, A. O., & Hamer, S. (2009). Knowledge brokering: Exploring the process of transferring knowledge into action. *BMC Health Services Research*, *9*, 1–6. https://doi.org/10.1186/1472-6963-9-12

Wasserman, S. & Faust, K. (1994). *Social network analysis: Methods and applications.* New York, NY: Cambridge University.

Weiss, C. (1979). The many meanings of research utilization. *Public Administration Review*, *39*(5), 426–431. https://doi.org/10.2307/3109916

8

WHAT IS THE RESEARCH BROKERAGE ROLE THAT CAN BE PLAYED BY SOCIAL RELATIONSHIPS?

Learning from a quantitative study from England

Chris Brown

Chapter overview

Research-informed teaching practice refers to the use of research evidence by educators to improve teaching and learning and, as a result, outcomes for students. The use of research by teachers is considered both beneficial and desirable; as a result, research-informed teaching should be both encouraged and facilitated. Within this book, we view one key aspect of brokerage as supporting practitioners to engage with evidence and to employ it locally. It is also clear, however, that the within-school conditions must be right for such brokerage to be successful. In light of the increasing focus on social influence as a driver of behaviour/behavioural change, with this Chapter I examine the extent to which social-influence affects teachers' take-up of research. Furthermore, I also examine the relative importance of social influence compared to other factors known to positively affect research use: (1) teachers' perceptions as to whether they work in a trusting work environment; (2) perceptions as to whether school leaders' encourage the use of research in their schools; and (3) teachers' perceptions regarding whether they are encouraged to innovate. To investigate the impact of social influence on teachers' research-use, a regression model using survey and social network data from 389 teachers from 42 primary schools in England was constructed. The findings of this analysis provide vital insights into the within school conditions most likely to support brokerage activity.

1. The power of social influence

It is now widely acknowledged that social influence can have a material impact on people's attitudes and behaviours: in other words, our choices and decisions and our opinions and beliefs are more often than not influencing others (Berger, 2016). It is also clear that social influence can assert itself a number of ways including: (1) through implicit norms and guidelines that govern our understanding of how to respond in specific situations (Berger, 2016); (2) individuals can rely on the judgement of others when they are uncertain, meaning that the views of groups in such situations can converge (Asch, 1956); (3) similarly individuals can also use the behaviour of others as a source of information to guide how to act – or as Berger observes, as "a heuristic that simplifies decision making" (2016, p. 29) (with Berger providing a myriad of examples to illustrate this point, ranging from where we park our car to how we decide which school to send our children to); and (4) that people often feel social pressure to confirm with the decisions or behaviour of the wider group (Berger, 2016).

But social influence doesn't always result in convergence: depending on the activity, social influence can also lead to individuals engaging in behaviour to differentiate themselves from others. Most notably once an item of clothing, a TV show or a make and model of car becomes 'too' popular, or is adopted by particular demographic groups, it can result in others then liking it less (again see Berger, 2016; for specific examples). Furthermore, similarities in the beliefs or behavior of connected individuals can actually represent a different phenomenon – that of homophily. Here shared similarities in relation to certain attributes simply occur because 'birds of a feather to flock together' rather than due to any inherent behaviour change (Daly, 2010). As such, when considering social influence, it is important to ascertain the both the direction and cause of correlated behaviour to determine what might be due to social influence, which way social influence is directing people and what role (if any) homophily is playing.

For the purposes of this chapter it is also important to differentiate between formal and informal forms of social influence that exist within organizations, with the latter involving alternative forms of influence and leadership (Daly, 2010). In particular, while formal relationships within organizations can be identified and mapped out though organizational charts, the informal organization should be conceived of more as a 'social network'. In other words, as an entity comprising groups of social actors "who are connected to one another through a set of different relations or ties" (Daly, 2010, p. 4). The presence of informal social networks within organizations provides an alternative means through which social capital, i.e.: "communication, ideas, knowledge, innovation, or any number of resources can flow through [the ties that exist] between actors" (ibid.). Since resources can flow through social networks, they can be accessed and harnessed. Often the influence deriving from these social networks is substantial as key aspects of an organization's culture is derived from them. Correspondingly, unlike formal hierarchies, where power results from one's position within the organization, with networks informal social influence accrues to those actors most able to successfully harness resource and/or control resource flow to others. The interplay between formal and informal influence is key to how change occurs within organizations. For instance, it is argued by Spillane, Healey and Kim (2010) that, given the influence that operates through social networks, it is informal leaders – those with connections to many other actors and most able to harness/control the resource flow that results – who are most likely to determine the fate of new initiatives or reforms. In this chapter, therefore, I focus on informal social connections and influence.

2. Research-informed teaching practice

Research-informed teaching practice (RITP) represents a collaborative process in which teachers and school leaders work together to access, evaluate, and apply the findings of academic research in order to improve teaching and learning in their schools (Walker, 2017). There is now a longstanding recognition by both teachers and policymakers that academic educational research can be used to improve practice but only limited evidence on how this might be facilitated at the school level (Graves & Moore, 2017). Furthermore, a systemic level gap appears to exist between research and practitioners which as yet shows little indication of narrowing (Buske & Zlatkin-Troitschanskaia, 2018; Coldwell *et al.*, 2017; Graves & Moore, 2017; Whitty & Wisby, 2017). As a result, this leaves only sporadic instances of RITP occurring within and across schools; with other factors such as intuition and experience instead solely driving much of the decision making undertaken by teachers (Buske & Zlatkin-Troitschanskaia, 2018; Vanlommel, Van Gasse, Vanhoof, & Van Petegem 2017). Yet at the same time RITP should be thought of as both beneficial and desirable and so both encouraged and fostered within schools. The benefits and desirability of RITP can be derived by exploring and utilizing the four factors established in Brown (2018) as relates to optimal rational positions. These are: factor (1) a robust and credible evidence base in relation to current or potential new behaviours; factor (2) a well-reasoned argument/theory of change that provides this evidence with meaning; factor (3) a social, moral or value-based imperative setting out the need for change based on this meaning; and factor (4) buy-in to this imperative from a range of credible stakeholders

Factor 1: Collaborative RITP can have positive benefits for both teachers and students. For example, correlational data reported by Mincu (2014) suggests that where research is used as part of high quality initial teacher education and ongoing professional development, it is associated with higher teacher, school and system performance (similar relationships are also reported in Godfrey, 2014). More recently Rose and colleagues (2017), using a randomized control trial across a sample of 119 schools, showed that increased levels of collaborative research use by primary school teachers had a significant impact on primary school student's exam results. CUREE (2010), meanwhile, lists a range of positive teacher outcomes that emerge from collaborative RITP including both improvements in pedagogic knowledge and skills, and greater teacher confidence.

Factor 2: A theory of change for why RITP should improve teaching and student outcomes is set out in Brown, Schildkamp and Hubers (2017). Broadly, this argues that there is a multitude of research that currently exists that can help teachers in a number of areas of their work. For example research can be used to: (1) aid teachers in the design of new bespoke strategies for teaching and learning in order tackle specific identified problems; (2) provide teachers with ideas for how to improve aspects of their day to day practice by drawing on approaches that research has shown to be effective; (3) help teachers expand, clarify and deepen their own concepts, including the concepts they use to understand students, curriculum and teaching practice, and; (4) provide teachers with specific programs or guidelines, shown by research to be effective, which set out how to engage in various aspects of teaching or specific approaches to improve learning. Thus, if teachers are able to engage with this research in a way that enables them to undertake any of 1–4 above, their teaching quality should be improved. Correspondingly, improved teaching quality should then lead to improved student outcomes.

Factor 3: Given that it is possible to use research evidence to improving teaching practices then teachers *should* engage in RITP. This imperative stems from advocates such as Oakley, who argues that evidence-informed approaches ensure that "those who intervene in other people's lives do so with the utmost benefit and least harm" (2000, p. 3). Oakley thus contends that there exists a moral imperative for practitioners to only make decisions, or to take action, when armed with the best available evidence. In other words that:

> we [all] share an interest in being able to live our lives as well as we can, free from ill-informed intervention and in the best knowledge we can gather of what is likely to make all of us most healthy, most productive, most happy and most able to contribute to the common good.
>
> *(2000, p. 323)*

More recently, Goldacre (2013) also argued that teachers *should* engage in RITP since it would lead not only to improved outcomes for children but also increased professional independence (resulting in teaching experiencing an 'enhanced' level of professionalization akin to that of doctors). Likewise, England's *Chartered College of Teaching* recently suggested that teachers' engagement with research should be viewed as the hall mark of an effective profession.[1]

Factor 4: It is evident that there now exists a general position in favour of teachers pursing collaborative RITP. For instance the direction of travel of recent educational policy in England and elsewhere (including, for example, Australia, Netherlands, Norway, Ontario, and the USA,) focuses strongly on promoting, assisting and requiring teachers to better engage with research (Coldwell *et al.*, 2017; Whitty & Wisby, 2017). It is also apparent from recent announcements by organizations, such as the Education Endowment Foundation (EEF), who in 2014 launched a £1.4m fund to improve the use of research in schools (EEF 2014) and in 2016 launched the *Research Schools* initiative.[2] In addition, this position can be associated with the rise of bottom up/teacher led initiatives, such as the emerging network of 'Teachmeets'[3] and 'ResearchED'[4] conferences (Whitty & Wisby, 2017) designed to help teachers connect more effectively with educational research. One recent prominent example of such teacher led initiatives was the 2017 launch of England's Chartered College of Teaching: an organization led by and for teachers in order to support the use of evidence-informed practice (Whitty & Wisby, 2017). In addition to the macro-environment influence we must remember there is a significant requirement for buy-in at an individual school level. The key for the success of this is related to the formal and informal power structures within each school. If those who are key social actors and influencers in the school (i.e. credible stakeholders) support the value of RITP its use will become an accepted part of the school's culture. This will support the longevity and sustainability of RITPs use and impact.

Although, as the above analysis shows, we have an understanding of why we should encourage teachers to engage in RITP, questions still remain as to how to make RITP an everyday reality in schools (Brown, 2018; Coldwell *et al.*, 2017). With this book we posit that effective brokerage has a role in closing the research to practice gap; but it is also clear that the conditions within schools must be right if efforts at brokerage are to be successful (in other words if teachers are to be receptive to brokerage efforts). As such I now explore the factors that influence these within-school conditions.

3. How social relationships might influence RITP

As Wentworth, Mazzeo and Connolly (2017) observe, schools are social structures in which norms and values help determine actions and behaviors. Recalling section 1 above (which examined the power of social influence), it seems likely that social factors could positively affect the take up of RITP. For instance if we know and witness our colleagues* engaging effectively in research use, we are likely to have more opportunity to see benefits of RITP, realize how to overcome any perceived costs, as well as possibly perceive that 'this is the way things should be done around here'. In other words if our colleagues are doing something, this is often likely to signal that this activity is something we ourselves can and should be doing. Conversely, the absence of these things could potentially make research-informed teaching practice less likely (Spillane *et al.*, 2010). This chapter therefore explores the importance of social influence on teachers' engagement in RITP. Specifically it explores whether teachers are more likely to use research to improve their practice depending on whether the teachers they have an informal social connection with engage in RITP (or not). In doing so it draws on analysis undertaken in a recent study by Brown, Zhang, Xu and Corbett (2018). The main hypothesis tested by Brown *et al.* (2018) was:

> **H1:** *There is a positive relationship between teachers' use of research to inform their practice and their colleagues'* use research to inform their practice.*
>
> *here the term colleague is referring to an individual a teacher has an informal social connection with

At the same time extant studies suggest a number of other factors could potentially affect teachers use of research (Coldwell *et al.*, 2017; Brown, 2018). As such, as well as examining the existence and direction of any relationship between teachers' use of research and that of their colleagues, Brown *et al.* (2018) also examined the relative importance of relational influence in comparison to the following factors:

3.1) a trusting work environment: In high trust schools, individuals feel supported to engage in risk taking and the innovative behavior associated with efforts at developing or trialing effective practice in a 'safe' learning environment (also Bryk & Schneider, 2002; Stoll, Bolam, McMahon, Wallace & Thomas, 2006; Mintrop & Trujillo, 2007). It is of no surprise therefore that trust between and amongst educators also likely to support professional efforts related to the use of research evidence (Brown *et al.*, 2016; Finnigan & Daly, 2012). For instance, a trusting work environment is instrumental to the type of 'double-loop' learning that is key to fostering RITP (Argris & Schön, 1996): that is, a trusting environment will be a prerequisite if teachers are to openly and collaboratively challenge and question their foundational assumptions as part of a process of seeking to continually improve teaching and learning. Furthermore, since effective research use is dependent on capacity (ability) to engage with research evidence, trust can mediate between those with and without such capacity. In other words, where teachers feel they do not have the knowledge or skills to challenge a research-informed position, trust enables that position to be widely adopted (Finnigan & Daly, 2012). As such it seems that high trust environments signal that it is okay to take risks, lowering the costs of doing so and making risk-taking a potentially more beneficial activity. The second hypothesis tested by Brown *et al.* (2018) therefore was that:

H2: *There is a positive relationship between teachers' use of research to inform their practice and their perception that they work within a high trust environment.*

3.2) an environment that encourages research-use: If it is to be 'the way things are done around here', research-use needs to become a cultural norm within schools. Such norms are likely to stem from a full commitment to research-informed practice from school leaders who, drawing on forms of transformational leadership, can establish a vision for their school that supports and encourages research use. In addition, school leaders should also provide the necessary resource and structures (e.g. time and space) for sustained, meaningful and collaborative research-use to become a reality (Buske & Zlatkin-Troitschanskaia, 2018; Coldwell *et al.*, 2017; Leithwood, Day, Sammons, Harris & Hopkins, 2006). Although these efforts are important, for a formal research use environment to have impact teachers must also possess mindsets that are specifically geared towards ways of working that support RITP: i.e. mindsets where there is a belief in the value of research-evidence and RITP, as well as valuing the systems and structures that are required to facilitate RITP (Wentworth *et al.*, 2017). Furthermore, teachers need to believe in the benefits of working collaboratively and the role of collaborative processes (such as learning conversations) in developing RITP (Brown, 2017; Wentworth *et al.*, 2017). An encouraging research-use environment is thus most likely to positively influence teachers' use of research through its effect on the signification associated with RITP (with the presence of time and space – if provided – potentially also reducing perceived barriers to engaging). If, despite this top down encouragement, teachers still do not believe in the benefits of RITP or its costs are still perceived to be too high, then RITP will still fail to take hold. Nonetheless a third hypothesis tested by Brown *et al.* (2018) was:

> **H3**: *There is a positive relationship between teachers' use of research to inform their practice and their perception that they are encouraged to engage in RITP.*

3.3) an innovative school environment: RITP is also more likely to materialize when school cultures are attuned to innovation. This may occur, for instance, through school leaders promoting the benefits of considering innovative ideas and normalizing the notion of experimenting with new ways of working (Coldwell *et al.*, 2017; Leithwood *et al.*, 2006). Likewise, RITP will be more likely to occur when school leaders facilitate a supportive environment within which new practice can be developed, trialed and evaluated (Stoll *et al.*, 2006). As with trusting work environments, innovative environments signal that it is OK to take risks, whilst lowering the costs associated with risk-taking activity. At the same time this does not automatically mean that RITP will be adopted – this again depends on the benefits, costs and signification that teachers associate engaging with research in comparison to other approaches to innovation (e.g. engaging in joint practice development activities such as lesson study or the use of alternative evidence bases such as school data). It is more likely that RITP will materialize in innovative environments than not, however, and so a fourth hypothesis to be tested is that:

> **H4**: *There is a positive relationship between teachers' use of research to inform their practice and their perception that they work in an innovative school environment.*

3.4) homophily: finally, it is argued that research use by teachers is unlikely to be caused by homophily as this would require teachers to actively chose their working environment based on whether other teachers hold similar research-use attitudes and behaviors to themselves. As has been shown in Brown (2018), however, individual schools as well as school federations can contain a myriad of teacher types as related to research use. This suggests that homophily is therefore unlikely to play a major role outside of our main hypothesis (H1, above). Correspondingly, Brown *et al.* (2018) did not examine its influence.

4. Methods and analysis

The research presented here forms part of a wider project examining the use of research by teachers (the *Research Learning Communities project* funded by the Education Endowment Foundation). As part of this study a social network survey was administered to all teaching staff within participating schools. A total of

TABLE 8.1 Sample demographics

	Mean or %	SD
School level		
Number of teachers	19.00	10.50
Number of students	320.00	194.38
Ofsted	2.86	1.17
Teacher level		
Years in current position	3.56	3.71
Gender (female)	82.0%	–
Serve as a subject leader	49.0%	–
Hold a formal senior leadership role	18.0%	–

828 teachers from 43 primary schools participated in the survey, resulting in an average response rate of 75%. Table 8.1 provides the overall demographics of the participating teachers from the 43 schools. As can be seen, schools involved had on average some 320 students (SD = 194.4) with approximately 19 teachers per school (SD = 10.5). The average schools' OfSTED grade[5] is close to the account-ability outcome level of "Good" (SD = 1.2). As for teacher data, of all the 828 teachers, 82% are female; approximately 49% serve as a subject leader (e.g., math lead or coordinator; and about 18% hold a formal and senior leadership position (e.g., headteacher). On average, the teachers have less than four years of experience working in their current position.

It should be noted that the demographic data does highlight a number of cave-ats in relation to how our analysis can be interpreted. First, all of the schools involved are primary schools, so no inference can be made about this analysis and England's 3,200+ secondary schools. Second, due to their desire to take part in the Research Learning Communities Project, it is possible that the schools involved are more predisposed to research engagement than the majority of England's pri-mary schools.[6]

In addition to the demographic data, to explore hypothesis 1, social network data were collected in order to determine the informal professional relationships that existed between teachers in the surveyed schools. Here participants were asked to assess the *frequency* of interactions with other colleagues of their school in rela-tion to a number of different interaction types, using a 5-point scale ranging from 1 (1–2 times a week) to 5 (Not at all) (see Table 8.3). In addition to the frequency of their teaching and learning-related interactions, we also asked participants to assess the *quality* of such interactions by reflecting the degree of usefulness on a 5-point scale, ranging from 1 (Not at all useful) to 5 (Very useful). Participants within each school received a roster with teachers from their schools in rows and the frequency of interactions for each relationship in columns. The number of nominations from the bounded list of nominees that participants could make was unlimited. This bounded method is a social network strategy that provides a more complete picture of the network and thus supports valid results (Scott, 2000).

TABLE 8.2 Survey questions employed

Hypothesis	RITP area	Survey questions	Shorthand reference
Dependent variable and hypothesis 1	Use of research	Information from research plays an important role in informing my teaching practice	r-practice
2	A trusting work environment	Staff in this school trust each other	Overall trust
3	An environment that encourages research-use	My school encourages me to use research findings to improve my practice	Encouragement
4	An innovative school environment	My school experiments with new ways of working	Experimentation

To understand participants' use of research to inform their teaching-practice, as well as to explore the three questions relating to hypotheses 2–4 above, the perception scales set out in Table 8.2 were employed. Each question in Table 8.2 employed a five-point Likert scale which ranged from 'Strongly Agree' to 'Strongly Disagree'.

To analyse the data it was assumed by Brown *et al.* (2018) that teachers' use of research (r-practice) was the dependent variable. The aim of the analysis therefore was to understand the interplay between r-practice and the factors that potentially influenced research-use represented in the hypotheses above), i.e.: (1) their colleagues' use of research (represented by the 'r-practice' scores for those individuals respondents had social ties with; (2) whether participants' perceived they worked in a trusting environment (Overall Trust); (3) whether teachers perceived that they worked in an environment that supports research use (Encouragement); and (4) whether teachers perceived their school encourages them to experiment with new ways of working (Experimentation). A regression model was developed (see Brown *et al.*, 2018) to examine the existence and nature of the relationship between dependent and causal variables. The model can be formally expressed as equation 1, below:

$$R-Practice\_I = f(R-PracticeC, Encouragement\_I, Experimentation\_I, Overall\_Trust\_I)$$

I: myself,

C: colleague.

To construct and evaluate the model, a Python program was written to process and generate the analysis result. Furthermore, to study social network structure, we

TABLE 8.3 Interaction categories used in the school survey

Prefixes	Description
ETL_F_	Expertise in teaching and learning frequency
ETL_Q_	Expertise in teaching and learning quality
SRBA_F_	Sought research based advice frequency
SRBA_Q_	Sought research based advice quality
ETM_F_	Exchanged teaching materials frequency
JEPW_F_	Jointly evaluated pupils' performance/work frequency
CWT_F_	Collaborated regarding improving teaching practice frequency
CF_F_	Regard as a close friend frequency
VT_F_	Vent to frequency
IN_F_	Consider to be an energy 'infuser' frequency

have programmed a function within our Python program using NetworkX library, which is an open-source software for complex networks, to create a social network graph model for each school based on the ten different interaction categories, which are listed in Table 8.3.

Based on these network graph models, 389 valid individual teacher data entries, which are illustrated in Table 8.4, were extracted by matching the teacher names from each school's social network data to the master survey results. In Table 8.4, the values from left to right in the first matrix are the other teachers' (neighbours) R-practice mean in the given teacher's individual school, the other teachers' (neighbours) R-practice standard deviation in the given teacher's individual school, the given teacher's own encouragement Likert scale point, the given teacher's own Experimentation Likert scale point and finally, the given teacher's own Overall-Trust Liker scale answer. In the second vector, the values is the given's teacher's own R-practice Liker scale point. All of the Liker scale points were transformed into numerical integers format with values range from -2 to 2.

The value from left to right in left matrix are: R-Practices_N_mean, R-Practices_N_STD, Encouragement_I, Experimentation_I and Overall-trust_I. The value in right vector is R-Practices_I

TABLE 8.4 Post-processed data samples.

$$
\begin{bmatrix}
1.57142857 & 0.53452248 & 2. & 2. & 2. \\
1.66666667 & 0.51639778 & 1. & 1. & 2. \\
1.6 & 0.54772256 & 2. & 2. & 2. \\
\vdots & \vdots & \vdots & \vdots & \vdots \\
0.75 & 0.46291005 & 2. & 2. & 1. \\
1. & 0.63245553 & 1. & 1. & 2. \\
0.90909091 & 0.70064905 & 2. & 2. & 0.
\end{bmatrix}
\begin{bmatrix}
1. \\
1. \\
2. \\
\vdots \\
1. \\
0. \\
1.
\end{bmatrix}
$$

TABLE 8.5 Feature importance scale

Rank	Features	Importances
1	Encouragement I	0.3725364
2	R-practice_C_STD	0.2363432
3	R-practice_C_Mean	0.2179004
4	Experimentation_I	0.1197469
5	Overall_trust_I	0.0534729

Because data was collected via Likert scale points and these types of data do not have a specified probability distribution, we therefore employed nonparametric statistical model and relevant data mining methods, i.e., Random Forests [Breiman, 2001] and Stochastic Gradient Boosting [Friedman 2002] for this analysis task and applied five-fold cross-validation technique on the data samples to evaluate these predictive models. After comparison, Brown *et al.* (2018) opted to use the Stochastic Gradient Boosting approach since it was able to provide higher prediction accuracy 0.601498 (by Gradient Tree Boosting classifier) vs 0.565601 (by Random Forests classifier) with similar standard deviation 0.072290 vs 0.065734 correspondingly. The result also indicates that the performance of this prediction model is stable and consistent due to low standard deviation among the 5-fold tests, and the accuracy of predicting unknown R-practices_I value by given new R-practices_C, Encouragement_I, Experimentation_I and Overall-Trust_I values is around 60%. Finally, Brown *et al.* (2018). computed the feature importance scale for each causal variables in the model to exam the previously defined four relationship hypotheses. The result is illustrated in Table 8.5.

5. Results

The results show that all of the factors tested (R-practices_C, Encouragement_I, Experimentation_I and Overall-Trust_I) do have some influence on R-practices_I. This means that all four of our hypotheses should be accepted. At the same time, however it is clear that the most influential factors by far are (1) perceptions by teachers that their school encourages them to use research findings to improve their practice; and (2) the extent to which an individual teacher's colleagues (i.e. those they have social ties to) report that research plays an important role in informing their teaching practice. Further investigating the significance of social influence, it can also be seen that the standard deviation score for R-practices_C is close to its mean suggesting that the strength of this relationship was common across all 42 schools.

6. Discussion

The principal argument of this chapter is that RITP is something to be encouraged and facilitated. Brokerage has a key role to play in increasing take-up of research, but brokerage efforts can only flourish in the right conditions (akin to the eco-system analogy of Godfrey and Brown, 2018). The aim of this chapter therefore was to examine these conditions and their implications for brokerage, in order to provide vital insights for brokers moving forward. Given the growing recognition that social influence can affect people's behavior, I drew on the work of Brown *et al.* (2018) to explore whether social influence affects the use of research by teachers. Furthermore to explore whether such influence is relatively more powerful than other factors thought to be associated with teachers' using research, i.e.: perceptions of a trusting work environment; perceptions of an innovative work environment; and perceptions that schools leaders are encouraging the use of research in schools (Coldwell *et al.*, 2017; Brown, 2018). The findings from Brown *et al.* (2018)'s regression model reinforce what was previous known about the importance of school leader encouragement for RITP if it is to become the 'way things are done around here' (Buske & Zlatkin-Troitschanskaia, 2018; Coldwell *et al.*, 2017; Leithwood *et al.*, 2006). They likewise confirm that trusting and innovative working environments do matter. Vitally, however, these findings also provide new understanding in terms of the importance of social influence in supporting the realization of RITP. Specifically they show that not only can social influence positively encourage RITP, but that such influence appears to be relatively important as a driver for teachers' use of research. These findings regarding the importance of social influence can be partially explained by previous qualitative work in this area (e.g. Brown, 2017; 2018). For instance, it seems clear that social and relational factors can help promote RITP by: (1) providing teachers with the opportunities to engage in research-informed learning conversations in which new innovations are shared and potentially ineffective practices challenged; (2) ensuring that teachers know who to turn to in order to access research or seek RITP related support; and (3) ensure RITP is regarded as a supported and meaningful endeavor that is regarded as personably desirable but also professionally expected. Furthermore, these findings can also be reflected by extant research into RITP which focuses the relational aspects of school improvement. For example, studies that highlight the roles of social structures, norms and values in helping determine effective and appropriate actions and behaviors (e.g. Wentworth *et al.*, 2017).

At the same time the analysis set out here also point to a key challenge for brokers, policymakers and school leaders if RITP is to become a reality in school systems. Namely, if our use of research is greatly influenced by our colleagues' use of research, then how can systemic and whole school research-use be 'kick started'? In other words, how do we switch on the idea that everyone is now using research? One way to address this may be to consider which individuals are best placed to influence perceptions as to the take up of RITP within a school. We note in section 1 that informal social relations within a school are often best thought of as a social network through which social capital resources (such as information and advice) flow. At the same time social capital tends to be unevenly distributed within networks (Spillane *et al.*, 2010). Correspondingly if we explore who it is that teachers turn to for work-related expertise, and then identify which of these individuals is turned to most, we will have likely pinpointed the teacher(s) most able to disseminate social capital resource to others. What's more, if these individual/s are also centrally positioned in other areas (e.g. in terms of a school's trust or support networks) then they can potentially also galvanize other teachers to adopt new practices such as RITP. As such, to mobilize RITP we suggest that, as well as encouraging research use from the top down, brokers should also begin to use social network approaches to identify teacher 'opinion formers'. Once identified these teachers should then by utilized as part of any drive to mobilize opinion and the adoption of RITP. In other words brokers (or others such as school and system leaders) should harness the social influence opinion formers possess in order to help make RITP a reality.

Notes

1 See: https://chartered.college/chartered-teacher-professional-principles
2 See: https://educationendowmentfoundation.org.uk/our-work/research-schools/
3 See: http://www.teachmeethants.co.uk/sample-page/
4 See: http://www.workingoutwhatworks.com
5 OfSTED is England's school inspectorate
6 20 of the schools in our sample were in a Teaching School Alliance, where there is a formal commitment to engage with research and development and another 20 were attempting to enter a research alliance.

References

Argris, C. & Schön, D. (1996). *Organisational learning II: Theory, method, practice, increasing professional effectiveness.* San Francisco, CA: Jossey Bass.

Asch, S. (1956). Studies of independence and conformity: A minority of one against a unanimous majority. *Psychological Monographs, 70,* 1–70.

Berger, J. (2016). *Invisible influence: The hidden forces that shape behaviour.* New York, NY: Simon & Schuster.

Breiman, L. (2001). Random forests. *Machine Learning, 45*(1), 5–32.

Brown, C. (2017). Further exploring the rationality of evidence-informed practice: a semiotic analysis of the perspectives of a school federation. *International Journal of Education Research, 82,* 8–39.

Brown, C. (2018). *How social science can help us make better choices: Optimal rationality in action.* London: Emerald.

Brown, C., Daly, A. & Liou, Y-H. (2016). Improving trust, improving schools: Findings from a social network analysis of 43 primary schools in England. *Journal of Professional Capital & Community, 1*(1), 69–91.

Brown, C., Schildkamp, K., & Hubers, M. (2017). Combining the best of two worlds: A conceptual proposal for evidence-informed school improvement. *Educational Research, 59*(2), 154–172.

Brown, C., Zhang, D., Xu, N., & Corbett, S. (2018). Exploring the impact of social relationships on teachers' use of research: A regression analysis of 389 teachers in England. *International Journal of Education Research, 89,* 36–46.

Bryk, A. and Schneider, B. (2002). *Trust in schools: A core resource for school improvement*. New York, NY: Russell Sage Foundation.

Buske, R. and Zlatkin-Troitschanskaia, O. (2018). Investigating principals' data use in school: The impact of evidence-oriented attitudes and epistemological beliefs. *Educational Management Administration & Leadership*, early online access.

CUREE, (2010). *Report of professional practitioner use of research review: Practitioner engagement in and/or with research* (Coventry: CUREE, GTCE, LSIS & NTRP). Available at: http://www.curee-paccts.com/node/2303, accessed on December 24, 2017.

Coldwell, M., Greany, T., Higgins, S., Brown, C., Maxwell, B., Stiell, B., Stoll, L, Willis, B., & Burns, H. (2017). *Evidence-informed teaching: An evaluation of progress in England*. London: Department for Education.

Daly, A. (2010). Mapping the terrain: Social network theory and educational change, In A. Daly. (Ed.), *Social network theory and educational change*. Cambridge, MA: Harvard Education Press.

Finnigan, K.S. and Daly, A.J. (2012). Mind the gap: Organizational learning and improvement in an underperforming urban system. *American Journal of Education*, *119*(1), 41–71.

Friedman, J. H. (2002). Stochastic gradient boosting. *Computational Statistics & Data Analysis*, *38*(4), 367–378.

Godfrey, D. (2014). Leadership of schools as research-led organizations in the English educational environment: Cultivating a research engaged school culture. *Educational Management Administration & Leadership*, early online publication.

Godfrey, D. & Brown, C. (2018). How effective is the research and development ecosystem for England's schools? *London Review of Education*, *16*(1), 136–151.

Goldacre, B. (2013). *Building evidence into education* (London, Department for Education). Available from: https://www.gov.uk/government/news/building-evidence-into-education, accessed on September 10, 2017.

Graves, S. & Moore, A. (2017). How do you know what works, works for you? An investigation into the attitudes of school leaders to using research evidence to inform teaching and learning in schools. *School Leadership & Management*, early online access.

Leithwood, K., Day, C., Sammons, P., Harris, A., & Hopkins, D. (2006). *Successful school leadership: What it is and how it influences student learning. Research report 800*. London: DfES.

Mincu, M. (2014). Inquiry paper 6: Teacher quality and school improvement – what is the role of research? In the British Educational Research Association/ The Royal Society for the encouragement of Arts, Manufactures and Commerce (Eds), *The Role of Research In Teacher Education: Reviewing The Evidence*, retrieved from https://www.bera.ac.uk/wp-content/uploads/2014/02/BERA-RSA-Interim-Report.pdf, accessed on November 8, 2017.

Mintrop, H., & Trujillo, T. (2007). The practical relevance of accountability systems for school improvement: A descriptive analysis of California schools. *Educational Evaluation and Policy Analysis*, *29*, 319–352.

Oakley, A. (2000). *Experiments in knowing: Gender and method in the social sciences*. Cambridge: Polity Press.

Rose, J., Thomas, S., Zhang, L., Edwards, A., Augero, A., & Rooney, P. (2017). *Research Learning Communities: Evaluation report and executive summary (December 2017)* Available at: https://educationendowmentfoundation.org.uk/public/files/Projects/Evaluation_Reports/Research_Learning_Communities.pdf, accessed on December 15, 2017.

Scott, J. (2000). *Social network analysis* (2nd ed.). Sage: London.

Spillane, J., Healey, K., & Kim, C. (2010). Leading and managing instruction: formal and informal aspects of elementary school organization, In A. Daly (Ed.). *Social network theory and educational change*. Cambridge, MA: Harvard Education Press.

Stoll, L., Bolam, R., McMahon, A., Wallace, M., & Thomas, S. (2006). Professional learning communities: A review of the literature. *Journal of Educational Change*, 7(4), 221–258.

Vanlommel, K., Van Gasse, R., Vanhoof, J. & Van Petegem, P. (2017). Teachers' decision-making: Data based or intuition driven. *International Journal of Educational Research*, *83*, 75–86.

Walker, M. (2017). *Insights into the role of research and development in teaching schools*. Slough: NfER.

Wentworth, L., Mazzeo, C., & Connolly, F. (2017). Research practice partnerships: A strategy for promoting evidence-based decision making in Education. *Educational Research*, *59*(2), 241–255.

Whitty, G. & Wisby, E. (2017). Is evidence-informed practice any more feasible than evidence-informed policy? Presented at the British Educational Research Association annual conference, Sussex, September 5–7, 2017.

9

BUILDING STUDENT TEACHERS' CAPACITY TO ENGAGE WITH RESEARCH

Georgeta Ion and Joaquín Gairín

Introduction

One of the main aspects related to the training of future teachers is the capacity of the university to contribute to the development of professional competences that can be transferred to future workplaces. The link between theory, practice and research in higher education is extensively discussed and represents a critical aspect in the process of teacher training due to its implications for teacher professionalism (Flores, 2018), however, more efforts have to be made in order to foster these dimensions in teacher education programmes and to move forward a real research culture (Flores, 2017; Valeeva & Gafurov, 2017). The gap between practice and research (and policymaking) is a recurrent topic in specialized literature and draws the attention to different conceptions of research and practice, the disconnections between knowledge producers and users (Dimmock, 2016; Brown, Schildkamp & Hubers, 2017, among others) and, in reference to teacher training, between the education understood as reproduction and education conceived as transformation (Vieira et al., forthcoming).

The presence of research in teaching (through mechanisms as research-led teaching or research-based teaching) is important to close the gap between theory and practice, research and practice and to contribute to bringing students closer to the 'supercomplex society' and its demands (Barnett, 2012; Healey & Jenkins, 2015). In addition, engaging students in research activities appears to be a useful strategy for enhancing their professional competences and can benefit them in several ways (Guilbert et al., 2015). Research activities support students in interpreting the research of others (Reis-Jorge, 2005); allow students to become more aware of their own learning (Todd, Bannister, & Clegg, 2004); and may lead to a deeper interest in and understanding of subjects (Turner, Wuetherick, & Healey, 2008). Research activities have also been shown to enhance undergraduate students' motivation for postgraduate studies (Lopatto, 2004; Ion & Iucu, 2016).

A more explicit presence of research in teaching appears to be a useful strategy for engaging students with research and leading to the development of high-level learning strategies that are directly transferable to professional life (Vereijken et al., 2016).

Connecting students with research takes on different forms and content—from inquiry approaches in initial teacher education (ITE), integration research into practicum (e.g. Qvortrup, 2016; Flores et al., 2016), action research projects (Cain, 2015), or conducting research studies (Niemi & Nevgi, 2014)—and each of these are associated with positive effects on professional competences for student teachers' training (Jyrhama et al., 2008).

In the process of connection between research and practice the knowledge is mobilized, transformed and used, through the "interactive, social and gradual nature of the connection between research and practice" which goes beyond a "one-way process" (Levin, 2013, p. 2). In this process different agents intervene, and the role of student teachers is crucial. Engaged in connecting research and practice, students become veritable knowledge brokers and, in this sense, a study conducted with postgraduate students reveals that studies provide teachers with an opportunity to link research conducted by faculties of education and their own work in schools (Ion & Iucu, 2016). In the same line, but in the context of bachelor studies, Practicum[1] appears to be an element with a high potential to ensure the link between research and practice, contributing to the redefinition of the role of university, moving beyond a view of teaching practice as a process of adaptation or of application of theory (Flores, 2017) to one in which student teachers and teachers are not only users of knowledge but also producers of their professional knowledge (Flores, 2018; Ion, 2014).

Despite the valuable benefits of research for the development of students' professional competences, students' engagement with research is not easy to achieve and is frequently associated with high levels of anxiety and negative feelings of students towards research studies (Ersoy & Çengelci, 2008), as well as a lack of motivation to conduct and interpret research (Ion & Iucu, 2014). In addition, students' engagement in and with research is mediated through different conditions and depends not only on personal factors but also on structural elements such as curriculum design and faculty strategic measures.

Starting from these premises, this study aims to investigate how research competencies are formed in initial teacher education through the integration of research in studies. We focus on understanding student teachers' perceptions of research integration and identifying the form of integration, students' motivation and participation in research during the bachelor's degree programme.

To approach these objectives, we begin with an overview of the different perspectives on the integration of research in undergraduate studies and the potential of these perspectives to form students' research competences. Second, we describe the study settings and methods. Finally, the findings and implications of the study for building research competencies in teacher education are addressed.

Perspectives of research integration in undergraduate studies and the role of students

The integration of research within study programmes is critical to the process of developing the research competencies of students (future educators); in this context, the relationship between teaching and research is assumed to be an important—or even a defining—feature of higher education, and the integration of research into teaching can be considered an important manifestation of that relationship (Taylor, 2007).

There are different models of the research-teaching nexus in teaching higher education, and Healey's (2005) diagram is of particular interest because of its relevance from the perspective of the role of students and curriculum design. Healy uses the diagram to present four different approaches to the teaching–research nexus using two axes. One axis classifies approaches to linking teaching and research according to the extent to which they are teacher-focused, where students are seen as the audience, or student-focused, where students are treated as participants. The second axis classifies the approach as emphasizing research content or research processes and problems.

In this model, four spaces are created that correspond to four distinct ways of integrating research and teaching in university curricula. Research-led teaching can be characterized as teaching with an emphasis on the research products or outcomes, without students engaging in inquiry or research activities. In research-oriented teaching, students have no active role in inquiry either, but the learning objectives are focused on the research problems and processes instead of research products, so in this quadrant, students focus on learning research methods. In research-based teaching, students actively participate in research or inquiry with an emphasis on the research processes and problems. In research-tutored teaching, students also play an active role, for instance, by critically analysing and discussing outcomes of academic research; meanwhile, teaching is mostly focused on research products.

The study of teaching-research relations reveals a series of formalities in this relationship. Visser-Wijnveen and her colleagues (2012) propose a list of four different approaches. The first is learning about research, including lecturing and reading literature. The second is inquiry learning, including analysis, assignments, discussions and reporting. Here, students learn in a research-like way without conducting actual research. A third approach is simulation, involving participation of students which can be an individual or group research project as part of course assignments, and the last approach is participation in the teacher's own research or in the academic world. These last two approaches imply students conducting research and taking part actively in research activity.

Other approaches to integrate research into studies is offered by Zimbardi and Myatt (2012). The authors offer a model in which research is integrated and has the objective of strengthening disciplinary knowledge and supporting understanding of how knowledge is produced in the discipline. The methods used are focused on understanding methodological approaches and developing research skills that offer students practical competences to solve practical problems.

If the previous models are focused on the integration of research into course design and curriculum, Flores (2018) makes a proposal based on the Practicum model in teacher education which aims at linking teaching and research, theory and practice. The model possesses a strong reflective component oriented towards student teacher professional development which enables teaching practice to become a space of transformation rather than an application of theory with a high potential to move toward a model of knowledge mobilization and research informed practice in schools. In this model students become not only recipients of research but knowledge producers and brokers of knowledge between university and school contexts.

Independently of the approach used, the link between research and teaching is a not straightforward process, but mediated by a series of factors, mostly connected to the curricular context. Verburgh (2013) identifies two primary factors that influence the research-teaching relationship in the integration of research into study programmes: the level and orientation of the programme. First, regarding the level of the programme, empirical studies suggest that the relationship between teaching and research differs either between different levels of programmes (bachelor/undergraduate versus master/postgraduate versus PhD students) or between first-year students and non-first-year students. Teachers perceive that teaching and research activities are more intertwined and that the distinction between the two becomes blurred at the postgraduate level (Neumann, 1992). Teachers consider research integration to be more natural (and hence more common) in the more advanced classes of bachelor's and master's programmes than in the earlier years (Elen & Verburgh, 2008). Second, the orientation of a programme can also be an influence. Higher education programmes can be more professionally or more academically oriented, with research integration assumed to be more prominent in academic than professional programmes (Verburgh, 2013). Research has shown that teachers of social sciences, such as the humanities, find it easier to integrate research into their teaching than their colleagues from other disciplines, such as sciences or mathematics (e.g., Coate et al., 2001; among others).

Method

Setting

The study was conducted in the Faculty of Education Sciences at the Universitat Autònoma de Barcelona (UAB), specifically with the bachelor's (BA) degree programme in primary teacher education (BA).

Regarding the methods of integrating research in study programmes, after reviewing the syllabus of the courses, we were perplexed by the fact that the research component in the curriculum of the BA programme in primary education is specified as such only in the course Planning, Research and Innovation (6 credits) offered in the third year. We also found a research component in the Bachelor's Degree Research Project (6 credits) planned for the 4th year of studies. The majority of the subjects up to approximately 65 credits (among compulsory and optional subjects) are general subjects in which the research is integrated in an implicit way in which students experience research through reading research papers, conducting small-scale inquiry projects linked to real practical situations and finally conducting an individual research project linked to a specific problem derived from practice.

However, we are aware that the introduction of the research component in teacher training also relies upon the methodologies and learning strategies applied by the professors to enhance research skills. These methodologies are not necessarily specified in the syllabus.

Instruments and techniques

To measure student perceptions of research integration in university courses, the *Student Perception of Research Integration Questionnaire* (SPRIQ) was constructed and validated by Visser-Wijnveen, Van der Rijstn and Van Driel (2016).

This instrument is a tool of 40 items scored on a five-point Likert scale ranging from very rarely to very frequently, while the four questions on the beliefs scale were scored on an agreement scale ranging from strongly disagree to strongly agree. The questionnaire consists of three constructs (Visser-Wijnveen et al., 2016, p. 6): "research integration", "quality of the course", and "beliefs about research integration". The research integration subscales are reflection (including items focusing on attention being devoted to the research process leading to research results), participation (including items on the involvement of students in and their contribution to scientific research), current research (is a combination of items concerning becoming familiar with the current research from their teachers and in general) and motivation (items concerning an increase in student enthusiasm and interest for the subject). Quality deals with items related to elements deemed important for good-quality teaching, and beliefs refer to students' beliefs about the importance of research integration for their learning.

The scale applied to our sample shows a high level of reliability with a Cronbach's alpha of .963, with values above .80 indicating good internal consistency of the scale.

Sample

For this analysis, we surveyed the students in the primary teacher education degree programme. In total, 240 students were enrolled in the degree programme, and the study sample consisted of 114 students (89.4% female; 9,7% male; 0.9% agender). The sample size calculation with a 95% confidence level for finite populations (p and q=0.5) indicated that the margin of error was ±6.72.

Table 9.1 shows the sample description regarding the level of surveyed students:

TABLE 9.1 Sample description: students by academic year.

Year of study	1st	2nd	3rd	4th	Total
N	39	24	17	34	114

Procedure

The questionnaire was completed in class at the end of a lecture class by members of the research team. Once the data were gathered, univariate and multivariate statistical analyses were performed using the IBM Statistical Package for the Social Sciences (SPSS v.20).

Results and discussion

Student perceptions of research integrated into studies

Overall, the findings (see Table 9.2) demonstrate that the scores for the subscale *reflection*, which includes items that reflect on the way research results are produced, tends to be higher than the rest of the subscale scores (m=2.97). However, the comparison of mean scores on the subscales between courses (Table 9.2) shows that the subscale reflection tends to be slightly higher during first-year (m_0=3.07) and third-year courses (m_2=3) and lower in second-year (m_1=2.92) and fourth-year (m_3=2.85) courses. Students tend to perceive research as both a product (Q1 m=3.19) and a process (Q2 m=3.12). In addition, students perceive research as a less integrated part of the curriculum (Q6 m=2.62), and the methodology of research is weakly integrated into their studies (Q9 m=2.96). These scores arise because during first- and third-year courses, most subjects focus on the discussion and comprehension of research content. Students are usually engaged in subjects in which theories are discussed, and the research is basically integrated into different disciplines through readings and text comments. Students are less engaged in carrying out their own research projects in these courses. However, the first courses are usually focused on creating an inquiry learning introducing students to literature and creating awareness on research as part of the disciplinary content, laying the foundation for future courses.

Second, higher scores are observed for the *motivation* for research, the subscale associated with increased interest and motivation for research in the discipline. Among items forming this category, students consider whether research made them "inspired to learn more about this discipline" (Q7, m=3.08), which has higher scores, together with the increased interest in the "understanding of the most important concepts in the domain" (Q8 m=3.48), as shown in Table 9.4. If this category is distributed by different academic years, we can see that students in the first year tend to be more motivated to conduct research than their peers from the next levels. The mean is considerably higher for students in first-year courses, which could be explained by the integration of research in theoretical disciplines at the beginning of education studies. As mentioned before, during the first course, students engage with theoretical-fundamental courses, establishing the foundation for the disciplines, so research is integrated as part of the curriculum.

The scores for the subscales *current research and student involvement* were below the scores for previous subscales, with considerably lower means overall, as shown in Table 9.2.

The current research subscale refers to the engagement of students with research carried out by their teachers, and student involvement concerns items related to the student's own participation in research-based projects. The items on both subscales highlighted the increased role of students in research, showing the link to an approach in which subjects are organized around inquiry-based learning.

Among items related to the *current research subscale*, students perceive that during their studies, "they learn what kind of studies have been carried out in my field" (Q23 m=3), and they made links between their studies and current research practices (Q30 m=2.66). However, research continues to appear as part of the discipline curriculum, and students play a passive role. When the different academic years are compared, higher scores are registered for first-year subjects (m_0=2.72); scores decrease during the second year (m_1=2.50), and then they recover slowly during the third (m_2=2.58) and fourth years (m_3=2.63). The results could be explained by the presence in the study programme during the third and fourth courses of Practicum activity in which student teachers mobilize and develop diverse types of knowledge such as: scientific knowledge related to the disciplinary content, pedagogical knowledge, and research related knowledge. During fourth course students have to carry out an individual research project linked to a topic derived from practice, which constitute a favourable context for them to mobilize knowledge to examine their practice, identify a problem, justify the focus of research and link the theory with research.

Student involvement in research is the subcategory with lower scores, which is proof that students are not integrated as active agents in conducting research and as members of research teams (m=2.41). However, among this subcategory, the item related to the involvement of students in research registered the higher score (Q28 m=2.69). If we analyse the distribution of this category across academic years, students in the first year perceive that they are more engaged in research at the beginning of their studies (m_0=2.64), and the perception decreases during the second year and the fourth year. Although the subjects in which students conduct research (especially during the research projects that students have carried out) are basically distributed during the last year, students perceive insufficient involvement. Despite students having to conduct research, their projects are conducted individually, and in most cases, they are not integrated into the tutors' research teams.

Quality of teaching is represented by items dealing with the elements considered important for good-quality teaching, such as excellence in instruction (Q34), effectiveness of lecturers' explanations (Q35) and clarity of expectations (Q36).

TABLE 9.2 Mean scores on the subscales

Subscale	1st Year (m_0)	2nd year (m_1)	3rd year (m_2)	4th year (m_3)	Mean general (m)
Reflection	3.07	2.92	3.00	2.85	2.97
Motivation for research	3.26	2.84	2.73	2.68	2.92
Current research	2.72	2.50	2.58	2.63	2.64
Student involvement	2.64	2.16	2.35	2.29	2.41
Quality	3.12	2.94	2.94	3.20	3.08
Beliefs	3.18	3.43	2.81	2.98	3.12

Overall, students perceive teaching as high quality, with a mean over the average (m=3.08) differences between the first- and fourth-year courses. The students perceive higher quality in fourth-year courses (m_3=3.20), followed by the first-year courses (m_0=3.12) and second- and third-year courses with an equal mean (m_1 and m_2=2.94). Although the fourth year is associated with the perception of fewer forms of contact with research, it tends to be valued more highly by students. As mentioned in the setting description, during the last year, the curriculum is basically composed of optional courses, and students have the possibility of choosing those closer to their interests.

The *beliefs* subcategory includes items reflecting the perception of students of research and its integration in the study programme: whether the inclusion of research stimulates learning (Q37), the perception of the importance of lecturers in engaging with research (Q38), whether research in education is stimulated for learning (Q39), and the culture of research in the school of education (Q40). Overall, this category registered a higher score among all the categories reported (m=3.12), and the scores for all academic years are higher than the average.

Role of students in research integration

Regarding the items conforming to the research integration scale overall, it is worth noting that at the UAB, students think that *during their studies, the teachers encouraged them to ask critical questions about their work*; this item's higher mean (Q27 m=3.72) highlights the academic disposition encouraged by research. Students also state that it is *important to them that teachers conduct research* (Q38 m=3.54), which relates to the beliefs about research integration in class.

On the other hand, among the lowest scored items, we found *during my studies, there were opportunities to talk with researchers about scientific research* (Q4 m=2.09) and *during my studies, I had opportunities to socially interact with researchers within the university* (Q29 m=2.10). These items related to the integration of students in the research community during their degree and to the contact they experienced with teachers' own research (see Table 9.3 for details).

TABLE 9.3 Means and Standard deviation for the Items of the Student Perception of Research Integration Questionnaire (SPRIQ)

Item	Min. 1 Max. 5	
	Mean (m)	SD
Q1. During my studies I assimilated knowledge about research findings	3.19	.822
Q2. During my studies I learned to pay attention to the way research is carried out	3.12	.933
Q3. During my studies I developed an academic disposition	3.30	.885
Q4. During my studies there were opportunities to talk with researchers about scientific research	2.09	.931
Q5. During my studies attention was paid to recent developments in the field	2.89	1.097
Q6. During my studies the scientific research process was an essential part of the curriculum	2.62	1.020
Q7. During my studies I was inspired to learn more about this discipline	3.08	1.045
Q8. During my studies my understanding of the most important concepts in the domain has increased	3.48	.917
Q9. During my studies attention was paid to research methodology	2.96	.944
Q10. During my studies I felt part of the university's academic community	2.89	1.072
Q11. During my studies I became familiar with the research carried out by my teachers	2.53	1.010
Q12. During my studies my teachers encouraged me not to be satisfied with an explanation too quickly	2.95	1.109
Q13. During my studies we searched for answers to unanswered research questions together with the teachers	2.41	1.107
Q14. During my studies I became enthusiastic about my scientific domain	2.61	1.081
Q15. During my studies my contribution to the research was valued	2.48	1.158
Q16. During my studies I came in contact with my teachers' research	2.32	1.029
Q17. During my studies my participation in the research was important	2.35	1.140
Q18. During my studies I got the opportunity to hear about current scientific research	2.78	1.041
Q19. During my studies I became familiar with the results of scientific research	2.77	1.009
Q20. During my studies I was stimulated to critically assess literature	2.95	1.109

(continued)

TABLE 9.3 *(continued)*

Item	Min. 1 Max. 5	
	Mean (m)	*SD*
Q21. During my studies I felt involved in the university's research culture	2.32	1.029
Q22. During my studies, my awareness of the research issues that scientific researchers are currently contributing to, was increased	2.70	.981
Q23. During my studies I learned what kind of studies have been carried out in my field	3.00	1.061
Q24. During my studies my interest in research in this area was increased	3.08	1.062
Q25. During my studies I made a contribution to development in my field	2.31	1.036
Q26. During my studies I learned the ways in which research can be conducted in this field	2.96	1.026
Q27. During my studies the teachers encouraged us to ask critical questions about our work	3.72	1.114
Q28. During my studies as a student I felt involved with the research	2.69	1.036
Q29. During my studies I had opportunities to socially interact with researchers within the university	2.10	.916
Q30. During my studies links to current research practices were made	2.66	.997
Q31. During my studies I became involved in my teachers' research	2.21	1.089
Q32. During my studies my teachers encouraged personal interest and enthusiasm for research in this field	2.92	1.151
Q33. During my studies the teachers had sufficient time to support me in my learning process	2.71	1.058
Q34. During my studies the teachers carried out their instruction adequately	3.06	.859
Q35. During my studies my teachers were able to explain the subject matter effectively	3.15	.858
Q36. During my studies I developed an accurate picture of what was expected of me	3.04	1.109
Q37. My learning is stimulated when education is grounded in research	3.20	1.070
Q38. It is important to me that my teachers conduct research	3.54	1.134
Q39. Education in which scientific research is central stimulates my learning	3.18	1.071
Q40. The research culture at the university stimulates my learning process	2.96	1.093

TABLE 9.4 Comparison of mean scores between groups

Item	Group 1 Students in 1st and 2nd year	Group 2 Students in 3rd and 4th year	Sig. (bilateral) P<.05
Q7. During my studies I was inspired to learn more about this discipline	3.40	2.69	.00
Q10. During my studies I felt part of the university's academic community	3.13	2.61	.01
Q12. During my studies my teachers encouraged me not to be satisfied with an explanation too quickly	3.15	2.71	.03
Q21. During my studies I felt involved in the university's research culture	2.50	2.10	.03
Q24. During my studies my interest in research in this area was increased	3.29	2.82	.01
Q27. During my studies the teachers encouraged us to ask critical questions about our work	3.92	3.47	.03
Q39. Education in which scientific research is central stimulates my learning	3.37	2.94	.03

Considerable differences were found when comparing means between the students' years of study. We applied an independent-samples t-test to compare the means among independent groups to determine whether there were statistically meaningful differences. Group 1 comprised students in the two first years of the degree, and Group 2 consisted of students in the two last years of the degree. The results indicate that the following items are significantly correlated (Table 9.4).

As shown in Table 9.4, students in group 1 (enrolled in first and second courses) perceive higher connections between theory and research as students in group 2. Student teachers in first courses feel encouraged to take an interest in research, feel motivated to use critical and inquiry approaches in their learning. Also, they perceive a higher degree of implication in academic culture and academic community within the university. This fact should be taken into consideration and used to determine the reasons why motivation decreases in students who are already in the last two years of their bachelor's degree, as it is those years when the practicum activities occupies more curricular spaces and they start and develop their final research project. However, the perception of integration of research into course design and curriculum in first years has the potential to create a positive environment sensible to research, which create the premises for students' disposition and commitment with research in the second part of their studies. As we can see in the table, students in first two years are engage in learning scenarios linked to the approaches of learning about research and inquiry learning, considered in the Visser-Wijnveen et al. (2012) model corresponds to the situation in which lecturers use research to illustrate their courses or to create the student's disposition towards research as a basis for the next phase, in which students conduct their own research projects.

Regarding students' perception of research integration, we can affirm that students agree that education in which scientific research is central stimulates their learning and that research culture helps their learning process. Therefore, research improves their academic disposition. Results also revealed many students felt that they do not contribute to development in the field, so they should be more involved in real empirical research in the primary teaching professional context.

Students affirm that there are not enough opportunities to be integrated within the research community because they do not have the opportunity to talk with researchers, to be involved in teachers' research, or to be made aware of research being conducted on the topics that relate to the curriculum subjects.

Existing data reveal that students perceive a number of benefits when research is integrated into teaching, as it contributes to a better understanding of the discipline (Neumann 1992; Turner et al. 2008). In addition, research contributes to developing student inquiry, which represents a way to develop the students' capacity for understanding knowledge (Nelson & Campbell, 2017), but it is also a way to contribute to creating knowledge in different contexts, both educational and social or professional (Goodyear & Zenios, 2007). Creation of knowledge forms part of the rationale for pedagogies based on inquiry and research that demonstrate that students are more likely to adopt deep learning strategies when engaged with tasks that are authentic to their field, using its techniques and tools (e.g., Levy & Petrulis, 2012).

In almost all research integration dimensions, students in the first year of study tended to rate their studies higher, but this perception decreased during the second year. Previous studies do not indicate clear connections between the year of study and the students' perception of integration of research; however, Verburgh and Elen (2011) found that first-year students tend to indicate more positive aspects.

Despite the need to expand research integration in education studies, the findings reveal higher scores for students' beliefs regarding research, showing that they value the quality of teaching; these are promising premises related to the use of research in future professional life. Research integration not only is linked to the direct involvement of students in research activities during studies (Verburgh and Elen, 2011; Vereijken et al., 2016) but also to a wider series of learning situations beyond research activities and curriculum integration. Therefore, a change in students' research attitudes and perceptions should be considered, for instance, as a mediating variable between research integration and research usage in practice

(Griffioen, 2018). The findings prompt a discussion about the role of research integration in instructional design as a way to engage students with inquiry and to make them more sensitive to the benefits of using research as a tool for professional development. To do so, teacher education programmes can promote initiatives that aim to educate autonomous and reflective teachers who are able to act as practitioner researchers and who can be characterized as pedagogically thinking teachers. The aim is not to produce researchers but rather to provide future teachers with the skills and knowledge through which they are capable of applying what they have learned, observing and interpreting professional realities, and making decisions based on scientific evidence (Krokfors et al., 2011).

Despite the topic of integration of research into studies experimenting an increasing interest in the last years, further developments are needed to improve the research dimension within teacher education programmes. Research has to be present in a more visible and coherent way underpinning student teachers' professional development, both creating learning situations in which research is included into curriculum in a transversal way as well as enhancing the students' training in conducting research projects. Teacher education programmes need to introduce students to research in a gradual way, engaging them in reading and understanding research findings, and stimulating their participation in research projects with schools (Afdal & Spernes, 2018). Students become in this way not only users but also creators of knowledge, and knowledge brokers ensuring the transfer of knowledge from academia to professional practice. In order for this to happen, higher education institutions need to refine and enhance their roles as partner with schools, opening them up to new forms of teaching and research, research about teaching and teaching research (Flores, 2018).

Acknowledgement

Research funded by: Spanish Ministry of Economy and Competitiveness (Ministerio de Economía y Competitividad) (Programa I+D Retos 2018–2020) Ref: EDU2017-88711-R

Note

1 We understand by "Practicum" the period of time students conduct their school placements during their teacher education study programme. In the Spanish context, this consists in practical activities student teachers develop under the supervision of a faculty tutor and a school tutor.

References

Afdal, H. W., & Spernes, K. (2018). Designing and redesigning research-based teacher education. *Teaching and Teacher Education, 74*, 215–228. doi:10.1016/j.tate.2018.05.011.

Barnett, R. (2012). Learning for an unknown future. *Higher Education Research & Development, 31*, 65–77.

Brown, C., Schildkamp, K., & Hubers, M. (2017). Combining the best of two worlds: A conceptual proposal for evidence-informed school improvement. *Educational Research*, *59*(2),154–172

Cain, T. (2015). Teachers' engagement with published research: Addressing the knowledge problem. *The Curriculum Journal*, *26*(3): 488–509. doi:10.1080/09585176.2015.1020820.

Coate, K., Barnett, R., & Williams, G. (2001). Relationships between teaching and research in higher education in England. *Higher Education Quarterly*, *55*, 158–174. doi:10.1111/1468-2273.00180

Dimmock, C. (2016). Conceptualising the research-practice-professional development nexus: Mobilising schools as 'research engaged' professional development learning communities. *Professional Development in Education*, *42*(1): 36–53. doi:10.1080/19415257.2014.963884.

Elen, J., & Verburgh, A. (2008). *Bologna in European research-intensive universities: Implications for bachelor and master programs*. Antwerp: Garant.

Ersoy, A. F. & Çengelci, T. (2008). The research experience of social studies pre-service teachers: A qualitative study. *Educational Sciences: Theory and Practice*, *8*(2), 541–554.

Flores, M. A. (2017). Editorial. Practice, theory and research in initial teacher education. *European Journal of Teacher Education*, *40*(3), 287–290. doi:10.1080/02619768.2017.1331518.

Flores, M.A. (2018). Linking teaching and research in initial teacher education: knowledge mobilisation and research-informed practice. *Journal of education for teaching*. https://doi.org/10.1080/02607476.2018.1516351

Flores, M. A., F. Vieira, J. L. Silva, & J. Almeida. (2016). Integrating research into the practicum: Inquiring into inquiry-based professional development in post-Bologna initial teacher education in Portugal. In Flores, M. A. and Al-Barwani, T. (Eds), *Redefining teacher education for the post-2015 era: Global challenges and best practice* (pp. 109–124). New York: Nova Science Publisher.

Goodyear, P., & Zenios, M. (2007). Discussion, collaborative knowledge work and epistemic fluency. *British Journal of Educational Studies*, *55*(4): 351–68.

Griffioen, D. M. E. (2018). The influence of undergraduate students' research attitudes on their intentions for research usage in their future professional practice. *Innovations in Education and Teaching International*, doi: 10.1080/14703297.2018.1425152

Guilbert, D., Lane, R., & Van Bergen, P. (2015). Understanding student engagement with research: A study of pre-service teachers' research perceptions, research experience, and motivation. *Asia-Pacific Journal of Teacher Education*, doi: 10.1080/1359866X.2015.1070118

Healey, M. (2005). Linking research and teaching exploring disciplinary spaces and the role of inquiry-based learning. In Barnett, R. (Ed.), *Reshaping the university: New relationships between research, scholarship and teaching* (pp. 30–42). Maidenhead: McGraw-Hill/Open University Press

Healey, M., & Jenkins, A. (2015). Linking discipline-based research with teaching to benefit student learning through engaging students in research and inquiry. Retrieved from http://www.mickhealey.co.uk/resources

Ion, G. (2014). Teachers as research promoters. In M. Schratz, M. Pecek, & R. Iucu (Eds.), *The changing role of teachers. European network on teacher education policies* (pp. 196–218). Bucharest: Ars Docendi.

Ion, G., & Iucu, R. (2014). Professionals' perceptions about the use of research in educational practice. *European Journal of Higher Education*, *4*(4): 334–347.

Ion. G., & Iucu, R. (2016). The impact of postgraduate studies on the teachers' practice. *European Journal of Teacher Education*, *39*(5), 602–615.

Jyrhama, R., Kynaslahti, H., Krokfors, L., Byman, R., Maaranen, K., Toom, A., & Kansanen, P. (2008). The appreciation and realization of research-based teacher education: Finnish students' experiences of teacher education. *European Journal of Teacher Education*, *31*(1): 1–16. doi:10.1080/02619760701844993.

Krokfors, L., Kynäslahti, H., Stenberg, K., Toom, A., Maaranen, K., Jyrhämä, R., Byman, R., & Kansanen, P. (2011) Investigating Finnish teacher educators' views on research-based teacher education. *Teaching Education*, *22*(1), 1–13, DOI: 10.1080/10476210.2010.542559

Levin, B. (2013). To know is not enough: research knowledge and its use. *Review of Education*, *1*, 2–31.

Levy, P., & Petrulis, R. (2012) How do first-year university students experience inquiry and research, and what are the implications for the practice of inquiry-based learning? *Studies in Higher Education*, *37*(1), 85–101, doi: 10.1080/03075079.2010.499166

Lopatto, D. (2004). Survey of undergraduate research experiences (SURE): First findings. *Cell Biology Education*, *3*, 270–277. http://dx.doi.org/10.1187/cbe.04-07-0045

Nelson, J., & Campbell, C. (2017). Evidence-informed practice in education: Meanings and applications. *Educational Research*, *59*(2), 127–135, doi:10.1080/00131881.2017.1314115

Neumann, R. (1992). Perceptions of the teaching-research nexus: A framework for analysis. *Higher Education*, *23*, 159–171.

Niemi, H., & Nevgi, A. (2014). Research studies and active learning promoting professional competences in Finnish teacher education. *Teaching and Teacher Education*, *43*, 131–142. doi:10.1016/j.tate.2014.07.006.

Qvortrup, L. (2016). Capacity building: Data and research-informed development of schools and teaching practices in Denmark and Norway. *European Journal of Teacher Education*, *39*(5), 564–576. doi:10.1080/02619768.2016.1253675.

Reis-Jorge, J. M. (2005). Developing teachers' knowledge and skills as researchers: A conceptual framework. *Asia-Pacific Journal of Teacher Education*, *33*(3), 303–319. http://dx.doi.org/10.1080/13598660500286309

Taylor, J. (2007). The teaching-research nexus: A model for institutional management. *Higher Education*, *54*, 867–884. doi:10.1007/s10734-006-9029-1

Todd, M., Bannister, P., & Clegg, S. (2004). Independent inquiry and the undergraduate dissertation: Perceptions and experiences of final-year social science students. *Assessment & Evaluation in Higher Education*, *29*(3), 335–355. http://dx.doi.org/10.1080/0260293042000188285

Turner, N., Wuetherick, B., & Healey, M. (2008). International perspectives on student awareness, experiences and perceptions of research: Implications for academic developers in implementing research-based teaching and learning. *International Journal for Academic Development*, *13*(3), 199–211. http://dx.doi.org/10.1080/13601440802242333

Valeeva, R. A., & Gafurov, I. R. (2017). Initial teacher education in Russia: Connecting theory, practice and research. *European Journal of Teacher Education*, *40*(3), 324–360. doi: 10.1080/02619768.2017.1326480.

Verburgh, A. (2013). *Research integration in higher education. Prevalence and relationship with critical thinking*. Leuven: Education and Training Research Unit Centre for Instructional Psychology and Technology.

Verburgh, A. L., & Elen, J. (2011). The role of experienced research integration into teaching upon students' appreciation of research aspects in the learning environment. *International Journal of University Teaching and Faculty Development*, *1*, 1–14.

Vereijken, M. W. C., van der Rijst, R., Jan de Beaufort, A., van Driel, J. H. & Dekker, F. W. (2016). Fostering first-year student learning through research integration into teaching: Student perceptions, beliefs about the value of research and student achievement. *Innovations in Education and Teaching International*, doi:10.1080/14703297.2016.1260490

Vieira, F., Flores, M. A., Silva, J. L., & Almeida J.. (Forthcoming). Understanding and enhancing change in post-Bologna pre-service teacher education: Lessons from experience and research in Portugal. In T. Al-Barwani, M. A. Flores, and D. Imig (Eds.), *Leading change in teacher education: Lessons from education leaders around the globe*, London: Routledge.

Visser-Wijnveen, G. J., van Driel, J. H., van der Rijst, R. M., Visser, A., & Verloop, N. (2012). Relating academics' ways of integrating research and teaching to their students' perceptions. *Studies in Higher Education*, *37*, 219–234. doi:10.1080/03075079.2010.536913

Visser-Wijnveen, G. J., van Driel, J. H., van der Rijst, R. M., Verloop, N., & Visser, A. (2010). The ideal research-teaching nexus in the eyes of academics: Building profiles. *Higher Education Research & Development*, *29*, 195–210. doi:10.1080/07294360903532016

Visser-Wijnveen, G.J., van der Rijst, R.M. & van Driel, J.H. (2016). A questionnaire to capture students' perceptions of research integration in their courses. *Higher Education*, *71*(4), 473–488. https://doi.org/10.1007/s10734-015-9918-2

Zimbardi, K., and Myatt, P. (2012). Embedding undergraduate research experiences within the curriculum: a cross-disciplinary study of the key characteristics guiding implementation. *Studies in Higher Education*, *39*(2), 233–250, doi:10.1080/03075079.2011.651448

10

KNOWLEDGE BROKERAGE THROUGH RESEARCH-PRACTICE-ADMINISTRATION PARTNERSHIPS

Learnings from Germany

Nina Bremm and Veronika Manitius

Background

The relevance of effective transfer and implementation processes for success in the implementation of reforms at systemic and school levels is uncontroversial in the school development debate (van Holt 2014). The Standing Conference of the Ministers of Education and Cultural Affairs (KMK) in Germany emphasizes this in its newly revised strategy on educational monitoring where it states,

> the duties of the federal state-level institutes and quality assurance bodies include conducting and disseminating research in cooperation with academic institutions targeted at schools, educational administrations and makers of educational policy. In order to have a sustainable impact in this field, further specific implementation and transfer strategies are required among the federal states.
>
> *(KMK 2015, 14)*

Thus, research and federal state institutes have been identified as central cooperation partners that should provide and translate knowledge and research for schools and administrations. It remains, however, unclear how such cooperation structures should be understood in concrete terms and what defines these "special" implementation and transfer strategies.

The research and educational development project *Potenziale entwickeln—Schulen stärken* (hereafter referred to as the Potential Project) builds on the recommendations of the KMK and its conceptual approach focuses on the close cooperation between academia (the Universities of Duisburg-Essen and Dortmund) and administration (the Quality and Support Agency of State Institute for Schools in North Rhine-Westphalia [QUA-Lis]) in knowledge management and transfer activities for the project. Further stakeholders in the project include the Mercator Foundation, 36 schools in disadvantaged regions of the Ruhr metropolitan area, and the educational administration.

The project follows the objective of developing a knowledge base and findings to support effective strategies, interventions, and processes among schools in disadvantaged regions. It also aims to compile recommendations (for educational administration and the regulatory system) from which other schools can profit independently of the project schools. These recommendations may take the form of: concepts and modules for school-related training; development concepts for coordinated pedagogical and organizational intervention elements for schools in disadvantaged areas; approaches for specific support and guidance for school development; network concepts for cross-institutional cooperation and school networks; and guidelines and materials for practical activities with and within schools. The aim is to track the knowledge of the school regulatory system during the term of an ongoing school development project (and not only during a typical phase of transfer of results at the end of a project) in order to enable a synchronization of timelines and system logics that are often very different depending on which reference system they fall within: academia, schools, administration or education policy (Bremm et al., 2018). As an outcome of such a synchronization process, receivers of transfer knowledge (policy, administration, intermediates etc.) built up structures and situations within their reference system over time in which transfer knowledge can be implemented more easily as in a situation where they are provided with a body of transfer knowledge at the end of a project. In this chapter, the design of the Potential Project will be introduced and then integrated into the concept of *cooperative knowledge management* as it materialized within the scope of the Project. Doing so enables us to provide practical insights into the concrete implementation of the project concept. Lastly, the concluding section will explore and reflect upon the potential and limitations of the selected approaches to knowledge transfer processes in the education system.

The Potential Project

The Potential Project was conceived as an integrated school research and empirical school development project. In total, 36 schools in challenging circumstances in the Ruhr metropolis, an urban and mostly deprived area in North Rhine–Westphalia a federal state in Germany, were included. The Potential Project provides an innovative approach that connects practice-driven research with development. The development component is intentionally open in its conception in order to provide a flexible means of addressing the needs of the participating schools as identified through accompanying empirical research concerning and integrating the structures and actors present in the school system.

The project design can be divided into four main phases (see Figure 10.1).

In the first phase of the project, a quantitative initial assessment was carried out that examined the contextual and process characteristics of the schools. Internal

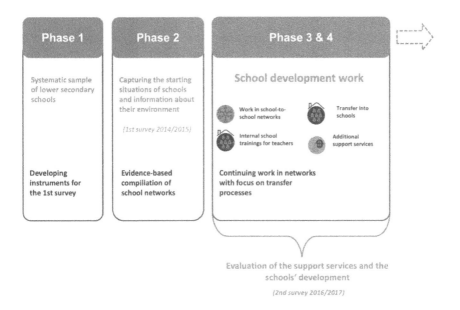

FIGURE 10.1 Design of the Potential Project

and external conditions were documented based on quantitative surveys of all school leaders and teaching staff of the schools as well as a sample of pupils and parents of all 6th and 8th graders in the schools. In this instance the quality of the performance results was recorded, as were the differentiated process characteristics of the individual schools. Characteristics were recorded that—according to recent research—could influence the effectiveness of schools, particularly schools in disadvantaged areas. These features were also characteristic of schools that were able to improve their process and output quality over a period of time.[1] Furthermore, with the help of a social index, differentiated markers of school-specific contextual factors were integrated. Developments within the schools were monitored through in-depth qualitative studies in six case study schools and through a longitudinal quantitative survey. All data from the baseline survey have been made available to the schools aggregated at the classroom or school level. A central structural element in the school development pillar of the project is the cross-school network approach, which follows the concept of network-based school development and incorporates empirical findings on the effectiveness of such networks (Manitius & Berkemeyer, 2015; Berkemeyer et al., 2015). Schools were sorted into networks based on data-driven criteria, so that schools with similar development profiles were able to work together on similar tasks. In addition to the network pillar of the project, schools were assigned development coaches who supported the schools in their development. QUA-LiS played a central role as a cooperation partner in this pillar by providing six "development coaches", with a contingent of five hours per week that allowed them to visit and consult schools during the school development process. These coaches participated in quarterly network meetings over a period of 3.5 years and accompanied development activities within schools. Schools were also offered thematically relevant network-level and cross-school development opportunities such as additional qualifications for school leaders as part of the "Potential Academy".

Cooperative knowledge management as a transfer strategy in the school system

Taking knowledge management as a possible pathway to support school improvement measures and transfer processes, raises the question of precisely what knowledge should be transferred to where and how it should be coordinated. The majority of the discourse related to education focuses on the discussion of the knowledge base in terms of evidence, with the aim of achieving a more strongly evidence-based or evidence-informed structuring of the practice (van Ackeren et al., 2013). With regard to the thematic focus of the project account supporting school development in challenging areas, the generation and coordination of *relevant* knowledge sources is of particular interest; these sources include research, internal school knowledge, administrative data, subject knowledge, and other expertise. This is with the intention to systematically secure the insights gained in a comparatively small exploratory project in order to—as a next step—evaluate how far these insights can be used in the further development of the wider school system in North Rhine–Westphalia (cf. Manitius & Groot-Wilken 2017). The determination of relevance is, therefore, a component of the sense-making process (Coburn, 2005) that can, in turn, act as an important prerequisite for successful transfer activities. This means that the transfer-related information, data, and knowledge must ultimately be recontextualized so that the knowledge base underpinning the support of school development work, for example, can be used. A precondition for this is, therefore, that an understanding and practical framework for knowledge management are implemented as part of the knowledge organization project.

Models of knowledge management focus mostly on the organizational level and the necessary interplay between organizational knowledge management and individual knowledge deployment, e.g. via individual learning that is also beneficial for the organization's development (Nonaka & Takeuchi, 1997). For knowledge management coordinated between the actors within a system the Munich model is of particular relevance (Reinmann-Rothmeier, 2001) because it takes account of the different dimensions of knowledge management as a process and questions the form in which knowledge management can be successfully achieved. In this model knowledge management is divided into four central categories: (1) *Knowledge representation* as the process for making knowledge transparent, comprehensive, and "tangible". (2) *Knowledge deployment* is the process by which the application of knowledge takes place, e.g. deploying knowledge as a foundation for decision-making and taking action. This is a highly demanding, notably complex stage of the knowledge management process because it often requires overcoming systemic inertia. (3) *Knowledge communication* is concerned with the direct activities of knowledge exchange, knowledge sharing, and dissemination. One of the challenges of this stage is creating effective communication processes for knowledge management that are characterized by a high density of interactions, trust between participants, and cooperative activities. *Knowledge generation* (4) is the final part, in which information is translated into practical knowledge and understanding. This requires the interrogation and modification of existing knowledge, as well as the addition of data, in order to create a new form of knowledge. From a management perspective it is valuable to bring the respective bearers of knowledge and expertise together with information providers in relevant communication settings.

The four process stages of knowledge management described here cannot be separated into strict, distinct categories but—taken together—they form an approximate picture of the important elements of knowledge management. In the Munich model these are seen as components of a properly functioning organizational structure upon which knowledge management is constructed to achieve organizational objectives and evaluation processes that, in turn, have an impact on knowledge management.

Here consideration is made of which constellation of individuals is best suited to this sort of knowledge management approach. This could include so-called *communities of practice* made up of individuals that work together on common interests and challenges, thereby operating in a way that is cooperative rather than competitive. The communities contribute to knowledge management processes by facilitating communication outside of hierarchical or organizational structures. They also support solution-driven exchange and expertise on common, connected problem points, and also provide motivational, trustworthy, identity-building frameworks that promote knowledge generation and learning processes that can spur innovation. A systemic perspective would also imply using less of a top-down approach to knowledge management, and more of a strategic approach based on well-targeted pilot projects that cover central leadership and decentralized activities (Willke, 2004). Evidence from experiences in the international context of transfer activities, for example, in the case of "knowledge mobilization" (Ng-A-Fook et al., 2015), has shown connected structures and cooperative strategies of knowledge transmission to be conducive to successful knowledge transfer.

Transferring these theoretical conclusions on knowledge management into the school system poses certain challenges. In the Munich model, for example, knowledge management is viewed from an organizational perspective and, therefore, presupposes an overarching organizational goal from which knowledge management activities flow. Within the school system the diversity of relevant organizations and stakeholders raises the likelihood of goal collision and divergent interests that carry with them the potential for conflict (Bremm et al., 2018). Therefore, transfer phenomena within the school system should be viewed thematically because this presupposes similar goals among the stakeholders. Assuming stakeholders in the school system have an interest in successfully supporting schools—in the case of this project, schools in socially disadvantaged areas—then the overarching systemic goal is that school development activities lead to qualitative improvements in the school's output (such as signifiers of school quality or pupil performance). If knowledge management is organized along this guiding principle, then it can be deployed accordingly in direct working relationships.

The concept of stakeholder constellations in the context of a community that operates outside of hierarchical structures of the school system is most relevant in the field of network-facilitated school development (Manitius & Berkemeyer, 2015; Rürup & Röbken, 2015). This specific school development strategy has enjoyed considerable resonance in Germany over the last ten years as can be seen in the context of the variety of programs and measures within the so-called educational landscape. Analogously to the concept of communities, the potential of school network activities lies primarily in acting as an intermediate organizational form that provides the possibility of exchange and learning; sparks innovation in structures and ultimately promotes the qualitative development of schools. In German-speaking countries the educational discourse focuses around how individual schools can benefit from networking activities as organizations (Berkemeyer et al., 2015).

From a systemic perspective it appears fruitful to draw upon the American work on *research practice partnerships* in school districts in which the concept of the community driving knowledge management becomes more tightly defined. Given their differing rationales, different actors within such partnerships need to work cooperatively in order to achieve their goals successfully. In the literature, the research practice partnerships approach has been defined as, "long-term, mutualistic collaborations between practitioners and researchers that are intentionally organized to investigate problems and solutions for improving district outcomes" (Coburn, Penuel & Geil, 2013, 2). The concept of *joint work*, in which the focus of the work is collectively agreed, and the responsibilities are shared, is important for direct cooperation (Penuel, Allen, Coburn & Farrell, 2015). This feature differs from typical cooperation between research and practice, for example, in which the research is traditionally intended to be advisory for an evaluation or has been commissioned to inform evaluation studies exploring applied practice. A further characteristic of such partnerships is the joint analysis of data is conducted, including on the basis of different data sources. This has proven compatible with the discourse participative genesis of the evidence base that is grounded in the discourse (Weiland, 2013).

A further characteristic of the research practice partnership is that confrontation with differing rationales is inherent in the *boundary crossing* aspects of the methodology, through which the operational logic and the professional area of the other are brought closer together (cf. Penuel et al., 2015). This can occur in communication settings, for example, that foster discussion and exchange between representatives from the academia and in-school practice, or in specific publication formats that cover the different viewpoints on a particular subject (Seidel et al., 2016). This contributes to a so-called "boundaries practice" when it accompanies and supports the appropriate reflection work and learning processes, which can ultimately lead to a change in norms (Penuel et al., 2015).

A form of knowledge management that can be applied from a systemic perspective as a transfer strategy to support schools in challenging environments offers some important pointers for the concepts mentioned thus far. The process dimensions described categorically in the Munich model of knowledge management demonstrate how knowledge management can be conceptualized as a project task. This covers the development and application of central instruments of knowledge management that support the generation and deployment of knowledge. In addition, knowledge communication is also of great importance, which, for successful knowledge management, means ensuring appropriate communication forms, settings, confrontations and—where necessary—constant proximity to the relevant actors.

In line with the project, in order to support school development work in challenging environments in an evidence-based manner that takes account of relevant resources from the most varied actors in the system (Bremm et al., 2017), a research practice partnership approach proved valuable because it allowed for a conceptually successful cooperation between the partners' different operational rationales. Studies on the effectiveness of such partnerships, between research and practice, support the positive impact of these attributes. Above all, their advantage lies in their contribution to the ongoing professionalization of participants regarding changes to their routine and behaviors, especially when these partnerships are centered around dialogue and long-term cooperation (Coburn & Penuel, 2016). Moreover, such partnerships have proven themselves to be significantly more transformative than classically conceived, linear transfer strategies (Penuel et al., 2015).

Knowledge management in the project

The cooperatively conceptualized structure of the project can be seen as similar to a research practice partnership. The constellation of actors in the landscape of practice and research is significantly broadened around educational administration, which takes an active role in the project-related cooperation.

The Project's goals around knowledge management are based on the desire of the relevant educational administration to generate insights from a school improvement project for 36 schools that can be evaluated in terms of their relevance for public support structures in the state of NRW and their transferability into regulatory structures. For a large territory such as NRW with over 5,500 schools, the approach is one of getting *practically* involved in a partnership between foundations, schools, academia and the public sector (the respective Ministry, State Institute, and the further education system in particular) in order to connect and provide results (research findings, experience, materials) that point to effective support for schools in disadvantaged areas that enable transformation in the support systems similar to that in the further education system.

This objective has been realized through a close, dialogue-driven cooperation of the partners steering the project from academia (University Duisburg-Essen and Dortmund), public administration (state institute for schools in NRW) and the Mercator Foundation. The strategy is followed using knowledge management instruments from academia as well as the state institute to provide a systematic enquiry into potentially meaningful knowledge bases, as well as to collate expertise and—in parallel—to initiate and cultivate a transfer-oriented dialogue with the further education system from the beginning of the project in order to take account of the actors in the further education system and to structure transfer activities on the basis of need. In addition, further types of knowledge, such as that generated through university research, are also incorporated.

Cooperative project structures

The partnership in the "Practice-, research-, administration-partnership" project (Manitius & Bremm, 2018) is structured in the following way in terms of the roles and responsibilities of the stakeholders (cf. Figure 10.2): the project implemented at the operational level by the relevant universities that receive the commensurate funding for this purpose through the Mercator Foundation. In doing so the universities assume a double role. One the one hand, they take responsibility for school improvement and support the project schools by coordinating project resources and facilitating school networks. On the other hand, they also carry out research into network activities and school development, e.g. through conducting or commissioning evaluations into the enacted measures.

An example of dialogue-based evidence gathering among a variety of knowledge types can be found in school-specific data gathered as part of a baseline survey of the quality of individual schools that is discussed with almost every school in a joint meeting between researchers, school leaders, steering committees and selected staff members where divergent viewpoints on the school's internal development are aired.

In addition, the participating universities have close exchange with the state institute through regular partner meetings. This is to ensure that a content-rich, transfer-oriented discussion of the project status, individual measures, and the academic findings that flow from them is embedded into the process. When it comes to transfer activities in the project, the state institute takes a central role. First, it provides the networks with school development coaches. Through these the state institute is able to stay in regular communication with the schools, deploy knowledge management instruments and use frequent meetings between teachers and researchers for the purposes of dialogue. Finally, the state institute provides information to the Ministry for Schools and Education and to local government. It also coordinates regular exchange to bring real-time results into the discourse with those responsible for qualifications and training. The coaches seconded by QUA-LiS play an important interfacing role in the web of diverse project partners. They are supporting individual schools in their improvement activities, e.g. by helping to finding suitable teacher-training, by performing documentation tasks and by providing feedback to the network on the work carried out. A further important task that these teachers fulfil is contributing to knowledge management within the project.

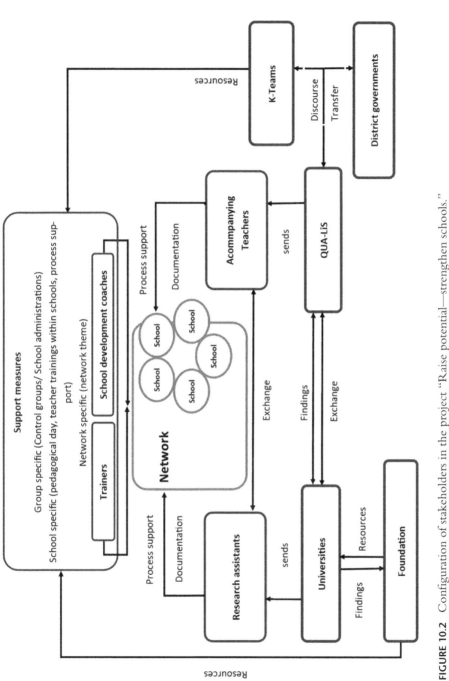

FIGURE 10.2 Configuration of stakeholders in the project "Raise potential—strengthen schools."

Originally published in Bremm, N. (2016). Kontextsensible Schulentwicklung. Das Projekt Potenziale entwickeln—Schulen stärken. *Neue Deutsche Schule*, 68(4), 20–21. Re-published with permission of Neue Deutsche Schule Verlagsgesellschaft mbH.

Knowledge management instruments

The knowledge management instruments[2] draw upon the relevant academic literature (Probst, Raub & Romhardt, 2012) that the state institute has developed, tested and adapted in coordination with input from researchers and the coaches after the first year of the project. The instruments were developed according the following heuristic structure (see Figure 10.3):

It is assumed necessary to gather data with a high narrative component in order to generate knowledge of complex processes. Assuming the purpose is to highlight the *problem* to be tackled (e.g. the necessity that there are problems with the individualization of tuition), then the *story* of greatest interest will be one which lays out exactly which steps were taken, which decisions were made and how, what the specific contextual characteristics were. This leads to examine which *insights* have been gained, e.g. not only into what is found to be applicable, but also what problems arose with implementation and which *conclusions* can be drawn. Finally, there is an exploration of the *follow-up questions* thrown up by the findings around the next steps to improve school development processes.

Three central instruments of knowledge management were used: (1) *Documentation tables* covering the lifecycle of development work; (2) *Micro articles* and (3) *Interviews*. In the (1) documentation tables the coaches record results, next steps, and events according to pre-assigned categories. These notes are made for each school and serve as a documentation as a basis for interviews between the state institute and the development coaches in which the processes in each school were discussed in depth afterwards. The documentation tables are made available to both the research teams and the state institute. The universities can triangulate this data with their other data. Every six months the coaches produce a (2) micro article—in line with the knowledge management structure in Figure 10.3—in

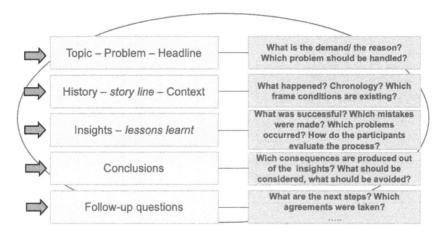

FIGURE 10.3 Structure for developing knowledge management instruments— adapted from Manitius and Groot-Wilken (2017)

which teachers record a "story" of their choosing from their experience working with project-schools. The micro article provides much more narrative material than can be drawn from the standardized documentation tables. Therefore, it provides a foundation for the half-yearly (3) interviews allowing a deeper understanding of the processes.

The data generated serve as a foundation for a systematic follow-on analysis, the essence of which can be fed back to the central stakeholders in the further education system and the relevant departments in the Ministry. Through interplay with qualitative and quantitative research findings from the project's scientific research part a multi-perspective, triangulated knowledge base is developed to support transfer work. In the project it was shown that the observed knowledge management instruments fulfil a reflecting function for development coaches serving in project schools. By writing short articles and providing detailed accounts of school development activities during interviews, coaches are able to reflect upon their individual contributions to supporting schools and even critically assess performance in the context of possible areas for professional development. These opportunities for reflection are further expanded through frequent meetings between the projects six development coaches, where colleagues can feedback on individual challenges in school development on a case-by-case basis.

Agreed transfer concept for knowledge transfer

In order to bring the different forms of knowledge and data together in a systematic way, while serving the transfer interests of the parties involved, the stakeholders agreed a so-called "transfer concept" that underpins the activities of knowledge management and transfer activities. The goal in negotiating this concept was to reconcile the different operating rationales of the participating partners. This was not about giving primacy to one central rationale over all others, rather it was about checking for overlaps between the different interests and how knowledge transfer can be organized according to its content while incorporating the various data sources and allowing for the different goal perspectives.

As part of the work on the transfer concept thematic clusters were defined that set out the content structure of the transfer concept. From this sprang the following clusters for the concept, which were in turn organized into sub-themes (cf. Figure 10.4):

Regarding the *practice research administration partnership* in the Project, the transfer concept is a result of a thoroughly resource-intensive negotiation and agreement process between the partners involved concerning what overarching shared transfer activities the partners should follow, given their varied interests and objectives. The concept addresses concrete content questions such as how different data sources relate to one another and what audience-appropriate transfer products should be. Thus, a commitment to the transfer work is developed, as is the awareness of areas where course correction is needed in real time, e.g. when data gaps appear in response to questioning that can be rectified through additional data gathering.

STRUCTURE OF THE TRANSFER CONCEPT	
TARGET AREAS	
1	**Intervention Strategies**
1.1	School-to school-networks
1.2	School development accompaniment
1.3	In house teacher training
1.4	Further teacher training & job shadowing
2	**Areas of impact**
2.1	Development of identified problem areas in the individual school
2.2	Development of other school quality areas in the individual school
2.3	Development of organizational and steering structures in the individual school (for systematic school development work)
3	**Conditions for success**
3.1	Leadership
3.2	Teacher cooperation
3.3	Organizational and steering structures
3.4	Professional self-concept of the teachers
3.5	Reflections on attitudes toward a socially disadvantaged student body, adaptive strategies in dealing with a socially disadvantaged student body
	…

FIGURE 10.4 Target topics for knowledge gathering as named in the transfer concept

Conclusion

Experience from the Potential Project shows that the configuration of actors in the practice-, research-, administration-partnership project provides a valuable basis for the transfer of educational innovation. The discursive negotiation of transfer goals, content, formats and target groups that together develop a unifying transfer concept as well as long-term acquisition, informing and incremental involvement of participants enables a systemic approach to preparing transfer processes that are shaped according to need and increase the likelihood of successful transfer. Concrete added value in the form of data-led operational and guidance strategies can be generated as a result of successful transfer processes. On the one hand, this increases the likelihood that the resources used will lead to concrete and sustainable change as well as better answers to pressing social questions. On the other hand, this approach demands considerable input not only in terms of time, but also in terms of the intense focus with which those involved must examine transfer content, above all with the system logic of the relevant operational partner in each case. This is no trivial achievement, because realistic estimates of the consequences of decisions are often hard for outsiders to a system to make because the internal logic and degree of interdependence is often difficult to discern at first or even second glance.

Personal cooperation structures that have grown among stakeholders over time are highly advantageous—if not indispensable—for achieving the transfer of project knowledge within systemic structures. Future school development projects should take account of the interdependence of content, structure and transfer. It should also invest in knowledge management as well as early-stage and continuous exchange throughout the lifecycle of the process. It is imperative that project carriers have the ability and the desire to equip such an investment with appropriate resources. Without the necessary level of human resources and time, the process (which demands intensive cooperation and relationship building) will not be successful.

In conclusion, a positive factor enabling a successful transfer process has proven to be a close and cooperative collaboration between steering project partners bringing different resources, networks and knowledge to the table. All the more so when these are focused not only on practical school development work and its study in the context of a school development research project, but also on knowledge management itself. This is also based on a shared understanding of transfer as a cooperative negotiation process through which different rationales—drawing on the most varied forms of knowledge—must first establish connectivity between different system logics, knowledge bases and communication styles.

Knowledge management must, therefore, occur systematically and requires agreement over which instruments can be used to generate and organize knowledge. Ultimately, this must come become embedded in the content of question setting and rationales. This content relationship is important to avoid the risk that unrealistic formulations and expectations are brought into the project or that knowledge management simply becomes self-serving. In the Potential Project it has proven valuable to address this content focus robustly as part of the negotiation and agreement processes of the steering partners in order to be able to relate the different operating rationales of the institutions involved to one another in a meaningful way that takes account of the diversity of their interests.

Notes

1 For example, teacher training, learning support and differentiation, classroom management, curriculum and learning management, internal and external cooperation, school improvement activities, and attitudes towards the heterogeneity of the school intake.
2 Further knowledge management instruments—developed by researchers—were implemented in the networks as part of the support offer to schools. These were also made available to other cooperation partners.

References

Ackeren, I. van, Binnewies, C., Clausen, M., Demski, D., Dormann, C., & Koch, A. R., et al. (Eds.) (2013). Welche Wissensbestände nutzen Schulen im Kontext von Schulentwicklung?: Theoretische Konzepte und erste Befunde des EviS-Verbundprojektes im Überblick. *DDS – Die Deutsche Schule, 12*, 51–73.

Berkemeyer, N., Bos, W., Järvinen, H.-S., Manitius, V. & van Holt, N. (Hrsg.). (2015). *Netzwerkbasierte Unterrichtsentwicklung: Ergebnisse der wissenschaftlichen Begleitforschung zum Projekt "Schulen im Team"*. Münster: Waxmann.

Bremm, N. (2016). Kontextsensible Schulentwicklung. Das Projekt Potenziale entwickeln - Schulen stärken. *Neue Deutsche Schule,* 68(4), 20–21.

Bremm, N., Eiden, S., Neumann, C., Webs, T., van Ackeren, I., & Holtappels, H. G. (2017). Evidenzbasierter Schulentwicklungsansatz für Schulen in herausfordernden Lagen. Zum Potenzial der Integration von praxisbezogener Forschung und Entwicklung am Beispiel des Projekts "Potenziale entwickeln – Schulen stärken". In V. Manitius & P. Dobbelstein (Eds.), Beiträge zur Schulentwicklung. *Schulentwicklungsarbeit in herausfordernden Lagen* (pp. 141–159). Münster, New York: Waxmann.

Bremm, N., Hillebrand, A., Manitius, V., & Jungermann, A. (2018). Wissenstransfer im Bildungssystem. Chancen und Herausforderungen kooperativer Akteurskonstellationen in Forschungs- und Entwicklungsprojekten. *Transfer Forschung <>Schule, 4*, 133–414.

Coburn, C. E. (2005). Shaping teacher sensemaking: School leaders and the enactment of reading policy. *Educational Policy,* 19(3), 476–509.

Coburn, C. E., Penuel, W. R., & Geil, K. E. (2013). *Research–practice partnerships: A strategy for leveraging research for educational improvement in school districts*. New York: William T. Grant Foundation.

Coburn, C. E., & Penuel, W. R. (2016). Research–practice partnerships in education: Outcomes, dynamics, and open questions. *Educational Researcher,* 45(1), 48–54 (7 Seiten), from http://dx.doi.org/10.3102/0013189X16631750.

KMK. (2015). *Gesamtstrategie der Kultusministerkonferenz zum Bildungsmonitoring. (Beschluss der 350. Kultusministerkonferenz vom 11.06.2015)*. Berlin: Sekretariat der ständigen Konferenz der Kultusminister der Länder.

Manitius, V. & Berkemeyer, N. (2015). Unterrichtsentwicklung mithilfe von Netzwerken. In H.-G. Rolff (Hrsg.), *Handbuch Unterrichtsentwicklung* (S. 595–608). Weinheim: Beltz.

Manitius, V. & Groot-Wilken, B. (2017). Kooperatives Wissensmanagement im Rahmen von Schulentwicklungsprojekten als Transferstrategie für die Unterstützung von Schulen in herausfordernder Lage. In P. Dobbelstein & V. Manitius (Hrsg.), *Schulentwicklungsarbeit in herausfordernden Lagen* (S. 266–282). Münster: Waxmann.

Manitius, V. & Bremm, N. (2018). Research–Practice–Partnerships als dialogische Transferstrategie? Zur Rolle des Wissensmanagements im Rahmen eines Schulentwicklungsprojektes in herausfordernden Lagen. In Eickelmann, B. & Drossel, K. (Eds.) *Does what works work? – Bildungspolitik, Bildungsadministration und Bildungsforschung im Dialog* (pp. 259–274). Munster: Waxmann.

Ng-A-Fook, N., Kane, R., Butler, J., Glithero, L., & Forte, R. (2015). Brokering knowledge mobilization networks: Policy reforms, partnerships, and teacher education. *Education Policy Analysis Archives*, 23(0), 122, from https://epaa.asu.edu/ojs/article/view/2090.

Nonaka, I., Takeuchi, H., & Mader, F. (1997). *Die Organisation des Wissens: Wie japanische Unternehmen eine brachliegende Ressource nutzbar machen*. Frankfurt/Main: Campus-Verlag.

Penuel, W. R., Allen, A.-R., Coburn, C. E., & Farrell, C. (2015). Conceptualizing research–practice partnerships as joint work at boundaries. *Journal of Education for Students Placed at Risk*, 20, 182–197.

Probst, G. J. B., Raub, S. & Romhardt, K. (2012). *Wissen Managen: Wie Unternehmen ihre wertvollste Ressource optimal nutzen (4. überarb. Aufl.)*. Wiesbaden: Gabler.

Reinmann-Rothmeier, G. (2001). Münchener Modell: Eine integrative Sicht auf das Managen von Wissen. *Wissensmanagement*, pp. 51–55.

Rürup, M., & Röbken, H. (2015). Kommunale Akteurskonstellationen in der Ganztagsbildung: Eine Fallstudie aus Niedersachsen. *Journal for educational research online: JERO*, 7(1), 125–151, from http://www.j-e-r-o.com/index.php/jero/article/view/549/236.

Seidel, T., Reinhold, S., Holzberger, D., Mok, S.Y., Schiepe-Tiska, A., Reiss, K. (2016). Wie gelingen MINT-Schulen? Anregungen aus Forschung und Praxis. Retrieved from: https://www.waxmann.com/?eID=texte&pdf=3571Volltext.pdf&typ=zusatztext [16.11.2018].

van Holt, N. (2014). Innovation durch selbstorganisierte Intervention—Eine Analyse von Transfer—und Implementationsprozessen am Beispiel des Schulentwicklungsprojektes Schulen im Team—Unterricht gemeinsam entwickeln. Technische Universität Dortmund. *Retrieved from:* http://hdl.handle.net/2003/33607.

Weiland, S. (2013). Evidenzbasierte Politik zwischen Eindeutigkeit und Reflexivität. *Technikfolgen—Theorie und Praxis*, 22(3), 9–15.

Willke, H. (2004). *Einführung in das systemische Wissensmanagement*. Heidelberg: Carl-Auer-Systeme Verlag.

11

THE ROLE OF BROKERS IN SUSTAINING PARTNERSHIP WORK IN EDUCATION

Kristen L. Davidson and William R. Penuel

Research–practice partnerships (RPPs) draw on the knowledge and experiences of researchers and educators to jointly define and address problems of practice over the long term (Coburn, Penuel, & Geil, 2013). Sustaining this collaboration involves learning about differences in the contexts in which researchers and educators work (Penuel & Gallagher, 2017). Partners often navigate boundaries defined by differing goals, timelines, language, and the types of disruptions to their work that tend to occur in each of their organizations (Farrell et al., 2017). In particular, when leaders in school district central offices experience common disruptions of leadership turnover, staff reorganization, or shifts in institutional priorities, the sustainability of their external partnerships might be threatened (Finnigan, Daly, & Liou, 2016).

In the case we share in this chapter, an intense district reorganization threatened the sustainability of a long-term RPP focused on creating a coherent district-wide system for improving the quality of mathematics instruction. Nevertheless, two key district partners were able to find ways to move the work of the RPP forward through a shared vision for mathematics instruction with the research team. In doing so, these district leaders acted as *brokers* who were able to translate the goals and perspectives of the members of the two organizations and cross boundaries between them (Burt, 2005; Obstfeld, 2005; Wenger, 1998).

These brokering acts are crucial to sustaining RPPs. Yet, little is known about how brokers cross boundaries in order to navigate major disruptions to partnership work. In a review of studies of boundary crossing, Akkerman and Bakker (2011) identify four ways in which learning occurs at the boundaries. For those involved, these sites of learning can lead to the development of new understandings and practices that transform their work. This process of learning and transformation is illustrative of the ways in which research and practice partners engage in boundary crossing in RPPs (Penuel, Allen, Coburn, & Farrell, 2015). Here, we use

Akkerman and Bakker's framework to make explicit the moves that brokers made when faced with a district reorganization. We show how these moves exemplified the learning processes that these authors named, and served to transform and sustain the partnership through a major disruption.

Theoretical framework

In order to work collaboratively in partnerships, researchers and educators must navigate differences in the nature of their typical work practices, such as those related to their goals, timelines, use of language, and organizational contexts (Coburn & Penuel, 2016; Farrell et al., 2017). These sociocultural differences can be understood as "boundaries" that research and practice partners must cross in order to move their joint work forward (Akkerman & Bakker, 2011; Akkerman & Bruining, 2016). In acts of "boundary crossing," partners on each side find themselves "encountering difference, entering onto territory in which we are unfamiliar and, to some significant extent therefore, unqualified" (Suchman, 1994, p. 25). In fact, because research and practice partners continuously negotiate boundaries in their collaborative work, Penuel and colleagues (2015) characterize the work of RPPs as "joint work at boundaries."

At times, boundaries can lead to "discontinuity in action" that can halt a partnership's work (Akkerman & Bakker, 2011, p. 133). In some cases, already-existing boundaries become more salient; in others, external disruptions—such as an institutional reorganization—can create new boundaries. Scholars of sociocultural learning emphasize, however, that moments of discontinuity offer important potential as sites of learning for those involved (Engeström, Engeström, & Kärkkäinen, 1995; Spinuzzi, 2011; Wenger, 1998). Specifically, as partners make boundary crossing moves in order to navigate discontinuities, they may develop new understandings, practices, and identities that transform their work together.

Drawing from studies of boundary crossing that evidenced these processes, Akkerman and Bakker (2011) suggest that *transformation* of the work at hand begins with a *confrontation* or disruption, in which partners "[encounter] discontinuities that are not easily surpassed" (p. 147). When this occurs, those involved might work toward *recognizing a new shared problem space* that will ground their continued work. From this space, new *hybridized* practices might be developed, and potentially *crystallized* or embedded into ongoing routines or practices. In the case of an RPP, this process might result in new practices that sustain the partnership.

In their framework, Akkerman and Bakker (2011) do not articulate how those who encounter a confrontation move to recognizing a new shared problem space in order to resume or transform their work while sustaining a collaboration. From other studies in their review, however, they identify three other types of learning mechanisms that can occur at the boundaries. First, in a process they call *identification*, those encountering boundaries might take a step back to redefine and reassert their own unique aims. Second, in a process of *coordination*, shared routines or practices might be developed that coordinate work across boundaries. Third, in a process of *reflection*, those involved expand their perspectives and identities by reflecting on their own work through the viewpoint of the other side.

While Akkerman and Bakker (2011) identify four types of learning that occur at the boundaries (transformation, identification, coordination, and reflection) through individual studies that evidenced each mechanism, these mechanisms are not discrete. In this study, we considered all of these sites of learning in documenting boundary crossing moves. Central to these processes were district leaders who acted as *brokers* through their ability to translate the work of each side of the partnership (Burt, 2005). The important role of brokers in facilitating relationships between groups has been well documented (Keast, Mandell, Brown, & Woolcock, 2004; Mandell, 2001; Pope & Lewis, 2008). In partnerships in particular, brokers are especially effective when they are committed to a shared vision with partners (Bevan, Penuel, Bell, & Buffington, 2018; Guile, 2011; Hammerness, 2001). As we show in this chapter, while the partnership evidenced each of the learning mechanisms that Akkerman and Bakker named, brokers' commitment to a shared "instructional vision" (Munter, 2014) with research partners grounded their efforts to enact boundary crossing moves that sustained the partnership.

Methods

This study draws from a larger qualitative study of three long-term research-practice partnerships (RPPs). Here, we focus on the "Math Partnership"[1] between a research university and a large urban school district. The partnership was collaborating to support the improvement of the quality of middle-grades mathematics instruction at the scale of the district. At the time of our study, the RPP was in its fifth year and had documented some evidence of progress in mathematics teachers' classroom practices and their students' outcomes. It also had shown that district coaches were considerably more accomplished than the teachers they were supporting, a key condition the team identified for improving the quality of instruction. Despite this progress, a recent district reorganization had threatened the Math Partnership's continued existence. Our interviews with researchers and district leaders therefore included discussion of the current state and perceived future of the RPP, which revealed boundary crossing moves enacted by researchers and district leaders most centrally involved in the partnership.

For the purposes of the study we present here, we analyzed data from 49 one-hour interviews with a team of five university-based researchers and 19 district leaders over 18 months. Informed by prior work on boundary crossing in RPPs (Penuel et al., 2015), a team of three researchers deductively coded interview data for: common *boundaries* in RPPs; *district reorganization* as a disruption; boundary crossing *moves*; and the *lines of work* that the partnership pursued. After the team established over 70% consistency in coding interviews for both researchers and district leaders, researchers individually coded the remaining interviews. The team met regularly to review coding, discuss questions, revise codes, and develop inductive codes that emerged (Miles & Huberman, 1994). For example, we added codes for *discontinuities* in the RPP's work and *shared vision* that emerged as a touch point.

Drawing on memos of coded data, data collectors' knowledge, and previous analyses of the dataset, we identified two district leaders who we considered to be *brokers*, Scott (the math specialist) and Talya (the mathematics project manager). These leaders fit the organizational definition of a broker as someone with strong ties between organizations who could serve either as a gatekeeper keeping outsiders from interacting with others within their organization or as someone who built bridges to others in their organizations (Burt, 2005; Obstfeld, 2005). In our focal RPP, leaders who were brokers were most involved in working with research partners, as described by themselves and others in interviews. In addition, our counts of the number of times that each participant had used the name of another participant in interviews revealed that Scott and Talya were most frequently named by both researchers and other district leaders, pointing to the extent of their work with others on both sides of the partnership. Participants also frequently mentioned Emmett (the chief academic officer) and Lauren (the director of curriculum and instruction), but their interview data did not include talk about navigating discontinuities. Rather, others mentioned these leaders as supportive of the district's vision and having authority to approve the partnership's work.

For this analysis, we focused on the boundary crossing moves made by researchers, Emmett and Lauren as district leaders with authority, and Scott and Talya as district brokers. To do so, we wrote short memos on the interview data for these participants, focusing on where we had coded for boundaries, discontinuities, and moves. We not only noticed evidence of all of the learning mechanisms that Akkerman and Bakker (2011) identified, but also discovered that brokers were central to the process of transformation.

Findings

When our study began, the Math Partnership had a five-year history with strong evidence of improving mathematics instruction. Yet, partners were debating whether the partnership could be sustained due to a recent and sudden district reorganization. In multiple interviews over 18 months, participants shared their evolving perspectives and, in the case of the most central brokers, the steps they were taking to move the partnership forward. Through these data, we identified the boundary crossing moves that participants evidenced over time and that led to the transformation of the partnership's work. Our interviews allowed us to get relatively contemporaneous accounts of boundary crossing, rather than retrospective accounts so distal in time that they would result in problematic "smoothing." Our analysis here focuses primarily on boundary crossing moves of district brokers, though researchers played important roles in brokering as well.

First, faced with the *confrontation* of the district reorganization, researchers and district leaders in positions of authority engaged in a learning process of *identification*, in which each took a step back from the partnership and reasserted their own unique visions. To sustain the RPP in the meantime, however, researchers were able to leverage previous efforts at *coordination* of the partnership's work, in which they had established regular routines of communication and feedback sessions with district leaders.

As mathematics leaders, Scott and Talya shared an instructional vision for mathematics with the research team. They saw the research team as a resource to pursue quality mathematics instruction during a time of intense transition in the district. As they proceeded to work closely with the researchers, they became key brokers for the partnership. Scott and Talya's brokering position afforded vantage points through which they were able to engage in a process of *reflection* that understood the visions and concerns of both sides of the RPP. Through this process, these brokers *recognized new shared problem spaces* for the partnership to address that connected the aims of the district's new vision for school-level autonomy and the research team's vision for high quality mathematics instruction. This gained the approval of district leadership and the research team, both of whom would be entering into new territory in planning standards-based professional development (PD) for principals and school-based coaches. The partnership leaders then collaboratively developed and implemented these *new, hybridized practices*, and in doing so, sustained their RPP through the reorganization. '

Together, these processes exemplified a *transformation* of the partnership's work. Below, we share the context of the initial confrontation that the district reorganization created, followed by the boundary crossing moves that demonstrate how brokers were able to sustain the partnership.

Confrontation: threatening a shared vision and creating multiple discontinuities

The district reorganization was a major confrontation that presented multiple discontinuities in the Math Partnership's work, threatening its potential to pursue their shared vision. The previous district leadership had actively supported the RPP's focus on developing a district-wide system to promote high quality mathematics instruction in the middle grades. The new leadership, in contrast, introduced a new district emphasis school-level autonomy in deciding on instructional methods and curricular resources, and it was skeptical of the partnership's value. The focus on school autonomy led to an abandonment of the district-adopted mathematics curriculum that supported inquiry-based instruction.

Instead of a district-wide system that supported a common curriculum and instructional supports, the new, more narrowly-defined role of the central office was to support schools in leading professional learning communities (PLCs) focused on data-based decision making and to hold them accountable in demonstrating improved student achievement on ambitious new state standardized tests. In addition, the roles of district-level coaches in the content areas were devolved into one cross-curricular instructional coach in each school ("school-based coaches"), who typically did not have expertise in mathematics.

This new district context created a sharp divide in the visions for instruction held by district leaders who were newly established in positions of authority and the research team, which created multiple discontinuities in the RPP's work. First, former district partners were reassigned or removed, requiring researchers to develop relationships and reestablish a shared vision with new mathematics department leaders. Researchers had to rely on these new partners to access district leaders with decision-making authority, who were skeptical of the partnership's value. Second, the loss of coaches with mathematics content expertise caused researchers to question whether the district had the capacity to lead and support a coherent system of support for high quality mathematics instruction. Third, the abandonment of the adopted mathematics curriculum removed a common resource through which to develop inquiry-based instructional practices across schools. Altogether, the district's new structure and direction halted the Math Partnership's plans for collaboratively designed PD based in the adopted curriculum and prompted partners to consider whether their joint work could continue.

Identification: taking stock of the research team's and district's differing visions

Such a major confrontation in the Math Partnership's work initially caused both sides of the RPP to engage in a process of *identification* (i.e., reasserting their unique visions). In individual interviews that captured their reactions to the reorganization, researchers emphasized their commitment to supporting high quality mathematics instruction at scale within regular classroom instruction. They contrasted this aim with the new district leaders' vision that deemphasized math-specific expertise and encouraged the creation of pull-out programs and interventions. Because of these seemingly incompatible visions, researchers expressed concerns about the RPP's viability. For example, Fran (a researcher) questioned whether the research team and district partners were two groups who were no longer aligned:

> . . .[I]f they're talking about improving student achievement in whatever way is appropriate then, the conversation is, sort of, it's like we're crossing. We're just shooting across one another. . . . [The district has] shifted their focus so they are not concerned with instructional quality at the moment. . . . [T]here's just been so much change that I think what they're doing is completely unaligned with what we're trying to do so . . . we have a lot of concern as to . . . how much we can learn from them and how much they can learn from us because, at the moment, we're just not speaking the same language.

Notably, Fran's use of metaphors such as "crossing" and "shooting across one another" signal a boundary that had become a discontinuity in the RPP's work (Kerosuo, 2004). She contrasts the research team's core interest in "instructional quality" with the district leadership's focus on "student achievement in whatever way is appropriate," i.e., without a clear and consistent focus on what instruction should look like in order to get there. Fran suggests that this discontinuity is detrimental to the researchers' and district partners' mutual learning and may be insurmountable for the partnership. In this way, she and other researchers took stock of the purpose of their work, asserting their own aims and considering whether or not they could be compatible with the district's new direction.

At the same time, Emmett (the new chief academic officer) and Lauren (the new director of curriculum and instruction) exerted their strong beliefs in the district's new vision centered on data-driven decision making and school-level autonomy. Emmett asserted that the research team's feedback was useful to the district, but that a previous focus on instructional programs was misguided. Further, in contrast to the research team's concern about the loss of mathematics expertise, Emmett claimed that content area expertise was not necessary for school-based coaching that would support teacher learning through data-driven decision making in PLCs. Lauren likewise expressed her support for the district's new direction that was shifting from district-wide PD—such as that co-designed with the research team around inquiry-based instructional practices—to school-based or regional PD determined through data and school surveys that indicated schools' individual needs. These district leaders' and the research team's visions for instructional improvement therefore differed starkly.

Leveraging established coordination of partnership routines and practices

In the first years of the Math Partnership, researchers and district leaders engaged in processes of *coordination* that clarified their joint aims and created routines through which they would pursue them. The research team and the district initially chose to work together because of their compatible visions for mathematics instruction. Their *shared vision* for high-quality instruction grounded their aims to develop a coherent, district-wide system of inquiry-based mathematics instruction. To pursue the RPP's aims, research and district partners first established a practice in which researchers observed mathematics classrooms and engaged in regular cycles of feedback sessions with district leadership about teachers' instructional visions and practices, which included written reports with recommendations. Researchers recounted how the practices of structuring timely feedback sessions and writing reports in accessible ways had emerged as a way to navigate boundaries related to differences in researchers' and education leaders' timelines and language use. In addition, partners engaged in regular communication related to both the feedback sessions and district leaders' efforts to act on researchers' recommendations. These practices represented processes of coordination by establishing routines that eased translation between research and practice, offered continuity in the RPP's work, and developed trust among partners. This foundation made the RPP well positioned to make a planned transition into researchers and mathematics coaches collaboratively designing professional development (PD) based in the adopted curriculum.

It was at this point that an outside evaluation of the district prompted the district reorganization, which helped to justify the replacement of the superintendent, along with a new focus on school-level autonomy and the removal of central office positions, including district-level mathematics coaches who had been key partners in the Math Partnership's work. During this time of transition, the established cycles of feedback sessions and communication offered an important anchor for the research team to continue its work with the district. As Usher, a researcher, explained,

> [W]e essentially really got the message from Emmett that they weren't interested in what we had to offer around co-planning a coherent instructional system and the supports around it. But they continued to be interested in us providing a feedback cycle.

While the partnership maintained a foothold in the district through these routines, central to its transformation was a shared vision for instruction among the researchers and two mathematics department leaders: Scott, who was a newly hired mathematics specialist, and Talya, who remained in her position as a mathematics project manager. Mirroring the research team's sentiments, Talya expressed her concern that

> we're abandoning all the inquiry-based programs that we had in place . . . that ensure really good high-quality instruction and learning. If we're going to abandon that way of teaching, I believe that's a huge challenge for us, and it's going to be a fear of mine.

These shared concerns and visions led Scott and Talya to work closely with the research team as key brokers who pushed the work of the partnership forward. Fran, a researcher, described the differences in the research team's relationships with these two brokers and other district leaders:

> With Scott and Talya, we're completely 100% transparent with the idea that we think [it's] a problem that their [school-based] coaches aren't math-specific, and they 100% agree. . . . We did give that same feedback in the feedback report to . . . all of the district leaders, but I don't think we would engage in conversation around that as easily as we would with Scott and Talya . . . I think it's honestly because of the nature of our relationship.

In this way, the Math Partnership not only was able to maintain its connection to the district, but also was able to carve new paths forward with Scott and Talya. Committed to the partnership's vision, these two district brokers worked together to identify new, shared problem spaces to continue the RPP's work in ways that would be both actionable and effective within the new district context.

Reflection: making sense of differing visions and finding shared problem spaces

While the research team and district leadership reasserted their differing visions, the two district brokers, Scott and Talya, offered more expansive perspectives that connected the new district context to the Math Partnership's vision for instruction. We considered this a process of *reflection* as the district brokers made sense of each side's visions through the lens of the other. Their unique position of being able to understand both sides of the partnership allowed them to hold this dual vantage point and act as brokers.

In light of the district reorganization, Scott expressed concern that the now-fragmented central office would not pursue the research team's recommendation to work toward a common vision for mathematics instruction in the district:

> The first step around mathematics does need to be that getting to a common vision. But I don't know that that's necessarily recognized by all the important parties. . . . If we're trying to get all students to a certain level, and that's the expectation, what do we have to do to get them there? What is our method of instruction? What materials are we using? . . . There's definitely not necessarily a consensus, nor has there really been a conversation around . . . what middle school instruction should look like in mathematics.

Scott reflected on the district context from a vantage point in which he identified with the district, yet saw the lack of a coherent instructional vision as a problem in the same way that the research team did. Similarly, the other district broker, Talya, reflected on how the research team was able to expand her own perspectives related to their shared vision:

> The [research team], they're great in the sense that they'll take an idea, and I'll just say something and they know exactly what I mean. It's like, I just formulate a sketch and they add all the clothes to it. It's phenomenal, it's awesome. . . . It's like, "Yeah, that's exactly what I meant." They make it so much better. . . . It's about understanding around mathematics instruction, what the pie in the sky mathematics instruction should look like.

Scott and Talya thus offered vantage points in which they could reflect on each side of the partnership in light of the other.

The combination of Scott and Talya's relationships with the Math Partnership researchers, their shared instructional vision, and their dual vantage point led them to be able to recognize new problem spaces in which the RPP could continue its joint work. Talya recalled how she and Scott worked together to find this common ground:

> . . . I worked with the math specialist, and we would brainstorm where the areas of need were and then how [the research team's] expertise could help

us, what they've done in the past and what they could offer to do now. We would brainstorm, "This is what our coaches need. This is what we've done in the past, but this is what they need now. This is what we could probably do." . . . We decided we wanted to focus on the math practices.

Although district leadership had expressed an interest in focusing on the state's "content standards" for mathematics, Talya and Scott decided here that they might be able to focus support for the coaches on the state's "practice standards" for mathematics that were consistent with inquiry-based instructional methods. The two brokers knew that they had to target the restructured district's needs related to mathematics instruction and reimagine how the research team's expertise could be useful to these ends.

Scott describes how he and Talya identified new shared problem spaces that they pitched to district leadership and to the research team:

> I had lots of conversations with Talya . . . We . . . came up with this three-pronged approach of working with principals, working with [school-based coaches], and [then] working with teachers. We had a conference call . . . myself and Talya and Lauren and Emmett on [the district's] end, and . . . Quinn [on the research end], and I put forth the plan, . . . and Quinn made sure to keep pointing out that it's a collaboration, that [the research team] wants to work in concert with us . . . Lauren and Emmett . . . approved the plan, and that's what got the ball rolling.

Situating the need to develop capacity for instructional leadership with principals and school-based coaches offered an important point of connection between district leaders' emphasis on school-level autonomy and researchers' emphasis on instructional quality. Importantly, Scott and Talya also pointed to the importance of building this capacity in order to respond to data and impact student achievement, in line with the districts' new vision. These moves thus allowed the brokers to gain approval from leaders with authority. In addition, this nudged the research team—who previously only had worked at the district level—to expand its sense of possible activities to offer PD based in the state's practice standards for principals and coaches based in schools. Once these new problem spaces were agreed upon, researchers and district brokers worked together to create new, hybridized practices that advanced the RPP's work.

Hybridization: co-creating new practices that sustained the partnership

As Scott shared above, he and Talya worked most closely with the research team in order to create new agreed-upon areas of work. Specifically, the research team found ways to connect their interest in developing a coherent system of instructional improvement to the district's focus on professional development (PD) for principals and school-based coaches. Quinn, the lead researcher, described how this type of work at the school level was new to him:

> [W]e, from our point of view, can do a small-scale thing around principal PD, which we're interested in, because we've got particular issues we want to explore . . . We [researchers] have a school leadership team, and I'm a member of that team, bizarrely, [but we have] some ideas around observational feedback. So that's one of the foci of PD. How can we support principals in giving feedback that's actually likely to support instructional improvement?

Quinn suggests that although the research team had to compromise its original vision of supporting instructional improvement at scale, they were able to find common ground in offering PD for principals. He and others had expressed concerns about the capacity of principals to suddenly become instructional leaders, and about the capacity of school-based coaches without mathematics expertise to develop and support high quality mathematics instruction with teachers. The hybridized practices of focusing PD on principals and coaches therefore addressed these concerns in a way that was amenable to district leadership.

In addition to the plans for PD based in the state's practice standards, researchers and district brokers recognized the importance of connecting their work to the district's emphasis on PLCs as the core site of teacher learning. As Laura, a researcher, noted, "Professional learning communities are the things that they're after, so we're going in with a set of questions about those that relate back to the theory of action, and we're going to try to answer those questions." Researchers therefore expanded the scope of their observations to include PLCs and offer feedback to the district on how the PLCs functioned. In addition, they focused PD for school-based coaches on building their capacity to support high quality mathematics instruction through their work with teachers in PLCs at their schools.

Finally, because school-based coaches had to support instruction in multiple content areas, district brokers and researchers worked together to ground the PD in ideas that could be applied broadly across the district. For example, Mara, a researcher, and Scott co-designed a PD grounded on "mindset" as an idea that could be applicable across content areas.

In this way, researchers and district brokers co-created new, hybridized practices of designing PD for principals and school-based coaches. These practices later crystallized into sustained forms through co-developed tools and routines. The Math Partnership indeed succeeded in pursuing this approach, and did so through the duration of the grant. However, the narrowed focus, limited authority of the partnership to effect change in instructional quality through curriculum, and leaders' continued pursuit of a district theory of change in which instruction did not figure meant that the partnership did not have the broad impact on practice that the researchers and original district partners had set out to accomplish.

Discussion

The story of how the Math Partnership navigated a substantial disruption sheds light on the important roles of district brokers who held a dual vantage point of understanding both the research and practice sides of the RPP. In the face of a disruption to their plans for future work, researchers and district leaders in positions of authority first engaged in processes of identification in which they reasserted the unique visions of each side of the partnership. In the meantime, however, the partnership was able to leverage the fact that the district valued the established routines of feedback sessions, as well as commitments to a shared instructional vision among researchers and two key mathematics leaders. During this time of transition, the two mathematics leaders emerged as key district brokers who were able to engage in a process of reflection that understood the visions and concerns of both sides of the RPP. From this dual vantage point, they defined new problem spaces for the partnership to address that connected the aims of the district's new vision for school-level autonomy and the research team's vision for high quality mathematics instruction. This strategic connection gained the approval of district leaders with authority and the research team, both of whom would be entering into new territory in planning standards-based PD for principals and school-based coaches. Researchers and district brokers then collaboratively developed and implemented new, hybridized PD practices, and in doing so, sustained their partnership through the reorganization.

By continually crossing boundaries between research and practice, navigating discontinuities that emerge, engaging in the expansive learning that these situations offer, and co-creating new hybridized practices that move the partnership's work forward, the work of RPPs can be understood as joint work at the boundaries. This case highlights the central role of brokers in this work, as they hold dual vantage points that can translate the work of each side in order to recognize new problem spaces. Importantly, the brokers held a shared vision with the research team that was a motivating factor in their efforts to engage in boundary crossing work, and they were able to leverage established partnership routines through the reorganization process.

Because partnership work is highly contextualized, the processes of transformation that might occur in response to a confrontation may vary in different RPPs and situations. However, it is important for those working in RPPs to consider foundational aspects of their partnerships that can contribute to its longevity and navigate disruptions. For example, established routines can help to maintain a partnership during shifting circumstances. Building trusting relationships with a variety of people in the partner organization who share a common vision can help the RPP to survive turnover and distribute knowledge of and support for the partnership. Multiple relationships likewise can lead to more partners who are able to access the types of vantage points that brokers in this case held and make connections that can lead to synergistic joint work.

Those who find themselves in brokering roles in RPPs can benefit from considering how their ability to understand both sides of the partnership can offer insights in connecting their work. From this vantage point, and grounded in a shared vision with partners, brokers can leverage established routines and points of commonality with leaders in positions of authority in order to advance partnership work in the face of a disruption. Existing tools can support researchers and education leaders in navigating this work, such as those offered by the Research + Practice Collaboratory (see researchandpractice.org/toolkit), the Design-Based Implementation Research (DBIR) website (see www.learndbir.org/tools), and a recent book on creating research-practice partnerships in education (see Penuel & Gallagher, 2017). Such discontinuities and the boundary crossing efforts required to navigate them are not to be avoided; they are intrinsic to the joint work and expansive learning that take place in research–practice partnerships.

Note

1 The partnership and participant names are pseudonyms. The titles of some professional roles also have been masked to protect anonymity.

References

Akkerman, S. F. & Bakker, A. (2011). Boundary crossing and boundary objects. *Review of Educational Research*, *81*(2), 132–169.

Akkerman, S. & Bruining, T. (2016). Multilevel boundary crossing in a professional development school partnership. *Journal of the Learning Sciences*, *25*, 240–284.

Bevan, B., Penuel, W. R., Bell, P., & Buffington, P. J. (2018). Learning, generalizing, and local sense-making in research–practice partnerships. In B. Bevan & W.R. Penuel (Eds.), *Connecting research and practice for educational improvement: Ethical and equitable approaches*. New York: Routledge.

Burt, R. S. (2005). *Brokerage and closure: An introduction to social capital*. Oxford, UK: Oxford University Press.

Coburn, C. E. & Penuel, W. R. (2016). Research–practice partnerships in education: Outcomes, dynamics, and open questions. *Educational Researcher*, *45*(1), 48–54.

Coburn, C. E., Penuel, W. R., & Geil, K. (2013). *Research–practice partnerships at the district level: A new strategy for leveraging research for educational improvement*. New York: William T. Grant Foundation

Engeström, Y., Engeström, R., & Kärkkäinen, M. (1995). Polycontextuality and boundary crossing in expert cognition: Learning and problem solving in complex work activities. *Learning and Instruction*, *5*, 319–336.

Farrell, C. C., Davidson, K. L., Repko-Erwin, M. E., Penuel, W. R., Herlihy, C., Potvin, A. S., & Hill, H. C. (2017). *A descriptive study of the IES Researcher– Practitioner Partnerships in Education Research program: Interim report (Technical Report No. 2)*. Boulder, CO: National Center for Research in Policy and Practice.

Finnigan, K. S., Daly, A. J., & Liou, Y-H. (2016). How leadership churn undermines learning in low-performing school districts. In A. J. Daly & K. S. Finnigan (Eds.), *Thinking and acting systemically: Improving school districts under pressure* (pp. 183–206). Washington, DC: American Educational Research Association.

Guile, D. (2011). Learning at the boundary: A commentary. *International Journal of Educational Research*, *50*(1), 55–61.

Hammerness, K. (2001). Teachers' visions: The role of personal ideals in school reform. *Journal of Educational Change*, *2*(2), 143–163.

Keast, R., Mandell, M. P., Brown, K., & Woolcock, G. (2004). Network structures: Working differently and changing expectations. *Public Administration Review*, *64*(3), 363–371.

Kerosuo, H. (2004). Examining boundaries in health care: Outline of a method for studying organizational boundaries in interaction. *Outlines: Critical Practice Studies*, *6*(1), 35–60.

Mandell, M. (2001). Collaboration through network structures for community building efforts. *National Civic Review*, *90*(3), 279–287.

Miles, M.B. & Huberman, A.M. (1994). *Qualitative data analysis: An expanded sourcebook* (2nd ed.). Thousand Oaks, CA: Sage.

Munter, C. (2014). Developing visions of high-quality mathematics instruction. *Journal for Research in Mathematics Education*, *45*(5), 584–635.

Obstfeld, D. (2005). Social networks, the *tertius iungens* orientation, and involvement in innovation. *Administrative Science Quarterly*, *50*(1), 100–130.

Penuel, W. R., Allen, A-R., Coburn, C. E., & Farrell, C. C. (2015). Conceptualizing research–practice partnerships as joint work boundaries. *Journal of Education for Students Placed at Risk*, *20*(1–2), 182–197.

Penuel, W. R., Fishman, B. J., Haugan Cheng, B., & Sabelli, N. (2011). Organizing research and development at the intersection of learning, implementation, and design. *Educational Researcher*, *40*(7), 331–337. https://doi.org/10.3102/0013189X11421826

Penuel, W. R. & Gallagher, D. (2017). *Creating research–practice partnerships in education*. Cambridge, MA: Harvard Education Press.

Pope, J. & Lewis, J. M. (2008). Improving partnership governance: Using a network approach to evaluate partnerships in Victoria. *The Australian Journal of Public Administration*, *67*(4), 443–456.

Spinuzzi, C. (2011). Losing by expanding: Corralling the runaway object. *Journal of Business and Technical Communication*, *25*(4), 449–486.

Suchman, L. A. (1994). Working relations of technology production and use. *Computer Supported Cooperative Work*, *2*(1), 21–39.

Wenger, E. (1998). Communities of practice: Learning, meaning, and identity. Cambridge: Cambridge University Press.

12

USING FRAMEWORKS AND MODELS TO SUPPORT KNOWLEDGE MOBILIZATION

Vicky Ward

Introduction

So far in this book we have seen an unwavering commitment to the principle of evidence-informed practice and the introduction of an array of approaches and methods designed to make this principle a practical reality within education systems. This commitment and approach is not unique to education, but is shared across diverse sectors from healthcare to criminal justice. As a result, knowledge mobilization is beginning to be recognized as a specialism in its own right. Roles for knowledge mobilization specialists are now relatively commonplace (see http://www.ktecop.ca/category/careers/) and research funders are increasingly expecting to see fully costed knowledge mobilization and research impact plans as part of grant applications (e.g. https://www.ukri.org/innovation/excellence-with-impact/pathways-to-impact/). The increase of such practical efforts to mobilize and share knowledge is mirrored by the rise of knowledge mobilization as a field of research.

The past 20 years have seen an explosion of academic literature on the topic. In 2012 Ferlie et al. identified 684 articles on knowledge mobilization work in the social sciences (Ferlie, Crilly, Jashapara, & Peckham, 2012) and by 2014 Davies et al. were able to identify 71 substantial *reviews* of knowledge mobilization research literature in the fields of health, social care and education (Davies, Powell, & Nutley, 2015). This period has also seen the establishment of the journal *Evidence & Policy*, which is dedicated to the relationship between research, policy, and practice, and the establishment of several specialist research units on the same topic such as the Research Unit for Research Utilisation (www.ruru.ac.uk).

We might expect that a field dedicated to enhancing the use of evidence in various forms of practice and policy would also be dedicated to practising what it preaches: that practical efforts to mobilize and share knowledge would themselves be rooted in research about how knowledge is and can be mobilized. Ironically, however, it appears that even here there is a gap between research and practice. Several studies have found that organizations with a recognized knowledge mobilization role or remit tend to make limited use of the research and latest thinking on knowledge mobilization and have difficulty connecting the complex concepts and jargon contained within the knowledge mobilization literature with their own knowledge mobilization practice (Powell, Davies, & Nutley, 2017; Smits & Denis, 2014).

This chapter is an attempt to address this issue. It focuses on one part of the knowledge mobilization research literature – knowledge mobilization frameworks and models – and explores how these can be used to support efforts to encourage evidence-informed practice. I begin by discussing the nature and scope of frameworks and models and why they might be a useful place to start when trying to get to grips with knowledge mobilization. I then introduce you to a range of frameworks and models from different fields of research and practice (health, education, management) and to a way of thinking about these that moves beyond the field in which they were developed. It ends by considering how these frameworks and models can be put to practical use by knowledge mobilisers.

The purpose of frameworks and models

There are a number of ways that frameworks and models can be understood but one of their main functions is that of simplification. This can be the simplification of an observable phenomenon or a disparate set of literature. Against the complexities of the knowledge mobilization landscape (with its vast and unwieldy literature), something that summarizes and simplifies key insights, processes, and activities is likely to have enormous value for those wishing to get to grips with or support it in practice. An added bonus is that this simplification often extends to a handy diagram that can provide an 'at a glance' presentation of key insights.

Within the implementation science literature (a specific sub-set of knowledge mobilization, which focuses on the implementation of well-defined programmes and interventions), models and frameworks comprise three distinct purposes:

1. To describe and/or guide the process of translating research into practice;
2. To understand and/or explain what influences implementation outcomes; and
3. To evaluate implementation.

(Nilsen, 2015)

These purposes inevitably drive both the content and focus of the models, with those in category 1 depicting the processes involved in mobilizing knowledge; those in category 2 describing the determinants of that process, and those in category 3 focusing on the key outcomes of knowledge mobilization. All three categories could be useful to those wanting to better understand knowledge mobilization but for those wanting to support it in practice, process models and frameworks (category 1) offer the most promise.

Early frameworks and models tended to depict knowledge mobilization as a linear process, but there is now general agreement that mobilizing knowledge is a complex social process that usually takes place in dynamic and complex systems (Holmes et al., 2016). This learning has led to an increasing recognition that determinant frameworks are often unable to sufficiently account for these complexities and hence provide limited 'how-to' support for knowledge mobilization (Nilsen, 2015). Instead, efforts to encourage knowledge mobilization and evidence-informed practice are more likely to be supported by frameworks which focus on how knowledge mobilization actually happens (i.e. processes) rather than what gets in the way (i.e. determinants).

Framework and model authors inevitably face challenges in adequately capturing the complexities of knowledge mobilization processes in a radically simplified form, but many have risen to this challenge. In a review of knowledge mobilization process frameworks conducted in 2014 I identified 47 distinct models from a range of fields and settings (Ward, 2017). The ongoing expansion of knowledge mobilization as a field of study and practical activity means that by the time you are reading this there are likely to be many more. Later in this chapter I will consider how you can make sense of these and, importantly, select one (or more) to use in your own practice, but before that I will introduce you to a small sample from three fields.

Knowledge mobilization frameworks

In this section I will introduce a range of knowledge mobilization frameworks from the fields of education, health and management. Some of these may be familiar to you, but some are generally lesser-known. Given the number and range of knowledge mobilization frameworks, this is certainly not an attempt to provide a comprehensive coverage of what is out there. And nor is the inclusion of certain frameworks any marker of quality, importance or popularity. Instead, my intention is to introduce a selection of frameworks that I consider interesting and could be useful for those seeking to support evidence-informed practice. Of course, you may disagree with me and find the frameworks presented here uninspiring and/or unhelpful. But I hope that this selection will inspire you to search for and identify your own favourites. It should be noted, however, that the frameworks presented here are all focused on the *process* of knowledge mobilization for the reasons outlined in the section above.

Education

Knowledge mobilization frameworks originating from the field of education are actually relatively few and far between. Those that do exist frequently fall into the determinant category and focus on the contextual features surrounding knowledge mobilization and research use (e.g. Levin, 2004). This is not to say, however, that there has been no work undertaken in education – as the rest of this book attests. Merely that there are fewer process frameworks than in other fields.

One of the earliest studies to consider knowledge mobilization processes in education was conducted in the context of the 'Research for Better Schools' programme in the United States (Donner, 1980). The study focused on five schools that were engaged in two educational development projects each of which involved developers, educators and 'linkage agents' (a form of knowledge broker). Having studied these development efforts over a period of two years, Donner concluded that the knowledge transfer process that the schools and developers engaged in consisted of four stages:

- In-house development – this stage involves developers drawing on a 'mixed bag' of research findings, their previous experiences and knowledge of school improvement work and their images and perceptions of teachers and schools.
- Presentation by linkers – this stage involves linkers drawing on their expertise in group dynamics, experiences of implementing projects in schools and knowledge about how to balance the integrity of the approach and materials devised by developers with the need to keep educators happy about the collaboration.
- Trial and use by educators – this stage involves teachers and administrators judging the utility of the approach and materials drawing on their experiences of classroom teaching and the interactional norms that characterized their schools.
- Feedback to developers for revision – this stage involves negotiating between the developers' knowledge of the content area and the educators' practical knowledge and experiences of classroom teaching resulting in the growth of knowledge and expertise on both sides and the revision of the approach and materials.

For those interested in supporting knowledge mobilization Donner's work highlights two further points. First, although the stages outlined above are analytically distinct, they actually overlap in time. Second, that practical knowledge at any one stage affects the knowledge introduced at another.

A more recent educational initiative which took a process approach to knowledge mobilization was the York Informed Practice Initiative (Sharples, 2015). Developed by the Institute for Effective Education at the University of York, the scheme was designed to generate meaningful research-based materials for schools and to develop and test an iterative process of engagement and dialogue. This process consisted of five stages:

- Setting the scene – this stage involves developing an understanding of the school's context, strategic targets and objectives.
- Digging deeper – this stage involves identifying areas for improvement.
- A way forward – this stage involves identifying a range of evidence-based strategies which could be used to bring about the desired improvements.
- Managing change – this stage involves supporting schools to apply evidence-based practices by providing practical information on implementation.
- Capturing outcomes and sustaining change – this stage involves encouraging a cycle of enquiry and review.

In a similar vein to Donner's work, Sharples and Sheard also found that ongoing dialogue and interactions were a crucial aspect of knowledge mobilization, leading them to conclude that knowledge mobilization is both a dynamic and social process.

Health

In contrast to the field of education, health-related research has produced a plethora of knowledge mobilization frameworks and models which have become more and more complex and detailed. One of the best-known models is the Knowledge to Action cycle developed by Ian Graham and colleagues (Graham, Logan, & Harrison, 2006). It was informed by a review of terminology and definitions related to the concept of knowledge translation and a review of planned-action theories, frameworks and models. The resulting model comprises two interlinked processes: knowledge creation and knowledge application.

The knowledge creation 'funnel' in the centre of this model depicts a four-part process through which knowledge becomes more distilled, refined and potentially useful. Whilst the authors point out that their conceptualization of knowledge encompasses both research-based knowledge and other forms of knowing (such as experience) their illustrations of the knowledge creation process tend to focus on the use of scientifically rigorous methods for identifying, appraising and synthesizing information. The action cycle comprises eight main phases or activities:

- Identifying a problem that needs addressing.
- Identify, reviewing, and selecting the knowledge or research relevant to the problem.
- Adapting the identified knowledge or research to the local context.
- Assessing barriers to using the knowledge.
- Selecting, tailoring, and implementing interventions to promote the use of knowledge.
- Monitoring knowledge use.
- Evaluating the outcomes of using the knowledge.
- Sustaining ongoing knowledge use.

Like others, the authors are at pains to emphasize the dynamic and complex nature of the knowledge to action process, suggesting that the boundaries between knowledge creation and action are fluid and permeable.

In 2012 colleagues and I produced another model designed to take the insights of Graham et al. and other framework authors in the healthcare landscape one step further (Ward, Smith, House, & Hamer, 2012). An initial review of 28 knowledge mobilization models enabled us to identify five common components of the knowledge mobilization process, which we subsequently tested and refined using empirical data (i.e. observational fieldnotes) from three healthcare teams. The resulting components were:

- Problem identification and communication – this component involves identifying, clarifying, focusing, reviewing and evolving the service-oriented problem.
- Knowledge development and selection – this component involves locating, tailoring, assessing, classifying and selecting knowledge that could help to address the identified problem(s).
- Analysis of context – this component involves exploring the potential influence of personal, interpersonal, organizational, and professional characteristics on the process and outcomes of knowledge mobilization.
- Knowledge mobilization activities – this component involves clarifying and discussing ways of mobilizing knowledge that could include knowledge management, linkage and exchange, capacity development, or decision and implementation support.
- Knowledge utilization – this component involves considering whether knowledge is to be used directly, conceptually or politically as well as dealing with the practical difficulties of using knowledge and spreading and sustaining knowledge use.

Our fieldwork also enabled us to empirically demonstrate the fluid and multidirectional process that Graham and many other authors had previously discussed since we found that the five components could occur separately or simultaneously and not in any set order. Our illustration of the process is shown in Figure 12.1.

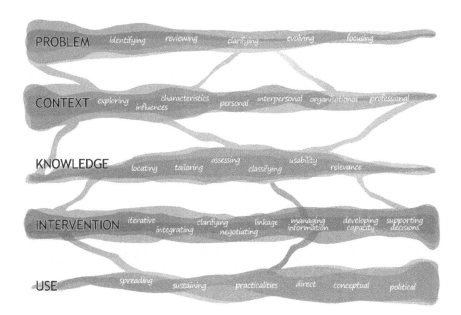

FIGURE 12.1   Ward et al.'s 'Knowledge Exchange Framework'

Originally published in Ward, V., Smith, S., House, A., & Hamer, S. (2012). Exploring knowledge exchange: A useful framework for practice and policy. *Social Science & Medicine, 74*(3), 297–304. Re-published with permission of Elsevier B.V. through PLS Clear.

Management

The field of management has an extraordinarily rich tradition of research on topics such as organizational knowledge creation, knowledge management, and organizational learning. It is perhaps unsurprising, then, that the management literature contains a wealth of potentially useful insights and frameworks relating to knowledge mobilization. These are often overlooked, however, thanks to the erroneous belief that insights from the world of private sector management are not applicable to the public sector (Rashman, Withers, & Hartley, 2009). To redress this the two frameworks I have selected were both developed in the context of private sector organizations.

The first framework describes the process by which knowledge is shared across boundaries for the purposes of solving problems (Berends, Garud, Debackere, & Weggeman, 2011). It is based on an empirical study of interactions within two industrial research groups where researchers were engaged in different practices and not involved in joint projects. By studying how these researchers interacted with one another Berends and his colleagues found that much of their problem-solving work was accomplished via what they term 'thinking along'. They describe this as an interactive process that allows a person with a problem to tap into someone else's knowledge base without becoming deeply involved in that new knowledge base. 'Thinking along' (see Figure 12.2) comprises four interrelated activities which are iterative rather than linear

- Initiating – this involves a 'problem owner' recognizing that they have exhausted their own theories, rules of thumb, and practical skills and requesting input from a 'contributor'.
- Connecting – this involves the problem owner and contributor exploring the problem using an iterative and interactive process of description and questioning.
- Contributing – this involves a contributor making suggestions which are further explored and evaluated (often leading to further description and questioning).
- Concluding – this is the stage at which the problem owner gains fresh insights and possible solutions or closes the interaction if it has not proved helpful.

The second framework I have selected focuses on knowledge mobilization in the context of new product development project teams. Whilst this may seem far-removed from education, I suggest that it is not difficult to imagine that a model of how knowledge is mobilized between product developers may also be relevant to teachers and schools who are trying to develop or implement new programmes. Frank and Ribiero's model was based on a comparison of 'knowledge transfer' models drawn from across the management literature (Frank & Ribeiro, 2014). They define knowledge transfer as 'the process of knowledge movement from a source to a recipient, and its subsequent absorption and use' and knowledge as 'a blend of experience, values, contextual information and insights' (Frank & Ribeiro, 2014, p. 216). In the paper they develop a view of knowledge transfer as a formal and structured process comprising several stages.

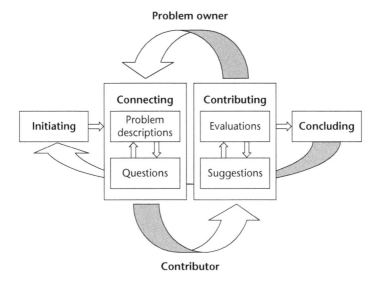

FIGURE 12.2 Berends et al.'s 'thinking along' framework

Originally published in Berends, H., Garud, R., Debackere, K., & Weggeman, M. (2011). Thinking along: A process for tapping into knowledge across boundaries. *International Journal of Technology Management*, 53(1), 69–88. doi:10.1504/ijtm.2011.037238. Re-published with permission of Interscience, which retains copyright of this image.

- Knowledge generation – this stage occurs when knowledge is created in the minds of team members during the project work and/or team members share their knowledge and learn together within a project.
- Knowledge identification – this occurs when an opportunity to apply the knowledge to other projects/teams is recognized and knowledge is abstracted so that it is applicable to other contexts.
- Knowledge processing – this stage applies when a 'formal' (i.e. technical) approach to knowledge management is taken and involves placing knowledge into a formal register, preparing and formatting the knowledge to be comprehensible to others and comparing and associating the knowledge with other knowledge sources.
- Knowledge dissemination – this stage involves distributing or disseminating consolidated knowledge to other teams that may use it.
- Knowledge application – this involves other teams studying and learning about how to apply the shared knowledge in their context and integrating it into their routines.

Although Frank and Ribiero's model represents an idealized and highly formal and structured approach to knowledge transfer, they do consider how the process applies to situations where knowledge is shared via face to face interactions. They suggest that whilst the 'knowledge processing' phase may not be applicable, the other phases could still occur but in a less sequential and structured way.

Making sense of knowledge mobilization frameworks

As we have seen, knowledge mobilization frameworks have been developed in a wide range of disciplines and fields. Thanks to a widespread view that 'context is everything', many of these frameworks have not made their way beyond the boundaries of the field in which they were developed. Few healthcare researchers, for instance, will be aware of frameworks from the management literature and few management researchers will be aware of those from the education literature. And yet, many of these frameworks share striking similarities. The 'problem definition' phase of the Knowledge to Action cycle, for instance, is remarkably similar to the initiating and connecting phases of the 'thinking along' process. And the subsequent phases of the Knowledge to Action cycle bear a marked similarity to the knowledge identification, processing and dissemination aspects of Frank and Ribiero's model. From this, perhaps we can conclude that the originating context of these models is less important than we might imagine, especially if we accept that sharing knowledge and learning are fundamental human processes.

This is not to say, however, that there are not important differences between the many knowledge mobilization frameworks which are out there. As Nilsen pointed out, when it comes to working out how to distinguish between and make use of frameworks and models characteristics such as their assumptions and aims matter far more than how an individual approach is labelled (Nilsen, 2015). A number of authors have attempted to categorize frameworks in ways that move beyond terminology and field. Best and Holmes (2010), for example, have proposed that conceptual approaches to knowledge mobilization fall into three distinct 'types'.

1. Linear models that depict a one-way process whereby researchers produce new knowledge, which gets disseminated to end users, and then incorporated into policy and practice. These models view knowledge as a product that is generalizable across contexts with use depending on effective packaging.
2. Relationship models that incorporate the principles of linear models for dissemination and diffusion but also focus on the interactions among people using the knowledge. These models view knowledge as coming from multiple sources with use depending on effective relationships and processes.
3. Systems approaches that recognize that diffusion and dissemination processes and relationships are shaped through the structures and systems that tie people with different worldviews, priorities, languages, means of communication, and expectations together. Knowledge use depends on the activation and linking together of the whole system

In a similar vein John Lavis and colleagues categorized three types of approach to knowledge mobilization – push, pull and linkage and exchange (Lavis, 2006). All of these approaches, however, are explicitly focused on increasing the use of research-based (as opposed to other forms of) knowledge.

It is this observation which goes to the heart of many of our persistent difficulties with making sense of and using knowledge mobilization frameworks. Many of them inherently contain hidden assumptions about fundamental principles such as the nature of knowledge, the relationship between knowledge and action and the value and purpose of mobilizing different forms of knowledge. It is such hidden assumptions which can make it difficult for those trying to support knowledge mobilization to select relevant frameworks and adequately communicate with one another and those they are seeking to support.

In 2017 I published a framework that was designed to surface many of these hidden assumptions (Ward, 2017). It was based on a review and thematic analysis of 47 knowledge mobilization process models and frameworks from the fields of healthcare, management studies, social care, public policymaking and evaluation research. I found that it was possible to understand and characterize these frameworks using four broad themes that could be expressed as four simple questions:

1.   The purpose of mobilizing knowledge (Why mobilize knowledge?)
2.   The knowledge source/donor (Whose knowledge?)
3.   The definition or understanding of knowledge (What type of knowledge?)
4.   The knowledge mobilization methods and techniques advocated (How is knowledge mobilized?)

Whilst these four categories operate as a broad organizing framework for thinking about knowledge mobilization, nested within them are a range of specific 'options'. These comprise:

1.   Why

- To develop local solutions to practice-based problems
- To develop new policies, programmes and/or recommendations
- To adopt/implement clearly defined practices and policies
- To change practices and behaviours
- To produce useful research/scientified knowledge

2.   Whose

- Professional knowledge producers
- Frontline practitioners and service providers
- Members of the public/service users
- Decision makers
- Product and programme developers

3.   What

- Scientific/factual knowledge
- Technical knowledge
- Practical wisdom

4. How

- Making connections
- Disseminating and synthesizing knowledge
- Facilitating interactive learning and co-production

The full organizing framework can be seen in Figure 12.3.

Using KMb frameworks in practice

Earlier in this chapter I suggested that knowledge mobilization frameworks could serve a variety of purposes. To conclude our journey into the world of frameworks and models I will briefly explore how they can be put to practical use by those interested in or tasked with encouraging evidence-informed practice.

As I see it, there are four main ways that frameworks and models might be best put to use. The first is to aid the planning and development of knowledge mobilization strategies and activities. Process frameworks, such as the Knowledge to Action framework, can provide a much-needed guide to the essential elements of any knowledge mobilization effort and help to focus attention on what to include. It was used, for example, to design a project which aimed to integrate and sustain the use of knowledge about how to support patient decision making within the undergraduate nursing curriculum at a Canadian university (Stacey et al., 2009). One of the most important aspects of any planning process is to decide on the main aim or goal of the activity. This is frequently more difficult that it at first appears and has led to the evaluation researcher Michael Quinn Patton famously describing it as the 'goals clarification shuffle' (Patton, 2008). This is where overarching organizing frameworks such as those outlined in the previous section might be most helpful by helping project designers to discuss and clarify the overall purpose or intended outcome of mobilizing knowledge in their given context.

The second use of frameworks is to evaluate the outcome of knowledge mobilization efforts. Evaluating and monitoring knowledge mobilization is a widely discussed topic with many lamenting the lack of evaluation tools and mechanisms and the ever-present difficulties of attributing change to knowledge-based interventions. In a review of knowledge to action literature, Sarah Morton and colleagues found that one of the key components of successful evaluations was a theory-based approach (Morton, Wilson, Inglis, Ritchie, & Wales, 2018). Knowledge mobilization process frameworks have the capacity to provide a common theoretical focus for evaluation work, ensuring that the focus remains on the activities and outcomes that are most likely to be achieved via knowledge mobilization. The value of applying such a framework was highlighted in a 2015 Canadian study of knowledge brokering (Dagenais, Laurendeau, & Briand-Lamarche, 2015). The authors found that retrospectively applying two conceptual frameworks to their observations of knowledge brokering in a public health context enabled them to develop a more thorough and nuanced critical analysis of the outcomes of the intervention, including a clearer evidence of the different forms of knowledge use which had been supported.

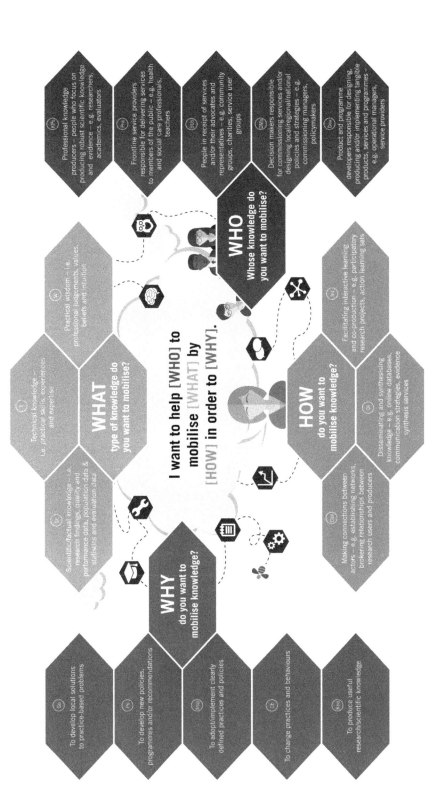

FIGURE 12.3 Ward's 'Why, whose, what, how' framework

Originally published in Ward, V. (2017). Why, whose, what and how? A framework for knowledge mobilisers. *Evidence & Policy: A Journal of Research, Debate and Practice*, 13(3), 477–497. doi:10.1332/174426416X14634763278725. Re-published with permission of Bristol University Press, UK

The third use of frameworks is more personal. As I outlined earlier, knowledge mobilization is a complex, complicated, and often-bewildering field, particularly for those who are entering it for the first time. It is also a rapidly growing area of work, meaning that many more people are finding themselves in knowledge mobilization roles and positions, often with relatively little training. For these individuals, it can be particularly difficult to make sense of and navigate the various options which are open to them. This is where frameworks that synthesize or organize key ideas are most likely to be helpful since they can act as mechanisms to prompt reflection and learning. Considering key questions such as 'what is knowledge?' and 'whose knowledge is important?' (Ward, 2017) can help individuals to move beyond the practical activities, tools and approaches that are traditionally emphasized in knowledge mobilization training schemes (Champagne, Lemieux-Charles, Duranceau, MacKean, & Reay, 2014) towards deeper and more meaningful insights that can help to sustain them in their work. An additional spin-off of such reflection is an increased ability to clearly communicate their own personal stance and find appropriate sources of support.

The final use of frameworks is in the context of developing a greater understanding of and knowledge about knowledge mobilization itself. Many knowledge mobilization efforts and activities are built on common sense rather than more formal types of evidence. Whilst this is not necessarily a problem (especially if we accept that knowledge and evidence come in many forms), it does hinder our attempts to evaluate and better understand how knowledge is mobilized and how practice can become more evidence-informed in general terms. As (Nilsen, 2015) pointed out, whilst the use of theory is not necessarily more helpful than common sense in terms of implementation, theory is at least explicit and open to question, examination and revision. It is through the interplay of theoretical frameworks and practical experiences that we are most likely to come to a clearer understanding of how best to support evidence-informed practice in education and beyond.

References

Berends, H., Garud, R., Debackere, K., & Weggeman, M. (2011). Thinking along: A process for tapping into knowledge across boundaries. *International Journal of Technology Management, 53*(1), 69–88. doi:10.1504/ijtm.2011.037238

Best, A., & Holmes, B. (2010). Systems thinking, knowledge and action: Towards better models and methods. *Evidence & Policy: A Journal of Research, Debate and Practice, 6,* 145–159.

Champagne, F., Lemieux-Charles, L., Duranceau, M.-F., MacKean, G., & Reay, T. (2014). Organizational impact of evidence-informed decision making training initiatives: A case study comparison of two approaches. *Implementation Science, 9.* doi: 10.1186/1748-5908-9-53

Dagenais, C., Laurendeau, M.-C., & Briand-Lamarche, M. (2015). Knowledge brokering in public health: A critical analysis of the results of a qualitative evaluation. *Evaluation and Program Planning, 53,* 10–17. doi: http://dx.doi.org/10.1016/j.evalprogplan.2015.07.003

Davies, H. T. O., Powell, A. E., & Nutley, S. (2015). *Mobilising knowledge to improve UK health care: Learning from other countries and other sectors – a multimethod mapping study.* Retrieved from https://www.ncbi.nlm.nih.gov/books/NBK299400/

Donner, W. W. (1980). *Research into use: The social contexts of knowledge transfer.* Philadelphia, PA: Research for Better Schools, Inc.

Ferlie, E., Crilly, T., Jashapara, A., & Peckham, A. (2012). Knowledge mobilisation in healthcare: A critical review of health sector and generic management literature. *Social Science and Medicine, 74*(8), 1297–1304. doi:http://dx.doi.org/10.1016/j.socsci med.2011.11.042

Frank, A. G., & Ribeiro, J. L. D. (2014). An integrative model for knowledge transfer between new product development project teams. *Knowledge Management Research and Practice, 12*(2), 215–225.

Graham, I. D., Logan, J., & Harrison, M. B. (2006). Lost in knowledge translation: Time for a map? *Journal of Continuing Education in the Health Professions, 26.* doi: 10.1002/chp.47

Holmes, B., Best, A., Davies, H., Hunter, D., Kelly, M., Marshall, M. N., & Rycroft Malone, J. (2016). Mobilising knowledge in complex health systems: A call to action. *Evidence & Policy, 13*(2), 539–560.

Lavis, J. N. (2006). Research, public policymaking, and knowledge-translation processes: Canadian efforts to build bridges. *Journal of Continuing Education in the Health Professions, 26*(1), 37–45.

Levin, B. (2004). Making research matter more. *Education Policy Analysis Archives, 12*(56). Retrieved from http://epaa.asu.edu/epaa/v12n56/

Morton, S., Wilson, S., Inglis, S., Ritchie, K., & Wales, A. (2018). Developing a framework to evaluate knowledge into action interventions. *BMC Health Services Research, 18*(1), 133. doi: 10.1186/s12913-018-2930-3

Nilsen, P. (2015). Making sense of implementation theories, models and frameworks. *Implementation Science, 10*(1), 53. doi: 10.1186/s13012-015-0242-0

Patton, M. Q. (2008). *Utilization-Focused Evaluation* (4th ed.). Thousand Oaks, CA: Sage Publications.

Powell, A., Davies, H., & Nutley, S. (2017). Missing in action? The role of the knowledge mobilisation literature in developing knowledge mobilisation practices. *Evidence & Policy: A Journal of Research, Debate and Practice, 13*(2), 201–223. doi: 10.1332/17442641 6X14534671325644

Rashman, L., Withers, E., & Hartley, J. (2009). Organizational learning and knowledge in public service organizations: A systematic review of the literature. *International Journal of Management Reviews, 11*(4), 463–494. doi:10.1111/j.1468-2370.2009.00257.x

Sharples, J. (2015). Developing an evidence-informed support service for schools – reflections on a UK model. *Evidence & Policy: A Journal of Research, Debate and Practice, 11*(4), 577–587. doi:10.1332/174426415X14222958889404

Smits, P. A., & Denis, J.-L. (2014). How research funding agencies support science integration into policy and practice: An international overview. *Implementation Science, 9.* doi:10.1186/1748-5908-9-28

Stacey, D., Higuchi Kathryn, A. S., Menard, P., Davies, B., Graham Ian, D., & O'Connor Annette, M. (2009). Integrating patient decision support in an undergraduate nursing curriculum: An implementation project. *International Journal of Nursing Education Scholarship, 6,* 1–16.

Ward, V. (2017). Why, whose, what and how? A framework for knowledge mobilisers. *Evidence & Policy: A Journal of Research, Debate and Practice, 13*(3), 477–497. doi: 10.1332/ 174426416X14634763278725

Ward, V., Smith, S., House, A., & Hamer, S. (2012). Exploring knowledge exchange: A useful framework for practice and policy. *Social Science & Medicine, 74*(3), 297–304.

13

CONCLUSION

The future of research use?

Christopher Lubienski

The question of the relationship between research and practice is significant concern that has occupied the attention of scholars in education for some time. This volume presents some of the best current thinkers focused on this issue, so I was excited to be asked to contribute a concluding comment to this outstanding set of chapters. However, somewhat in contrast with the tone of much of this volume, and with the encouragement of the editors who are seeking different perspectives, I am offering a more critical and cautionary take on the issue of research use. While this may partly be due to my natural inclinations as a skeptic, there is also some empirical basis for my tone. Although I do not focus on the relationship of research and practice in my work, for the last decade or so I have been immersed in investigating research use in education policymaking. This has strengthened my skepticism of research use overall for two reasons. First, quite obviously, much policymaking in education is fact-free and willfully ignores research evidence, or research is "used" in ways that do not really inform policy (Lubienski, 2019). Second, the rise of intermediary organizations—which play a key and positive role in several of the chapters in this volume—has often been problematic in shaping policymakers' use of research evidence, more so than in the research-to-practice equation (Lubienski, Brewer, & Goel La Londe, 2016). These intermediaries can play a useful role in identifying and translating research evidence to inform policy. But quite often in the policy arena they have a perverse effect of curating evidence around a particular agenda (to the exclusion of good counter-evidence), and then packaging and promoting that "research" in ways that are detrimental to the ideal of evidence-based policymaking (Lubienski, Scott, & DeBray, 2014). Thus, this concluding chapter takes a more critical approach in considering some of the concerns around research use.

The idea of tying research more closely to practice is attractive on its face, and appeals to the pervasive technocratic impulse that assumes we can "tinker"—to borrow Tyack and Cuban's (1995) apt term—toward individual, organizational, institutional, and social improvements by empirically identifying the most effective remedies to problems of practice and policy. Indeed, not only is this general approach alluring in its promise of addressing obstacles that impede educational effectiveness and equity, but it also undergirds a common, overriding assumption that things *can* be made better by simply paying better attention to the facts—a relatively easy task. However, as I will go on to argue in this concluding discussion, such a focus on improvement through evidence also has an appeal in that it draws our attention to what we think we can fix, while safely diverting attention from the painful fact that much of the ills that plague educational efforts may be beyond our ability to address through evidence-based educational improvement strategies.

Thus, in this chapter, I offer a summary discussion of some of the lessons gleaned on research use from the evidence provided in this book. But I then go further and highlight some of the continuing and in many cases intractable challenges facing education systems striving to improve. As I note, part of these continuing challenges can be addressed by advancing and extending the research lines highlighted in this volume. Yet, unfortunately, I also see significant structural impediments that call into question strategies celebrating the use of research evidence to guide practice and policy. I not only consider such obstacles, but I also examine the underlying assumptions behind the basic premise of seeking to enhance connections to cross the research–practice divide, concluding with some admonitions regarding the role of research in the current, fact-averse climate.

Linking research to practice in education

The questions undergirding this volume highlight the related concerns: (1) why is there not a tighter link between education research and practice? and (2) what can be done to improve that link? Before considering the multiple challenges and possibilities shaping the potential ways of addressing those questions, it is worth asking whether education is particularly exceptional in this regard, at least relative to other comparable fields. In fact, it is quite common to see education as being rather loosely coupled with the body of knowledge assumed to serve as its empirical basis. Unlike, say, medicine, where there are more direct—although hardly perfect—channels and dynamics tying research to practice, education lacks important factors that make that tie similarly strong. For instance, compared to professions such as medicine or law, education, as a semi-profession, has less of a defined body of expert knowledge guiding practice. Preparation for educators is often criticized as being too abstract, based in theory rather than empirical foundations of good practice. Moreover, education has myriad, often conflicting goals that reflect multiple constituencies and fragmented accountability systems (Labaree, 1997), which complexifies the idea of a unified body of research informing classroom practice. Thus, at least in some ways, education is somewhat unique in its weak links between research and practice.

Nonetheless, public policymakers and private philanthropists have—often rather bluntly—been pushing to tighten research-practice links in education. Ironically (using policy levers that themselves are often not based in research), these advocates have been promoting measures to encourage the use of "what works" in education with the presumption that by simply identifying and then inducing the use of effective practices, educational improvements will follow. Too often, though, such desires to strengthen the connection between research and practice gloss over important questions that confound efforts to enhance the research-practice link. Following the arguments set out in this volume, here I review and discuss just a handful of considerations that may help shape—and in many cases weaken—that link in education.

Demand: While we can improve the quality and availability of research pertinent to classroom practice, that in itself is no guarantee that such information is desired, much less that it will be utilized. While many practitioners certainly seek to use evidence to improve the efficacy of their efforts, that does not mean that the evidence they seek is "research"-based. Instead, such evidence can also come from experience, anecdotes, or the apprenticeship of observation from their own time as students.

Literacy: Even if practitioners seek research evidence to inform the improvement of their work, it does not necessarily then follow that they are in a position to translate the findings in ways that are useful for then meaningfully shaping practice. Certainly, researchers often present their work in ways that are unnecessarily arcane and inaccessible to wider audiences. Still, much research is, by its very nature, highly sophisticated, and written for other researchers rather than for practitioners, with methods and findings fraught with caveats and qualifiers that make the implications and applicability difficult for non-experts in that field to assess.

Sources: Unlike, say, pharmalogical research that must undergo stringent peer-review and clinical trials before earning the stamp of approval from federal authorities in the US, education research has no monolithic source for standards of approval. Instead, education is a site with multiple, often conflicting (and often politicized) sources of research evidence, including universities, think tanks, advocacy organizations, non-profit organizations, and for-profit vendors. In that way, the field is closer not to pharmalogical research but to the wide-open market for supplements, alternative medicine, and other shams.

Expertise: Related to the number of sources is the issue of varying views on expertise in education. Again, unlike in some other fields that focus almost exclusively on training in research methods to determine expertise, education offers the imprimatur of credibility through multiple avenues, including practitioner experience, institutional affiliation, or simply having an audience as with a substantial media or social media presence (Malin & Lubienski, 2015). The relative ease of entry into education offers a range of "experts" the expanded opportunity to shape practice.

Information: In a functional marketplace, access to useable information on the relative quality of a good or service is widely distributed, with providers having no special advantage over consumers regarding knowledge of what they are offering. Of course, with professions such as law or medicine, the information asymmetries enjoyed by experts are tempered by professional responsibilities to act in the best interests of the client. In education, information asymmetries are endemic, with knowledge about the (in)effectiveness of various practices often more apparent to providers and not practitioners, while providers such as for-profit vendors may lack the same professional guidelines evident in other fields.

Of course, there are many other issues in addition to the five outlined above. For instance, there are cultural considerations such as respect for scholarship, and ideas about what constitutes "good" or "real" schooling (Metz, 1990) that can shape practice. But as I indicate, some of the major obstacles for more closely connecting research to practice have to do with knowledge and expertise on research and practice. There needs to be channels through which preferences for information on research evidence can be articulated and recognized. Is knowledge on alternatives and their effectiveness available? Is it transparent? Objective? Trustworthy? Relevant? Applicable? Understandable?

While I have highlighted some issues on the demand side, the supply of research is also important. For research to matter, it must be relevant, timely, and applicable to the problems facing practitioners. Researchers have to ask the right questions, and adopt understandable language. Given that many researchers—especially those at universities—are focused on other forms of impact in research and policy rather than practice, this suggests the importance of enhanced channels of communication between the supply and demand sides of the equation.

Discussion: research and practice in a post-truth era

I began this chapter by posing two questions that animate this volume: Why is there not a closer link between research and practice in education? And, thus, what could be done to strengthen that link? While this book offers a number of fascinating insights into these questions, the preceding discussion also indicates that, despite the best intentions of policymakers and researchers, there are still some structural impediments that further complexify efforts to make a tighter connection between research and practice. However, here I go beyond those two motivating questions to examine some of the assumptions undergirding them. Particularly given the current socio-political climate, where evidence is often a politicized factor, I raise four questions about approaches to strengthening ties between research and practice in education that may be useful in thinking about ways forward on this important issue.

First, inasmuch as there are impediments to tighter connections between research and practice, as I just discussed, it may be useful to consider not just the cause or remedy, but the nature of the distance between research and practice. Indeed, schooling largely emerged as an institution of practice in response to perceived social problems, not as a research-based remedy to empirically diagnosed issues. That is, it was largely a political endeavor, which suggests appeals to a different set justifications such as commonsense, popular sentiment, and party alliances, rather than to a strong evidentiary rationale. Consequently, the idea that education practice should be closely tied to a vibrant apparatus producing empirical evidence is a relatively new idea. Yet while the field of education research has grown and become more sophisticated, it has never been organically affiliated with areas of education practice it might be expected to influence. Instead, for the most part, research and practice represent distinct institutions with unique assumptions and incentives shaping them.

Yet, second, at the same time, the notion that there are stark boundaries than need to be bridged between research and practice may also not always be as true as is often assumed. While there are certainly distinct institutional origins for research and practice in education, they are not always discrete institutions consisting only of the separate functions thought to be at their core. That is, as evident in this volume, there are countless cases of organizations of practice created with a research component expected to have a more direct, if not immediate, impact on educational practice in that organization. For instance, professional development schools are primarily about teaching, but also place a strong emphasis on generating new evidence to inform that teaching. Alternatively, there are numerous examples of research organizations, such as laboratory schools, that also have one foot set squarely in practice. The pertinent point is that while we can talk of the need for boundary spanners to bridge the gap between research and practice, it is not always the case that such divisions are as stark as supposed, as evidenced by the long history of what we might see as institutional trespassers that defy such categories.

A third concern, and perhaps a rather uncomfortable one, is the question of whether practice is actually deserving of the attention we bestow on it in discussions of strengthening the tie between research and practice. Certainly, as I have noted, there are also questions about the importance, influence, and impact of research as well. But, without wishing to oversell the point, there is also a long line of evidence in education that calls into question the impacts we might have from improving practice. While some research highlights the promising possibilities of leveraging more effective practitioners (Chetty, Friedman, & Rockoff, 2011), there is also an established empirical basis for noting the limitations of what can be accomplished through improved practice. Going back for decades, researchers have documented the importance of non-classroom and non-school factors in shaping student outcomes. While this does not then necessarily mean that there is little point in trying to improve practice, it certainly underscores the limits and challenges to such a focus, and points to other factors outside of educational practice as being at least as important areas for attention (Rothstein, 2004).

Fourth and finally, much of the discussion around enhancing ties between research and practice appears to assume—more or less—a rational model of problem diagnosis and treatment identification, not completely unlike a medical model. But, as noted above, the models informing this field are not that simple and clear. When we talk about evidence informing educational practice, it begs the question as to whose evidence. Is it that of expert researchers? Is it that of practitioners who are closest to the concerns? Should we attend to the evidence that parents utilize in forming their ideas about what their children need (but may not be getting)? Indeed, schooling is the site of conflicting models for organizing the educational enterprise, models that variously privilege different actors, such as the parent, the practitioner, or the "objective" expert.

This is a particularly salient question in an increasingly post-truth age where evidence is questionable, malleable, or often just irrelevant. Just as policymakers can advance policy based upon manufactured crises, regardless of actual facts, evidence can be easily ignored in determining how to change educational practice. Researchers can be dismissed for their ideological agendas and methodological choices. Policymakers can be perceived as being beholden to special interest agendas. But if we denigrate technocratic and democratic models of education, that leaves schooling largely in the realm of market forces to determine what policies and practices to adopt. Indeed, in considering the various claims to improve practice, private vendors may epitomize that market model for education in this regard. Still, as they seek to sell educators on what they have to offer, it raises important questions for how we understand efforts to bridge the research-practice divide. Are particular practices promoted based on evidence of their effectiveness, or on self-interestedness of organizations seeing to expand their market share? To enhance the research-practice connection, do educators need better vehicles that can convey the best thinking on alternate options, or will we see simply better packaging used to sell particular practices? Will we see an increase in "boundary spanners" that bridge the research-practice divide, or just "spinners" that promote a practice based on image more than evidence? Will networked connectors play the role of match-makers or marketers in connecting educators to new, perhaps not-so-promising or empirically-based, practices?

While I dislike ending such a useful volume on such a cautionary note, these questions point to problems inherent in promoting the use of research, whether for policy or practice, particularly in an era where prominent decision-makers are quite comfortable in ignoring or undercutting empirical evidence that challenges, or is simply inconvenient to, their political or personal wellbeing. As the *New York Times* notes, we live in

> an era when so many of the people who put on the trappings of authority and peddle pearls of wisdom don't actually have the goods. When so many opinions come with a swagger inversely proportional to their worth. When social media, cable channels, webcasts, podcasts, blogs and more have created an environment in which everybody's an expert and nobody's an expert—in which it's sometimes impossible to tell.
>
> *(Bruni, 2019, p. SR3)*

Moreover, not only disregard over expertise, but too often the callous disregard for the truth as incentivized by political and profit motives, has meant the rise of organizations that have a "loose" relationship with facts, whether in the news business or education reform, and make it their business to assert agendas over evidence.

Thus, researchers would do well to keep in mind not only the institutional impediments noted above, but the very ideas of "research" and "evidence," in an increasingly post-truth environment.

References

Bruni, F. (2019, February 3). The meaning of Tony Romo, Super Bowl psychic. *New York Times*, p. SR3. Retrieved from https://www.nytimes.com/2019/02/02/opinion/sunday/super-bowl-2019-tony-romo.html

Chetty, R., Friedman, J. N., & Rockoff, J. E. (2011). *The long-term impacts of teachers: Teacher value-added and student outcomes in adulthood* (17699). Retrieved from http://www.equality-of-opportunity.org/assets/documents/teachers_wp.pdf

Labaree, D. F. (1997). Public goods, private goods: The American struggle over educational goals. *American Educational Research Journal, 34*(1), 39–81.

Lubienski, C. (2019). Advocacy networks and market models for education. In M. Parreira do Amaral, G. Steiner-Khamsi, & C. Thompson (Eds.), *Researching the global education industry: Commodification, the market and business involvement* (pp. 69–86). Cham: Springer International Publishing.

Lubienski, C., Brewer, T. J., & Goel La Londe, P. (2016). Orchestrating policy ideas: Philanthropies and think tanks in US education policy advocacy networks. *Australian Education Researcher, 43*(1), 55–73. doi:10.1007/s13384-015-0187-y

Lubienski, C., Scott, J., & DeBray, E. (2014). The politics of research production, promotion, and utilization in educational policy. *Educational Policy, 28*(2), 131–144. doi: 10.1177/0895904813515329

Malin, J. R., & Lubienski, C. (2015). Educational expertise, advocacy, and media influence. *2015, 23*(6). doi: 10.14507/epaa.v23.1706

Metz, M. H. (1990). Real school: A universal drama amid disparate experience. In D. E. Mitchell & M. E. Goertz (Eds.), *Education politics for the new century* (pp. 75–91). New York: Falmer Press.

Rothstein, R. (2004). *Class and schools: Using social, economic, and educational reform to close the Black–White achievement gap*. Washington, DC: Economic Policy Institute.

Tyack, D. B., & Cuban, L. (1995). *Tinkering toward utopia: A century of public school reform*. Cambridge, MA: Harvard University Press.

INDEX

Page numbers in *italics* refer to figures. Page numbers in **bold** refer to tables.